The Pilgrimage Series

THE CANTERBURY PILGRIMAGES

THE MARTYRDOM OF ST THOMAS.

From a Copy, preserved in Canterbury Cathedral, of the almost obliterated Painting
at the head of the Tomb of Henry IV.

THE CANTERBURY PILGRIMAGES

BY

H. SNOWDEN WARD

EDITOR OF "THE PHOTOGRAM"; AUTHOR OF "SHAKESPEARE'S TOWN AND TIMES,"
"THE REAL DICKENS LAND," ETC.

WITH FIFTY FULL-PAGE ILLUSTRATIONS, PHOTOGRAPHED
BY **CATHARINE WEED BARNES WARD**, AS WELL AS
THREE SKETCH MAPS AND MANY WOOD-CUTS
IN THE TEXT

CAPUT THOMAE
One of the leaden Pilgrims' Signs.

LONDON
ADAM AND CHARLES BLACK
1904

" .   .   .   From every shirés end
Of Engéland, to Canterbury they wend,
The holy, blissful martyr for to seek.'

CONTENTS

" For him was liever have at his bed's head
Tweénty bookés clad in black or red
Than robés rich, or fiddle, or gay psaltrie."

LIST OF ILLUSTRATIONS

PRINTED SEPARATELY FROM THE TEXT

Photographed by C. W. Barnes Ward

vii

PRINTED IN THE TEXT

From the Ellesmere MS.

INTRODUCTION

THE breath of Spring blows fresh and sweet, the leaves grow soft and green, while high in heaven the hawk stoops to strike the lordly heron. Year after year it is the same, while Thomas of London climbs to towering heights—and falls.

Pilgrims loiter through the Kentish fields and gardens, over the soft, short sward of the open Surrey downs; while summoners, pardoners, and other mountebanks win their way by fraud. Century after century it is the same, while the Cult of Thomas the Martyr rises to towering heights—and falls.

The interest of this book centres around two great tragedies, the fall of Thomas the Archbishop; and the fall of the worship of Thomas the Martyr. These are bound up with a part of a still greater tragedy; the collapse of a grand religious movement, which, with all its human imperfections and shortcomings, had done a noble work for those who needed it most—the poor, the weak, the sorrowing.

It is well that we should view these disasters under the guidance of that man who was essentially the poet of the Springtime, whose puppets move serenely under the very shadow of impending doom, and whose verse breathes of birds and sunshine, daisies and open air. He helps us to see how eternal and how indifferent to incidents are nature and human nature. He shows us that his monk and his pardoner, his wife of Bath and his prioress, his gentle knight and his poor parson are people we meet to-day under other names. And he preaches the resurrection and the life: not only for individuals, but for ideas, for thoughts, and for aspirations. He shows that though forms and circumstances change, though truth be veiled at times, the noble man will always be noble, the pure will always be pure.

THE CANTERBURY
PILGRIMAGES

CHAPTER I

THOMAS OF LONDON

THOMAS was born in London, on December 21, 1118, in a house standing upon the site now occupied by the chapel of the Mercers' Company, on the north of Cheapside. It was the Feast of St Thomas—which determined the name of the infant—and he was baptised at evensong on the day of his birth, in the church of his parish, St Mary Colechurch. His name is here given as Thomas, because there is no contemporary authority for the surname "à Becket" by which he is generally called, and because although the surname Becket or Beket was applied to his father, it did not necessarily descend to the son, for in that day such a name was a personal, and not a family possession. In only three cases are contemporaries recorded as speaking of him as Becket. In the enormous majority of instances he is simply called Thomas, or, as he attained position, Thomas of London, Thomas the Chancellor, or, Thomas the Archbishop.

His father was Gilbert Becket, the Norman, son of a Norman settler who came from Rouen, and of Matilda, a native of Caen. The mother's name is sometimes given as Rose (Roesa or Rohesia), but the probability seems to be that Gilbert and Rose were the grandparents, and Gilbert and Matilda the parents of Thomas. The name of Rose was given to a sister of Thomas, who survived him until about 1167, and to whom Henry II. granted a pension at the time of his penance at the tomb of her murdered brother.

Around the name of "Thomas à Becket" many interesting legends have arisen. The most persistent is that which tells the romantic adventures of his father in the Holy Land, and how on his return to England he was followed by the daughter of his paynim captor, who crossed the whole of Europe and the narrow seas guided by the two words—Gilbert ; London. This story of a maidenly devotion which had scarcely been deserved by Gilbert's desertion of his fair convert, was apparently unknown to the contemporaries of Thomas, and it seems to have been based upon a statement, made after his death, that he united the churches of the East and the West, and because of his adoption as the patron saint of the knights of Acre.

There are stories—recorded not long after his martyrdom — of many miraculous occurrences accompanying the birth of Thomas. The story of the Saracen maiden is accompanied by an enthusiastic prophecy, said to have been spoken by the Bishop of Chichester when sitting with six other bishops, to decide whether Gilbert might conscientiously marry the converted pagan; there are tales of wonderful dreams which came to the mother of the child before his birth, and of a fire which broke out in his father's house on the day he was born, destroying not only his birthplace but also a good part of the city. All these things—including the very unfriendly omen of the conflagration—were supposed to have been sent especially to show that the child was to be a burning and a shining light, and a builder of churches. Fortunately he knew nothing about these things, so that they did not affect his life; and this is probably true of another story, although his friend and biographer, Herbert of Bosham, records it as from the lips of Thomas himself;—that when as a boy he lay sick of a fever, the Virgin Mary appeared unto him, promising recovery from the illness, and giving him two golden keys, which she said were the keys of paradise, thereafter to be in his keeping. These keys have also been connected with the churches of the East and the West, of which mention has been made.

When ten years old, Thomas was taken to the Priory of St Mary's, at Merton, in Surrey, where he made one of his most valued and life-long attachments; for Robert, the prior who was charged with his education, became his private confessor, and was one of the very few who stood by him to the last on the day of his murder. This Robert of Merton has told us that the personal life of Thomas was pure and upright, and that as a schoolboy he was bright and intelligent, with a great memory, but also with a preference for idleness and sport rather than for study. The facts, that when Thomas was consecrated archbishop he made Robert his chaplain, and that the Priory of Merton was visited and materially helped by Henry II. at Thomas's suggestion, show that the bright boy long retained pleasant memories of his first school, and that gratitude had a place in his character.

An occurrence which has a natural explanation, but which the chroniclers consider miraculous, was connected with the lad's love of sport. In this he was encouraged by Richer de l'Aigle, a wealthy knight or baron of Pevensey Castle, who stayed at the house of Gilbert Becket on his visits to London, and who took the boy to his Sussex home for at least one considerable visit. On one such occasion, while the two were hawking, "they came to a mill-stream spanned by naught save a plank. Richer, who went first, passed across the plank. Thomas came after, all hooded. But the foot of his horse slipped, and he, with the horse as well, fell into the stream. Torn from his horse, he was drawn fast toward the mill-wheel. Just as he was bound to be dragged under the wheel, the miller turned off the water. The knight and his retinue followed with cries along the bank. Hearing their voices the miller came out, and dragged out Thomas half dead."

This account is taken from two of the chroniclers, whose records supplement each other in certain small details. As showing how a simple incident may become miraculous, it may be well to quote the same story from a third chronicler, Edward Grim, who was with Thomas at his death, and who is notably and exactly accurate whenever recording matters within his own knowledge. He writes: "On a certain day, when Thomas was hawking with [Richer], the hawk, chasing a wild duck, and seizing it just as it dived, was itself pulled into the water. The young man, sorry that the hawk should perish, leapt from his horse and threw himself into the stream. At once he was in danger, now sinking under the water, anon rising to the surface, and none was able to stretch him a hand. Toward the mill-wheel he was drawn by the rushing water, but just as he approached the outflow, the wheel stood, and moved itself no more until, alive indeed, but greatly injured, the young man was pulled out. But the unfortunate youth was cherished by the healing hand of the Saviour, who in this time of danger would not allow the future light in Israel to be extinguished, from whose precious death we have seen so many benefits appear."

From Merton, Thomas went to one of the great schools in London, where the recognised sports of the boys included cock-fighting and the roughest of football, and thence to Paris, where he remained until he was twenty-one. To this season in Paris has been assigned an occurrence which is probably only a later version of a vision already mentioned. It is told that when one of the fashionable feasts of love occurred, and all his school-fellows received presents from friends and sweethearts, Thomas alone had no such gift. He prayed to his Lady the Virgin for a token of her favour that might be shown to his fellows, and thereupon appeared on the altar a casket con-

taining ecclesiastical ornaments, while a voice
bade him use the gift when he should become a
priest.   One of the chronicles records the name
of one of his school-fellows, Everlin, afterward
Abbot of St Laurence, Liege, who dedicated an
altar to St Thomas in memory of their school-
days, while another old writer says that Ludolf,
who became Archbishop of Magdeburg in 1194,
was taught by Thomas, in Paris.   Another man
who was to become a fast friend and biographer—
John of Salisbury—was studying in Paris during
part of the time that Thomas was there, and it
is possible that their acquaintance began in those
student days, although the fact is not recorded.

Of the instructors we are even more ignorant
than of the fellow-students, though we know that
one, Robert of Melun, "taught dialectic and the
sacred page" in Paris at the time.   He had John
of Salisbury as one of his pupils, and at a later
date he was invited to England by Henry II. at
the instance of Thomas, who afterward preferred
him to the Bishopric of Hereford.   This was
probably a second instance of gratitude to a
teacher.

When Thomas was about twenty-one, his
mother died.   His father had been much reduced
in worldly circumstances as the result of various
fires, and the son became a clerk to one of his
relatives, Osbern Huitdeniers, a very wealthy
and influential merchant.   He seems also to
have been clerk in the portreeve's office, and it
is recorded that he was for some time notary to
Richer l'Aigle, his sporting friend, but this part
of the career is not very certainly known.   Probably the supposed engagement with l'Aigle is an

error, founded on the story of their earlier friendship, and it is possible that Huitdenier held the office of portreeve during part (at least) of Thomas's service with him. From 1140 to 1143 he was engaged in commercial work, but shortly before November in the last-named year he had a stroke of good fortune which paved the way to his ultimate immense success.

Amongst the visitors to the house of Gilbert were a certain Master Eustace of Boulogne, and his brother the Archdeacon Baldwin, who noted the ability of Thomas, and suggested that he should find a position in the service of Theobald, Archbishop of Canterbury. The application seems to have been made by Gilbert in person, who reminded the archbishop that they were both Normans, and natives of the same city.[1] The candidate was further supported by a friend already in a lowly position in the archbishop's service, and, on the strength of this multiple recommendation, Thomas obtained a position in what was at the moment the most powerful and influential household in the kingdom. In those days of trouble between Stephen and Matilda, both claimants for the throne, only Henry, Bishop of Winchester, rivalled Theobald in political importance.

Natural ability, added to the experience of affairs gained in the service of Huitdeniers and in the companionship of men like l'Aigle and the Archdeacon Baldwin, had fitted Thomas to be

[1] "Tierrici villam" or Thiersy, in the account of Fitzstephen. But it is also suggested that the reminder was really of their connection with Bec Hellouin, where Theobald first became a monk, and from which Gilbert may have taken his surname, since Becket is the diminutive of Bec. In any case, Thiersy is close to Bec.

useful in a political household; but for the first
few years he owed more to his wonderful personal
power of attracting those with whom he
associated than to his recognised usefulness, for
twice he was dismissed from the service owing to
the malice and false representations of Roger
Pont l'Evêque (afterward Archbishop of York),
who seems to have become jealous of his
popularity, but on each occasion was reinstated
through the friendship of Walter, Archdeacon
of Canterbury, brother of the archbishop.
Theobald had drawn around him many young
men of great ability, so that his palace has been
described as the "home and training College of
a new generation of English scholars and
English statesmen," and although Pont l'Evêque
was unfriendly, at least two other members of the
household in addition to Walter the archdeacon,
soon recognised the sterling qualities of their new
companion.   These were Richard, then chaplain
to Theobald, and afterward successor to Thomas
as Archbishop of Canterbury, and John Belmeis,
afterward Archbishop of Lyons. At first,
Thomas, John, and Roger (Pont l'Evêque) had
banded themselves together for mutual aid in
securing those ambitious aims which they frankly
admitted; but as we have seen, Roger soon
became jealous, and his enmity and emulation
lasted through life, just as did the friendship of
those whom Thomas attached to himself.
Amongst such companions, and others who
afterward occupied many of the most important
sees in England, only supreme personal ability
could find much recognition, yet very soon after
joining the household Thomas was employed

PORTION OF REMAINS OF ARCHBISHOPS' PALACE AT OTFORD.

upon diplomatic services demanding great skill
and tact. His personality was all in his favour.
Unusually tall and powerful, handsome and
manly, with strongly-marked features, fine
prominent eyes, large, slightly aquiline nose, and
hands of unusual softness and whiteness, he had
abnormal quickness of sense, in sight, hearing,
touch, and smell; a peculiarity which remained
with him to the last. His bearing was naturally
majestic, his voice clear and resonant, his conversation alert and fluent, with great command of
language, and his expression quickly changing
from the animation of debate to an impressive
calm in repose.

Thomas early took minor orders, for he saw
that the path to power lay through the Church,
and his support was amply provided for by the
gift of the livings of St Mary-in-the-Strand, and
of Otford, in Kent, in 1143; and of prebendal
stalls in St Paul's and in Lincoln before the end
of 1154, in which year he was appointed Archdeacon of Canterbury, and Provost of Beverley,
to which were added many lucrative posts,
actually filled, as was the custom, with ill-paid
deputies.

Some time before this, however, Thomas had
found the results of his partially neglected education, and had applied himself with great earnestness to such studies as should make him, at
least, the equals of his companions.

About 1145, with the assistance of Theobald,
who took great interest in Roman Law and who
afterward established a lectureship at Oxford, he
spent more than a year on the Continent, at
Bologna and Auxerre, studying ecclesiastical and

civil law. In view of the fact that he was to become the great champion of the legal powers of the Church as opposed to those of the Crown, this experience was most important, for upon it were based the phenomenal success and the tragic end of one of the strongest and most rugged characters in England's history.

At this time the administrative authority of the Church was very great, and its labour in matters of litigation was constantly increasing. Diocesan courts had to be supplemented by many archidiaconal courts, and, to quote Dr Stubbs, "there was a vast increase in ecclesiastical litigation, great profits and fees to be made out of it; a craving for canonical jurisprudence . . . and with it the accompanying evils of ill-trained judges and an ill-understood system. . . . The archdeacons were worldly, mercenary, and unjust; the law was uncertain and unauthoritative; the procedure was hurried and irregular." To remedy this state of affairs, Theobald imported his masters of law, and established lectures in Oxford; but he also found them useful in his embittered contests with King Stephen; with Henry, brother of the king, and Bishop of Winchester, who, as legate of the pope, superseded the archbishop in certain matters, even in his own see; and with Hugh, Abbot of St Augustine's, Canterbury, who successfully maintained that he was independent of the archbishop, and subject only to the pope. In these involved intrigues Thomas soon took a part, and there can be no doubt that his sound judgment and quick appreciation of subtle points were highly valued by Theobald, who had the tact and self-control which were sometimes lacking when Thomas became his own master.

An early recognition of his services is shown by the fact that Thomas of London accompanied Theobald to Rome in November 1143, to oppose the claim of Henry of Winchester to be legate of the new pope, Celestine II., as he had been of Innocent II.   In 1144, Lucius II. succeeded Celestine, and the case was reheard, as was also the quarrel between Theobald and the Abbot of St Augustine's, which was decided in favour of the archbishop.   In June 1144, Theobald returned to England, confirmed in his position, without a rival or active opponent, and at some later date he was appointed papal legate.

In 1148 there was a convocation at Rheims by the pope, Eugenius III., to consider, *inter alia*, the election of William, nephew of the king, to the Archbishopric of York, which was opposed as illegal by Theobald.   The king forbade Theobald to leave the country, and threatened that if he did so he should be permanently banished. The ports were watched lest he should escape in disguise, but eventually, accompanied by Thomas of London and Roger of Canterbury (Pont l'Evêque) he crossed in a small boat, and was heartily welcomed by the pope as one who for the honour of St Peter had crossed the sea, though it was "more like a swim than a sail." For a long time Theobald and his companions were obliged to remain abroad.   Confiscations by the king were met by threats of excommunication by the archbishop, who carried on much of the business of his see from St Omer, and who impressed English and Normans alike with his

dignity, firmness, gentleness, and generosity to
the poor.   After a time, Theobald and his
companions returned to England, and he was
reconciled to the king.

At the council of Rheims, Theobald and
Thomas almost certainly met John of Salisbury,
who was to become one of the best friends, and a
biographer of the younger man ; and who came
to England in 1150 to take the position of
secretary to Theobald.

Soon after this a most important piece of
political business was undertaken by Theobald,
who is said to have employed Thomas as his
envoy to the pope.   As was to be expected, after
his quarrel with the king, the archbishop favoured
the party of Henry, Duke of Normandy (later
Henry II.), to whom he had pledged or renewed his
promise of support when at St Omer.   Theobald
opposed the succession of Stephen's son, Eustace,
and sent Thomas to Rome for letters from the
pope, forbidding his coronation.   In consequence,
when the nobles had sworn fealty to Eustace
at a great council in 1152, and Theobald and the
bishops were called upon to crown the young
man, Theobald refused.   He and his companions
were imprisoned in a house until they should
decide to obey the king, and when many of the
bishops protested against the refusal, Theobald
and those who sided with him escaped from the
house, dropped down the Thames in a small boat,
and took ship for Flanders.   Again there was
confiscation on one side, and threat to excommunicate the king and lay the country under a
papal interdict on the other side.   Stephen
relented, and recalled the archbishop, who in the

next year, when Henry, Duke of Normandy, was in England, arranged a treaty whereby the duke was to succeed Stephen. In 1154, during Lent, he entertained the king and the duke at Canterbury, when he oppointed Roger, one of the companions of his wanderings, to be Archbishop of York, and the other, Thomas, to succeed Roger as Archdeacon of Canterbury and Provost of Beverley, with other posts, as already mentioned.

On the death of Stephen on October 25, 1154, Theobald took the lead in inviting Henry of Normandy to occupy the throne, and during the weeks in which he was delayed at the siege of a castle in Normandy, Theobald acted informally as regent, and was very successful in maintaining peace amongst a very turbulent lot of almost independent nobles, and of mercenaries who were practically leaderless.

The new king landed in Hampshire, hastened to Winchester, and thence had a magnificent progress and triumphal entry into London, where he was crowned by Theobald on December 19. The king doubtless realised that the policy of the archbishop had been latterly guided by the keen brain of Thomas of London, and showed sound judgment in accepting the services of Thomas when recommended to him by Theobald. From the archbishop, patient, tenacious, wise and good, rather than brilliant, we must now part for awhile, but this chapter cannot close more fitly than with a quotation from a letter of several years later (1161), dictated on his deathbed, and written by John of Salisbury. It reproaches the king and Thomas for their long absence from the country, but it shows the feeling of love and trust with which Thomas was still regarded, after several years in the king's service, and it throws a pleasant light upon the character of the archbishop, of whom our record has been mostly of quarrel and stubbornness.   He writes to the king : " Let your loyalty move you, together with the affection for your children, from whom the sternest parent could hardly bear so long a separation.   Let the love of your wife move you, the beauty of the country, and that union of delights which it is impossible to enumerate—not to forget my own case; let my desolation move you, for my age and sickness will not enable me to wait long for your coming.   In this hope I wait.   With many a sigh I say, Will not my Christ give me to see him whom, at my desire, He gave me to anoint?"   And of Thomas he says : " He is the only one we have, and he is the first of our council.   He *ought* to have come without a summons, and unless your need of him had excused him, he had been guilty of disobedience to God and man.   But since we have ever preferred your will to our own, and have determined to further it in all that is lawful, we forgive him his fault.   We wish him to remain in your service as long as you stand in need of his services, and we order him to give his whole zeal and attention to your wants.   But permit him to return as soon as ever you can spare him."

CHAPTER II

WHOM THE KING DELIGHTETH TO HONOUR

THE new king had more than once had good opportunities of noting the abilities of Thomas. His earnest partisanship, his fidelity, his courage and resource under difficulties and temporary defeat, his quickness and clearness of judgment, and his power of swaying men, were qualities marking him as a most valuable assistant in the great work of settling and managing a disorganised kingdom. There are differences of opinion as to the extent to which Henry or Thomas was the real leader in the many important works they carried out, but it seems clear that however much he may have been helped and influenced by Thomas, Henry, who was brilliant, capable, and persistent, knew and initiated his own policy, and deliberately chose for his chancellor the one man in the kingdom who had proved his capacity for the work to be done. He probably overlooked one very important feature in the strong character of Thomas, one which was to cause great trouble between them, ending in the terrible death of one, and the almost equally terrible humiliation of the other. This was that curious fidelity to the master or the cause of the moment which was perhaps the strongest point, while, at the same time, it was in a sense the weakness, of a very fine nature. To a large extent it took the place of any theory of right or wrong :—when serving Theobald, the interests of Theobald were the only guide ; when serving the king, no personal preferences were allowed to stand in the way ; when serving the Church, not even his affection for the king, which was probably a far stronger influence than any fear of death, could make him deviate from the path he believed to be right in the interests of the Church. Thomas has been lauded as a saintly paragon, a man of unblemished perfection, and he has been decried as an unprincipled self-seeker, with a career of success checked only by his own overweening vanity and obstinacy. In reality, he stands between the two estimates—a strong, manly man, but very human, with the faults that correlate and in part spring from the very virtues that made him great.

We have seen how Theobald, the first great employer of Thomas, longed for his presence, even when at death's door, and we may be sure he felt that he was giving of his best when he offered his faithful and favoured archdeacon to the new king. This was quite in line with Theobald's general character. He had worked and waited, not only for the predominance of his see in ecclesiastical matters, but for the maintenance of peace in England, and for the consolidation of the royal power. Supporting Stephen on the throne, even while opposed by him in certain church matters, he had refused to recognise Eustace, because in the compromise whereby

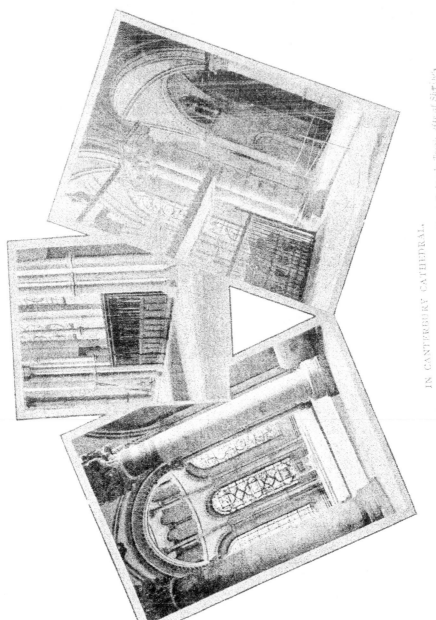

IN CANTERBURY CATHEDRAL.

Back Laing's Tomb, site of Shrine,
and Watching Chamber.

Antiquary.

Becket's Crown, with Chair of
St. Augustine.

Stephen was to be maintained during his life, with succession to Henry, the son of his rival the Empress Matilda, he saw the one hope for peace in the country of his adoption. By fidelity to this idea Theobald had become the leader of the Angevin party; the cause for which he had worked and waited, and even suffered, was established by the accession of Henry II., and it was only a step in the same course when he recommended to the king the very best man he knew.

It has been charged against Thomas that in deserting the Church for diplomacy, he was in some way untrue to his allegiance, but this is one of the very last accusations that should be brought against such a man. Though miracles and devotion, and the divine call have been embroidered upon the story of his early life by writers who wished to represent him as wholly saintly, the fact is that he deliberately chose "affairs" for his avocation. When he left his studies in Paris he did not enter into holy orders, but began business with Huitdenier. When he joined Theobald it was not to seek ecclesiastical preferment, but as a member of the household, and he soon took to the study of law. Even when Theobald was prepared to confer upon him the Archdeaconry of Canterbury—the most lucrative position below a bishopric in the whole Church of England—it was necessary to first make him a deacon. Thus diplomacy and politics were his proper, chosen sphere, and although his life was always chaste and regular, and became austerely religious after he was made archbishop, even in the Church his own proper work was guidance

B

and government rather than spiritual mini-
stration.

We do not know exactly when Thomas of
London became Thomas the Chancellor, but it
must have been immediately after the king's
accession, for a certificate issued in January 1155
bears his attestation with the new title.   Though
nominally the chancellor yielded precedence to
the lord chief-justice and a few other officials,
practically he was the most influential man in the
kingdom when he had the ability (as in the
present case) to make the most of the position.
His duties were a peculiar mixture.   He was
superintendent of the Chapel Royal, custodian of
all sees, abbacies, and baronies that might be
vacant, keeper of the great seal, and responsible
for all royal grants.   He had the right of attending all royal councils without summons, and had
access at all times to the private ear of the king.
In fact, he was the prime minister of an active
sovereign, taking a leading part in every act of
the king, and the intimacy that sprang up between
Henry and Thomas at once appears natural and
inevitable if we look through any collection of the
deeds, grants, and charters of the time.   For
while the great names attached as witnessing the
documents are constantly changing, one name
—"Thomas the Chancellor," or sometimes
"Thomas the King's Chancellor," appears in
every one.   Thus, while archbishops, bishops,
constable, chamberlain, nobles, and gentles of
varying degrees are frequently with the king, the
chancellor is ever at his hand.

The king began his reign with some active
travelling to various parts of his new kingdom,

visiting Oxford, Silveston, Northampton, King's Cliffe, Peterborough, Ramsey, Thorney, Spalding, Lincoln, York, Scarborough, Nottingham, Burton-on-Trent, Alrewas, and Radmore, all of them (almost certainly) during January and February; and while the great men in attendance are constantly changing, one man, Thomas the Chancellor, travels and sojourns ever with the king.

In the recreations, as well as in the more serious work of the court, the new chancellor took a foremost part. His keen senses and nice judgment gave him a refined and even a fastidious taste in matters of food and drink, of art, and of personal appointments and surroundings, in these respects forming a striking contrast to the king, who was almost ostentatiously vulgar in his personal tastes. The attractive personality of Thomas was briefly described in the last chapter, and a short description of the king, from a contemporary source may be of interest here. He was "a man of florid complexion, with red hair and grey eyes; careless in dress; hurrying over his meals; with hands and feet livid with wounds received in the hunting-field; restless at home; scarcely ever sitting down, except when engaged in business." He made the chancellor take his place in presiding over the royal banquets, at which he himself would sometimes take only a cup of wine before returning to his field sports, or after sitting awhile and wearying of the feast, would vault over the table as the easiest means of leaving the room.

In the hunting and the hawking loved by his royal master, Thomas notably excelled, for his natural abilities had been well trained in his holidays with Richer de l'Aigle and other sportsmen, and he could always render a good account of himself without allowing livid scars to mar the unusual whiteness and beauty of his hands, which remained one of his characteristics until his death. And even in the evening amusements of the king the chancellor took a leading and an intimate part, for Henry was a lover of "the game and play of chess," in which Thomas was also very skilful.

Before very long the king and the chancellor became inseparable friends, so that his old friend, Theobald, wrote to him, "it sounds in the ears and mouth of the people that you and the king are one heart and one mind." Another, writing to him, asks, "Who is ignorant that you are the next person to the king in four kingdoms?" while contemporaries spoke of him as one who "seems to be a partner in the kingdom," as "the king's governor, and, as it were, master," and as "a second Joseph, set over the land of Egypt."

It was not to be expected that such notable success could be secured without exciting envy and opposition. As on entering the household of Theobald, he met with unprincipled petty annoyances as well as more serious attack; and although his strength and energy crushed or his magnanimity ignored those whom he was unable to win by his fascination, he was often greatly depressed by the struggle. He told his intimate friends that he was weary of life, and eager to leave the court, if it were possible to do so without disgrace. As time passed, however, the country

and the courtiers alike saw that Thomas was a
man of strong purpose and wise intent, and
opposition was overwhelmed by the hearty
support and personal attachment of men who
had at heart the real good of the land.

The daily allowance to the chancellor as a
member of the royal household was far from
being extravagant. It consisted of one plain
and two seasoned simnel cakes; one sextary of
clear, and one of household wine; one large wax
candle, with forty smaller pieces; and five
shillings in money. But, fortunately, Thomas
had no need to attempt to live within these
means. He retained his various church benefices,
to which others were added, including the
deanery of Hastings, which was a royal chapel
with a college of secular canons. Far more he
might have had, for so popular did he become
with the patrons who had the gift of great
preferments, that "by merely asking for things
as they fell vacant, he might have become in
time the one sole encumbent of all ecclesiastical
preferment." From the secular side, at the hands
of the king, he received the wardenship of the
castles of Eye and Berkhampstead, the former
including the service of 140 knights. The
great income thus secured was largely spent
in maintaining great pomp and state with "so
great a multitude of soldiers and serving-men
which followed him, that the king himself
sometimes seemed deserted by comparison."
Fitzstephen, one of his personal friends and
biographers, dilates at length and with much
enthusiasm upon the troops of attendants and
servitors; the wealth of gold and silver table-

ware ; the lavish and luxurious provision, regard-less of cost ; the crowds of nobles, knights, and gentles who enjoyed its unparalleled hospitality ; the voluntary homage of many barons ; the innumerable and valuable gifts of horses, hawks, hounds, garments, gold and silver plate, and money ; and the great emulation between men of rank who strove to introduce their sons into the household which was considered the best school of manners and high breeding in the country, and of which even the heir-apparent to the throne was willing to be a cadet.

When he travelled abroad, the chancellor was as gorgeous as in his appointments at home, and we shall see one instance in which his bravery well served his royal master ; but, meanwhile, had the king been of a jealous disposition he might well have said, as John is supposed to have done to the Abbot of Canterbury : " Thou keepest a far better house than me."

By dwelling too much upon these luxuries and extravagances, it is possible to obtain quite a false idea of the character of the chancellor. Even his ostentation was undoubtedly a part of his deeply and wisely laid plan for securing influence and power, and well he used it in the interests of his king and country.

During the troubled reign of Stephen the country had fallen very largely into a state of anarchy. Violence, robbery, and imposition had been rampant. The greater cities maintained armed forces to protect their people, the wealthy men built castles (many hundreds were erected in Stephen's reign) to help in defending their own rights, and too often to help them to encroach upon the rights of others. The Church built religious houses for the succour of "the poor and them that have no helper," and by her divine authority and sanctity offered a stronger shield than the stone walls and deep moats of the barons could afford. Further, she healed the sick, fed the hungry, employed many of the industrious, and became the law-giver and peace-maker of the country for all private quarrels. At a time when the noblemen refused allegiance to the king, when the national parliaments failed to meet, when the judges were irregularly appointed and their sittings were irregularly held, when even the royal warrant was seldom backed with power for its enforcement, the Church was the one body in the land possessing unity and continuity of purpose, permanent organisation, wealth, influence, and a connection with all parts of the country and all classes of the people. The great princes of the Church indulged in political intrigue. Henry of Winchester openly worked and fought against his brother Stephen, and built a great castle in Windsor ; Roger of Salisbury, Alexander of Lincoln, and Roger of Ely built castles even more important, and more menacing to the peace of the realm than those of the barons. But stronger than the castle-building of these men was the influence-building and the law-making of Theobald, the wise archbishop.

William the Conqueror had separated the jurisdiction of the Church from that of the State at the time when he proclaimed the voice of the king to be the supreme law; for he saw that although the subdued people might submit to the loss of their rights of representation and popular law-making, the Church would not long be content with a final court of appeal other than that of Rome. Stephen's reign allowed the judicial power of the Church to grow abundantly, while that of the Crown was in obeyance; but Henry meant to be king in his own land. In this intention he was fully supported by his chancellor.

The first important act toward settling the kingdom was the disbanding of the foreign mercenaries who had served to prop Stephen upon his throne and to protect him from, though they could not overawe, his rebellious nobles. These irregular troops, often unpaid by their royal master, had degenerated into freebooters whose excesses were only checked when likely to arouse the active opposition of some noble or some city, and they were content to stay under Henry's rule on similar terms. But he drove them from the country, respecting the terrible William d'Ipres, who had been made Earl of Kent by Stephen, no more than he respected the draggle-tailed camp-follower. Thomas the Chancellor carried out the order, and robbers and cutthroats, whether they claimed to be soldiers or not, were forced to leave the land or take up legitimate occupations. " Then fled the ravening wolves, or they were changed into sheep; or if not really changed, yet, through fear of the laws, they remained harmlessly among the sheep."

The king required his earls and barons to meet him in council; at which times they were magnificently entertained, with Thomas the Chancellor as the king's delegate, presiding at the board. Castles which were deemed likely to

SOME PILGRIMS' RESTING-PLACES IN CANTERBURY.

St. John's Hospital.   St. Thomas' Hospital.   Ruins of Archbishop's Palace.   The Grey Friars.

be used against the interests of the king and his people, were levelled to the ground, and those who were tempted to resist the orders for such demolition might take warning from the activity and determination with which the king spent his first summer in besieging Cleobury, Wigmore, and Bridgnorth, and suppressing the rebellion of Hugh de Mortimer.   The chancellor restored the Tower of London, which was greatly dilapidated, employing so many men that the work was finished between Easter and Whitsuntide, which was considered almost miraculous.

Meanwhile, the common people began to breathe freely once again.   Crafts and industries flourished anew, fields that had long lain untended smiled in harvest, and travelling merchants were once more able to use the highways without fear of pillage.   In 1156 the king "relied upon the great help given by the chancellor" in suppressing the rebellion in Anjou; and in the same year Thomas was justice-itinerant in three counties.   In the spring of 1158, when Henry wished to arrange a marriage for his eldest son, Thomas was the ambassador to the court of Louis VII. of France, and his style was such that the description is worth condensing :—Carriages, each drawn by five horses; numberless clerics, knights, men - at - arms, falconers and huntsmen with their hawks and hounds, servitors arrayed in new and brilliant liveries; a menagerie of strange beasts; fierce mastiffs, each strong enough to conquer a bear or lion, guarding every carriage; on every sumpter-horse rode a monkey; enormous wealth of plate, bedding and utensils; sacred vessels and furniture for the chapel; huge cases of provisions, books, clothing, and money; and above all, iron-bound casks of English ale, so pure, sparkling, delicious, and wholesome as to charm every Frenchman who should taste it, and to fill him with envy of the islanders who could brew such exquisite liquor. From far and wide the French people, noble and simple, crowded to see the great procession, wondering whose train it might be, and when they were informed, they exclaimed, "If this be the state of the English chancellor, what must the king be!"

The habit of the King of France was to pay all the expenses of ambassadors, and Louis gave orders to the people of Paris to sell nothing to the visitors. But Thomas had anticipated this, and sent many purveyors, who bought great store in all the country round, so that when he reached his lodging he found three days' provisions for a thousand men.

His next expedition to France was a warlike one, when he accompanied the king to make good his claim to the fortresses of the Norman frontier, to the earldom of Nantes, and to the lordship of Brittany. On this occasion, in addition to managing the finances and introducing the method of scutage instead of the personal service of the vassals, Thomas equipped and maintained at his own expense 700 knights, and later, over 2000 knights and 4000 men-at-arms. In helmet and cuirass he rode at the head of his men, and led them in their assaults on castles and cities. Moreover, in single combat he defeated a valiant French knight, in addition to showing many other proofs of personal skill and daring. Other important events connected with the chancellorship demand our notice, but they properly belong to the next chapter, and it is only necessary here to mention a charge made against Thomas, that he had purchased the chancellorship as a step towards the archbishopric. This was made in a letter to Thomas himself, after he had been for some time archbishop, by Gilbert Foliot, Bishop of Hereford, and afterwards Bishop of London, who was the only man to openly oppose the election of Thomas to be archbishop. Although indeed the charge seems to have been groundless as regards the purchasing, such a transaction, *per se*, would have been considered perfectly legitimate at that day, and erelong it became universal. But that any wise man should have taken the chancellorship as a step to great church preferment, is quite unthinkable, for until Thomas made it, there had been no association between the two offices. Moreover, in his actual policy as chancellor he often, in the king's cause, rode roughshod over the prejudices and cherished privileges of the churchmen, so much so that he was spoken of as "a despiser of the clergy," a "persecutor and destroyer of holy Church"; and when the time came for his election to the archbishopric, Henry of Winchester, who performed the consecration could say no better than that he trusted the wolf would be turned into a shepherd of Christ's sheep, the persecuting Saul into an Apostle Paul. It was even rumoured that his old friend and master, Theobald, had threatened his excommunication. All this arose because Thomas treated the great lords of the Church just as he treated the feudal vassals of the king, in the matters of claiming their military subjection, razing their fortresses, imposing scutage, and in pressing what the king considered his legal claims in regard to alienated property and usurped rights.

And Thomas was much too wise to have done these things had he been a mere time-server, aiming at the archbishopric.

CHAPTER III

THE CONTEST IN THE KINGDOM:
CHURCH *versus* CROWN

IT was said of Thomas that "when he put on the chancellor, he put off the deacon," and there can be no doubt that he entered into the gaiety and frivolity of the court, into its political intrigues and its sports and recreations, in a way that could not be approved by monks and churchmen, who still maintained the profession of austerity. Yet he kept his court (for the king's court was practically his) pure and moral —to which fact there is ample contemporary testimony.

He was not regarded as a friend of the Church, and doubtless even his old patron Theobald, who did not fully understand his character of firm loyalty to the master of the time being, felt some grievance at the apparently ungrateful conduct of one whom he had advanced to great position.

Mention has been made of the great extension of church jurisdiction in civil matters. This had been a special care of Theobald, and as the power of the church courts grew, there is no doubt they sometimes tended to favour

29

claims of the Church as against any or all outsiders. An important case in point was that of Battle Abbey and its dependencies, over which the Bishop of Chichester claimed full jurisdiction. The Abbot of Battle resisted this on the ground of a special exemption granted by William the Conqueror, when he founded the abbey. The case had long remained unsettled, and in 1157 the king ordered it to be argued before himself, at Colchester. In attacking the Conqueror's exemption, the Bishop of Chichester argued that it was not lawful for "any lay man, no, not for a king, to confer ecclesiastical liberties and dignities upon churches, or to take them away when once they had been conferred; unless by the permission or with the confirmation of the Pope." At this Henry flew into ungovernable rage, and with a terrible oath, said to the bishop: "You imagine, by your craft and subtlety, to overturn those royal prerogatives with which God has been pleased to invest me; but, on your oath of fealty, I charge you to submit to correction for these presumptuous words against my royal crown and dignity; and I charge the archbishops and bishops here present to do me justice upon you, agreeably to the rights of the crown granted me by God Most High. Nothing can be clearer than that you are acting directly against my royal dignities — that you are labouring to deprive me of the privileges due to me of ancient right."

The excitement in the court was enormous. Those who were present included the Archbishops of Canterbury and York, the Bishops of London, Chichester, Lincoln, and Exeter, the Abbots of St Augustine's (Canterbury), of Hulme, and of Battle, the Earls of Leicester and Salisbury, Henry de Essex, constable, William, the king's brother, and many other nobles. On the storm that followed the king's words, broke the calm, persuasive voice of the chancellor, warning the Bishop of Chichester to guard his tongue more carefully, for that he had violated his oath of allegiance. When the Abbot of Battle rose to defend his cause, the king refused to hear him, saying, "It is not for your prudence, henceforth, to make good your claim ; it is my part, and my own royal prerogative to defend it. The decision of the business is my concern." Thereupon the court was adjourned for a space, and on its re-assembling, Thomas the Chancellor pronounced a long and eloquently-argued judgment against the Bishop of Chichester. He stated that the Abbot of Battle had but striven to maintain privileges granted to his abbey by William the Conqueror, amongst them, the exemption from episcopal jurisdiction.

It was the pleasure of the king to confirm all the privileges, "not" (as he turned to the bishop) "for the purpose of setting you at naught, but with a view to defending by sound reason those royal rights which you have been pleased, in our hearing, to call frivolous."

Later, in his capacity as archbishop, Thomas was to oppose and defy the king in matters very similar to those in which he now supported him, and this instance, typical of many, is given in some detail simply to show the contrast between the action of the chancellor, and the action of the same man when he became archbishop. It has been said, in explanation of his apparent inconsistency, that the circumstances were not precisely parallel, and that the later attitude was due to increased knowledge of the facts and a conscientious change of opinion. This may be true to a large extent, but it does not explain the objections raised by Thomas himself when the king wished him to become archbishop, and his argument that if he took that post he would be obliged to oppose certain projects of the king which, as chancellor, he could support.

When Theobald pressed the claims of Thomas for the chancellorship, although he was largely swayed by a wish to serve the king and country, he doubtless also thought that he was placing in a most influential position, one who would be a friend to the Church. And when the king urged and almost forced the acceptance of the archbishopric, we know that he believed he was thus securing the help of the Church in transferring judicial powers from itself to the Crown. Both Henry and Theobald misjudged their man, and failed to appreciate his unswerving loyalty to the master of the moment. With many of the personal qualities that would have made a splendid knight-errant, Thomas had that kind of fidelity which was the finest quality in the good mercenary soldier. He fought not for any abstract principle, and worked upon no personal theory of what was right, but with whole-souled earnestness strove even to the death, for the cause to which he was pledged. As Theobald's man, he was prepared to use his best efforts

CANTERBURY CATHEDRAL, AND PART OF MONASTIC BUILDINGS,
FROM PRIOR'S GREEN.

against even the king : as Henry's man, even his personal love for Theobald did not make him swerve from his duty to the king : and when the affairs of the Church were entrusted to his care, the Church became his one mistress, to whose interests not even the king should make him disloyal.

It is possible, by casuistry and subtle twisting of the evidence here and there, to show that Thomas was conscientious and consistent all through. It is possible, also, to show that he was an ungrateful, inconsistent, self-seeking adventurer. Either demonstration requires forced special pleading, and probably no just estimate of his character can be formed without full realisation of his loyalty to the master, rather than to any abstract "cause."

It is difficult to say how far the establishment of our present system of courts of justice was influenced by Thomas the Chancellor. He is commonly credited with being the founder of the Court of Chancery; and, during Henry's reign the Courts of Exchequer, of Common Pleas and of Chancery were formed to take definite departments of legal work, leaving to the original Court of King's Bench all matters not definitely assigned to one of the others. The growth of these courts was gradual, and although it began early in the reign, when Thomas was chancellor, we do not know exactly how far it was the gradual unfolding of a prearranged scheme, or how far it was the outcome of increasing pressure of work. At any rate, during the first eight years of the reign, great strides had been made in the direction of increasing the power of the

Crown, and the efficiency of its courts of law, and something had been done to check the pretensions of the Church.

But Henry saw that the first *great* opposition to his plans was to come from the ecclesiastical power, and when the death of Theobald, in 1161, left the primacy vacant, the king thought he saw his way to a step of the greatest political importance, a means of placing his own personal friend and strongest supporter at the head of the Church in his kingdom. The step was opposed by Thomas even more strongly than it was by the churchmen, who largely smothered their real feelings; but the king was imperative. He was in no hurry about the matter, for he was actively campaigning on the Continent, and found his chancellor so useful that he could not spare him to attend the dying bed of his old friend Theobald, though the poor lonely prelate wrote those piteous letters from which an extract has already been made (p. 14).

It is hard to believe that the king had not fully discussed the succession to the archbishopric with his trusted chancellor, either during the illness or after the death of Theobald, but contemporary writers assure us that when the king approached Thomas on the subject, a year after the see had become vacant, the suggestion came as a complete surprise. In his astonishment, pointing to his own finery, and scarce believing the king to be in earnest, he said: "A pretty saint you wish to put over that holy bishopric and that famous monastery." That the matter had been discussed by churchmen and politicians, we know, and that it had even been raised in the presence of Thomas himself, for, during an illness when he was visited by the Prior of Leicester, he had stated that he knew three poor priests in England whose promotion to the office he would rather see than his own; and that if he were appointed he must forfeit the favour either of God or the king. After this, he had evidently dismissed the matter, and when the king stated his wishes, treated them, first without seriousness, and then with firmer opposition. The king was supported by the strong representations of the Cardinal of Pisa; and after solemnly warning the king that his election to the see would mean the rupture of their friendship, Thomas reluctantly assented.

Though the king had much authority, he did not even pretend that he had the right to appoint an archbishop. The see was filled by election, by the bishops and abbots, and the monks of Christ Church (the Cathedral); and to persuade them to accept the man of his choice the king sent Hilary, Bishop of Chichester, and his old opponent, Walter de Luci, Abbot of Battle, Richard de Luci, his brother, Bartholomew, Bishop of Exeter, and Walter, Bishop of Rochester, brother of the late primate. To Richard de Luci, Chief Justiciary of the realm, the king was especially impressive. "If I were lying dead on my bier," he said, "would you endeavour that my first-born, Henry, should be raised to the throne?" and on receiving the expected assurance, he added, "Then I wish you to have no less care for the promotion of the chancellor to the See of Canterbury."

There was some real opposition to the election,

first by the monks of Christ Church, who urged that only a monk ought to have been suggested, and according to some of the chroniclers freely and unflatteringly discussed the tastes and habits of the chancellor. Eventually their scruples were overcome, and then came a second election, at Westminster, at which there were further objections, although only one man, Gilbert Foliot, Bishop of Hereford, had the courage to voice his opinion openly. The justiciary, de Luci, had been provided with very great powers by the king, and according to a declaration made by Foliot himself in later years, his opposition was met by a threat of banishment for himself and all his relatives. Thus all objection was silenced, and Thomas was elected to the most important post in the Church of England, although he was not even a priest.

His consecration caused difficulty. The Archbishop of York, as the highest official in the Church; Henry of Winchester, as precentor of the province; Walter of Rochester, as archbishop's chaplain, and one of the Welsh bishops in right of seniority, all claimed to perform the rite. Eventually, Thomas was ordained a priest by the Bishop of Rochester, on June 2, and consecrated archbishop on the following day by the Bishop of Winchester, in the presence of the Bishops of Ely, Bath, Salisbury, Norwich, Chichester, Chester, Exeter, Lincoln, Rochester, Llandaff, St David's, St Asaph, and Hereford.

Meanwhile, the new archbishop meant that there should be no misunderstanding as to where his allegiance lay. He had already personally warned the king that his election to the archbishopric would mean a breach between them, and on the day of his election he arranged for Henry of Winchester, in the name of all the electors, to request of the young Prince Henry, who was representing his father, that Thomas should be discharged from all obligations contracted during his chancellorship; and to this the prince agreed.

Thus Thomas the archbishop ceased to be the king's man, and became God's man; and his first official act was to arrange that the Feast of the Holy and Undivided Trinity, which had been irregularly held, and on different dates in different places, should in future be always held on the octave of Whitsun Day, the day of his consecration.

His outward habits underwent little change. He still spent extravagantly, entertained lavishly, and gave generously. Even when at court, his personal life had been pure, his tastes refined, and his influence very strong upon what one of his biographers calls "the wild beasts of the court." We have a little evidence that personal simplicity was combined with much display, for at the time when his private band of music had been the admiration of both the French and the English armies, a curious host, surprised that night after night his bed was unused, found him sleeping for choice on the boards of the floor. Some of the biographers tell of his mortifications and austerities after becoming archbishop, but he never paraded them; it was not until after his death that they were known to more than a few intimates, and we shall see in a later chapter that even his nearest friends had no idea of the extent of his self-mortification until they stripped his body for burial. Outwardly he was still somewhat ostentatious, not only when in his own country, but even when in banishment; so much so that some of his truest friends remonstrated with him, suggesting that his style and extravagance gave hold to the enemy.

The young warriors who had surrounded the chancellor were replaced by a court of scholars and clerics around the archbishop; and as he need not now lavish his means upon private armies for the king's wars, he gave great sums to the relief of the poor and to the building of churches and religious houses. Theobald had doubled the subscriptions of his predecessor to charitable funds, and Thomas doubled the charities of Theobald.

Not long after his own election, Thomas translated Gilbert Foliot from the See of Hereford to that of London, and addressed to him letters of praise and commendation which either indicate very great magnanimity, or a very subtle desire to conciliate the one enemy who had dared to speak openly. Probably Foliot thought the latter was the object, for, in 1166, he returned to the charge, stated that the electors of the archbishop had been coerced by the king's people, in spite of "the loud protest of the whole realm, and the sighing and groaning of the Church of God so far as she dare give voice to her complaint." He said, further, that fear of the chancellor had swayed them greatly. He had already "plunged his sword into the heart of his mother Church, and drunk deep of her blood" (in the matter of scutage), and a second blow was feared, unless the churchmen forwarded his ambition. And in conclusion: "Thus did you enter into the sheep-fold, not by the door, but by climbing up another way." This opposition, in which the bishop was supported by many of the clergy, shows that the archbishop was believed to have been no friend to the Church when in the king's service, and that even after he had made the change of allegiance his path was far from smooth. Foliot's remonstrances were frankly addressed to himself, and show that here was the same sort of opposition, misunderstanding, and jealousy as had been met in the household of Theobald, and in the early days of the chancellorship.

No opposition, no difficulties were allowed to change the purpose of the archbishop, and before long he was to come into conflict with his late master on many points.

The friction that arose out of confiscated church property and alienated rights, produced bitter feeling enough, and we shall have occasion to notice some particular instances; but the stern fight occurred on important matters of principle, where there was much to be said for both sides, and where each party may well have been convinced of the absolute justice of its contention.

In the early Christian theory, all Christians had been amenable to the Church, whether they were civil or ecclesiastics; and this had only been modified by the command that Christians should submit themselves to "the powers that be." Thus, in a Christian country, all the people (being Christians) must be fully subject to the

law of the Church as well as to the law of the
land.   But as the law of the Church was one of
brotherly love, and as Christians who had aught
against each other had been commanded to "tell
it to the Church," it was felt that while a
Christian must submit to anything the civil court
might inflict, he could not consistently take
matters before a civil court.   Gradually the
Church allowed this principle to become dis-
torted.   Christians applied to the civil courts in
spite of clerical objections; and eventually,
though the Church could not prevent its
members being plaintiffs, it adopted the theory
that clerics could not be parties to any civil court
proceedings, nor subject to the civil jurisdiction.
As the clerics were very numerous, including
great hosts of choristers, parish clerks, monks,
and friars, as well as the regular clergy, an
enormous number of people were shielded from
the action of the common law.   If these people
had really been devout children of the Church,
willing to abide by her great principles of love
and charity and uprightness, all would have been
well, but unfortunately many a churchman made
his religion a cloak for heinous crimes, cared
nothing for the highest punishment the Church
could inflict (excommunication), and was safe
from the arm of the law of the country.   This
was the state of affairs as it appeared to Henry
II., and this he proposed to radically alter.

There can be no reason to believe that
Thomas wished to encourage or protect evil
livers.   Even when chancellor, he had shown the
greatest possible severity to one of his household
who had betrayed the wife of a friend.   At the

CHRISTCHURCH GATE, CANTERBURY.

same time, while probably fully aware of abuses in the Church, he felt that they ought to be remedied by strengthening, and not by weakening the authority of the Church over her own children. Further, the Church still claimed the right to judge all cases where (*a*) the plaintiff was a widow, or an orphan under age; and (*b*) where the action dealt with usury, breach of faith, payment of tithes, or any matter relating to a church benefice; and this Thomas was prepared to maintain.

The king was, perhaps, a little tactless in his first step against the Church, for it involved an objection to the archbishop's retention of his archdeaconry after obtaining the higher office. The holding of many enormously lucrative offices by one man was doubtless very wrong from many points of view, but perhaps the objection might better have been raised during the years of the chancellorship, when the great revenues of the archdeaconry had helped to furnish soldiers for the king's wars and entertainment for his courtiers. It was an attack personal to Thomas, and he felt that it was just one of those matters of pure Church government with which the king had no right to interfere. On the other hand, the king probably felt that the system of pluralities was recognised by all honest church-men (not themselves pluralists) as a fault, and that in defending it in his own case Thomas would have to face a charge of being actuated by selfishness and covetousness rather than by any love for the Church. One reason suggested for the retention of the archdeaconry is unwillingness to allow it to be filled by a partisan of the king, and however this may be, when at last the archbishop submitted, such a partisan was appointed.

Meanwhile, under cover of an authority from the king, which his majesty afterward refused to support, on the ground that it was not used as intended, the archbishop proceeded to eject by force many illegal holders of lands belonging to the Church, thereby rousing a host of enemies, and annoying the king, who wished all such causes to go through the regular courts. Though he raged at the moment, however, Henry was willing to forgive; and when he landed at Southampton at Christmas 1162, and Thomas took the young Prince Henry (who was still living in his household) to meet his father, the king opened his arms and embraced his old friend most heartily, and they conferred together long and familiarly.

For some time in the next year the king and archbishop travelled together. "Thomas, Abp. of Canterbury" appears as the first name attesting many deeds, and on March 17 the king was in Canterbury, magnificently entertained by the archbishop, and together they attended the procession of the monks.

In July 1163, at a council at Woodstock, the king proposed to transfer certain customary fees of the sheriffs, consisting of or including the "Danegeld," to the royal treasury; and this was successfully opposed by Thomas, firstly, because he contended that the sheriffs earned the fees; and, secondly, because they were only paid by custom, not by legal right, and therefore might at some time be remitted, but if made into a charge for the royal treasury they would become a fixed tax for all time. Of course, such opposition was annoying to the king; but worse was quickly to follow, for in the same month a direct conflict arose between church and lay jurisdiction, when Simon Fitz Peter, recently a justiciary, complained that he had been insulted in the court at Dunstable by Philip de Broc, canon of Lincoln, who had been acquitted on a charge of homicide by the diocesan court, and had resisted arraignment by the justiciary. The king declared that there must be a new trial, to which Thomas agreed on condition that it should be before a Court Spiritual, and shortly afterward de Broc was tried at Canterbury, when he was acquitted on a charge of homicide, but received heavy sentence for resisting the king's officer.

At the same time Thomas was pressing claims for the restoration of church property, proceeding against small and great, including a suit against the Earl of Clare for the recovery of lands at Tonbridge; but these actions were in accordance with the law, and for the moment the king was friendly. But busy tongues were whispering all manner of accusation against the archbishop. As the old chroniclers say: "Nothing could now be said or done by him without being perverted by the malice of the wicked—insomuch that they even persuaded the king that, if the archbishop's power should go forward, the royal dignity would assuredly be brought to naught;— that, unless he looked to it, for himself and for his heirs, the crown would be at the disposal of the clergy, and kings would only reign so long as pleased the archbishop." Probably this persuasion of the king is a little over-stated, and in any case the royal suspicion was a plant of slow growth.   But it was constantly growing ; and even some of the king's speeches, which may have been intended as defence of the archbishop's loyalty, were twisted to sound like royal boasts of the churchman's servility.   For instance, it is recorded that at Windsor, in August 1163, the king made "an ungracious speech about Becket's having absolved William de Eynsford, to gratify the king."

In October of the same year, the question of principle was first raised upon which the great division and struggle between Church and Crown was to occur.   A great council was held in London, called for the purpose of formally acknowledging the Archbishop of Canterbury as the primate of all England.   This was pressed by Thomas and his friends, and strongly opposed by the Archbishop of York (the old opponent, Roger of Pont l'Evêque).   The king also raised the immensely important question of the "Customs of the Realm."   He was moved to this course by a case which had come before him in York five years earlier, wherein a Scarborough man complained that a certain rural dean had extorted from him a bribe of twenty-two shillings to withdraw an unsupported charge of adultery against the complainant's wife.   The royal edict had forbidden any criminal charge to be brought on the evidence of less than two witnesses, and the king summoned the rural dean, who made a defence which he was unable to substantiate. The king ordered him to be regularly tried, but the Archbishop of York, the Bishops of Durham

and Lincoln, and the treasurer of York contended
that as the dean was a cleric he could only be
tried by churchmen, and gave a sentence which
the king refused to recognise, stating that he
would appeal the matter to Theobald, Archbishop
of Canterbury. He also roundly accused the
archdeacons and deans of extorting from the
people by these means—more money than was
received by the royal treasury. A hurried
summons to Normandy caused the king to drop
this particular case, but the whole subject was
reopened at the first convenient opportunity: the
council in London. The king then roundly
charged the archdeacons and their courts with
venality, excessive severity to lay offenders, and
excessive leniency to clerics, and demanded that
churchmen accused of crimes should henceforth
be amenable to the lay courts.

To this, both the archbishops and all the
bishops, with the exception of Hilary of Chichester,
were resolutely opposed, and after long argument
the churchmen promised to obey the "Customs
of the Realm," *salvo ordine suo* (excepting our
order), while Hilary promised to obey them *bona
fide*. The king was greatly incensed at the
opposition, removed his son from the tutelage of
Thomas, resumed the custody of the castles of
Eye and Berkhampstead, and left London at
once. The archbishop soon followed, and over-
taking the royal train near Northampton had
an interview outside the city, for the king said
that the town was not large enough to hold
their two great retinues. The king insisted on
the submission of Thomas, demanding of him,
"Are you not the son of one of my villeins?" to

which the archbishop replied that even "the blessed Peter, prince of the apostles," was of lowly birth. The king reminded him that Peter died for his Master. "And I, too," answered Thomas, "will die for my Lord when the time shall come," a remark which was treasured in after years as having been prophetic.

Neither arguments nor threats moved the archbishop, and for some time the bishops continued to support him resolutely; whereupon the king employed Arnulf, Bishop of Lisieux, and others, to convert the bishops one by one, and to try to induce the pope to compel the obedience of Thomas. The Archbishop of York and the Bishop of Lincoln (though they had been parties against the king in the original case in 1158) were the first to submit to the royal will, and they were quickly followed by others, who were prepared to harass the Archbishop of Canterbury when they had the support of the king and a chance for their own aggrandisement. The claim of York to a position of equality with Canterbury was revived and pressed, Gilbert Foliot declared that the See of London was independent of Canterbury, and the Abbot of St Augustine's, Canterbury, a Norman, forced upon the monks by the king, contended that his abbey was also completely independent.

Late in the year, Hilary, Bishop of Chichester, as a special envoy from the king, met Thomas at Lenham, in Kent, but with unavailing arguments; the pope urged Gilbert Foliot to mediate in the matter; and in December the pope sent special envoys with expostulatory letters from himself and the cardinals. At length a meeting was arranged at Oxford, when the archbishop agreed to obey the king "in bona," or so far as was right.

To celebrate and ratify this royal success a great council was called at Clarendon, near Salisbury, and attended by the two archbishops, twelve of the bishops and a very large company of nobles. At this time Thomas was satisfied that the papal commands had been misrepresented, and refused to confirm the consent he had verbally given. For three days he stood alone, resisting alike the threats of his enemies and the entreaties of his friends. At length he submitted, and is quoted as saying, "It is my lord's will [probably meaning the pope] that I forswear myself. I must incur the risk of perjury now, and do penance afterward, as best I may." Even then the matter was not settled, for when the king had drawn up sixteen "Constitutions," which he said embodied the "Customs of the Realm," the archbishop denounced them as contrary to canon law, and refused to seal them. Even this determination, however, seems to have been over-ruled ; three copies of the Constitutions were sealed, and the archbishop rode away from the conference covering himself with reproaches. The council broke up, and further informal conferences followed, but resulted in nothing.

These Constitutions are so important to a proper understanding of the quarrel between the archbishop and the king, that they may well be given in full, in spite of the space they will occupy.

I. Of the advowson and presentation to churches : if any dispute shall arise between laymen, or between clerics and laymen, or between clerics, let it be tried and decided in the court of our lord the king.

II. Churches of the king's fee shall not be given in perpetuity without his consent and license.

III. Clerics accused of any crime shall be summoned by the king's justice into the king's court to answer for whatever the king's court shall determine they ought to answer there; and in the ecclesiastical court for whatever it shall be determined that they ought to answer there; yet so that the king's justice shall send into the Court of holy Church to see in what way the matter shall be there handled; and if the cleric shall confess or be convicted, the Church for the future shall not protect him.

IV. No archbishop, bishop, or exalted person shall leave the kingdom without the king's license; and if they wish to leave it, the king shall be empowered, if he pleases, to take security from them, that they will do no harm to the king or kingdom, either in going or remaining, or returning.

V. Persons excommunicated are not to give bail, *ad remanentiam*, nor to make oath, but only to give bail and pledge that they will stand by the judgment of the church where they are absolved.

VI. Laymen shall not be accused, save by certain and legal accusers and witnesses in presence of the bishop, so that the archdeacon may not lose his rights, or anything which accrues to him therefrom. And if those who are arraigned are such that no one is willing or dares to accuse them, the sheriff, on demand from the bishop, shall cause twelve loyal men of the village to swear before the bishop that they will declare the truth in that matter according to their conscience.

VII. No one who holds of the king in chief, nor any of his domestic servants, shall be excommunicated, nor his lands be put under an interdict, until the king shall be consulted, if he is in the kingdom; or if he is abroad, his justiciary, that he may do what is right in that matter, and so that whatever belongs to the king's court may therein be settled, and the same on the other hand of the ecclesiastical court.

VIII. Appeals, if they arise, must be made from the archdeacon to the bishop, and from the bishop to the archbishop; and if the archbishop shall fail in administering justice, the parties shall come before our lord the king, that

REMAINS OF THE MONKS' INFIRMARY, CANTERBURY CATHEDRAL.

by his precept the controversy may be terminated in the archbishop's court, so that it may not proceed further without the consent of our lord the king.

IX. If a dispute shall arise between a cleric and a layman, or between a layman and a cleric about a tenement which the cleric wishes to claim as eleemosynary, but the layman claims as lay fee, it shall be settled by the declaration of twelve qualified men, through the agency of the king's capital justice, whether the tenement is eleemosynary or lay fee, in presence of the king's justice. And if it shall be declared that it is eleemosynary, it shall be pleaded in the ecclesiastical court ; but, if a lay fee, unless both shall claim the tenement of the same bishop or baron, it shall be pleaded in the king's court ; but if both shall claim of that fee from the same bishop or baron, it shall be pleaded in his court, yet so that the same declaration above-named shall not deprive of seizin him who before was seized, until he shall be divested by the pleadings.

X. If any man belonging to a city, castle, borough, or king's royal manor shall be summoned by the archdeacon or bishop to answer for a crime, and shall not comply with the summons, it shall be lawful to place him under an interdict, but not to excommunicate him, until the king's principal officer of that place be informed thereof, that he may justify his appearing to the summons ; and if the king's officer shall fail in that matter, he shall be at the king's mercy, and the bishop shall forthwith coerce the party accused with ecclesiastical discipline.

XI. The archbishops, bishops, and all other persons of the kingdom who hold of the king in chief, shall hold their possessions of the king as barony, and answer for the same to the king's justices and officers, and follow and observe all the king's customs and rectitudes ; and be bound to be present, in the judgment of the king's court with the barons, like other barons, until the judgment proceeds to mutilation or death.

XII. When an archbishopric, bishopric, abbacy, or priory of the king's domain shall be vacant, it shall be in his hand, and he shall receive from it all the revenues and proceeds, as of his domains. And when the time shall come for providing for that church, our lord the king shall recommend the best persons to that church, and the election shall be made in the king's chapel, with the king's consent, and the advice of the persons of the kingdom whom he shall have

D

summoned for that purpose. And the person elected shall there do homage and fealty to our lord the king, as his liege lord, of life and limb, and of his earthly honours saving his orders, before he is consecrated.

XIII. If any of the king's nobles shall have refused to render justice to an archbishop, or bishop, or archdeacon, for himself or any of his men, our lord the king shall justice them. And if by chance any one shall have deforced our lord the king of his rights, the archbishops, bishops, and archdeacons shall justice him, that he may render satisfaction to the king.

XIV. The chattels of those who are in forfeiture to the king shall not be detained by the church or the cemetery, in opposition to the king's justice, for they belong to the king, whether they are found in the church or without.

XV. Pleas for debts which are due, whether with the interposition of a pledge of faith or not, belong to the king's court.

XVI. The sons of rustics shall not be ordained without the consent of the lord in whose lands they are known to have been born.

Meanwhile the pope himself was weakly endeavouring to avoid a breach with any of the parties. Refusing to give to York the "legation of all England," which was demanded by the Archbishop of York and the king; he offered to give the legation to the king, with power to give it to any one he chose, subject to the consent of the Archbishop of Canterbury. At the same time he wrote to Thomas, telling him of the useless concession he had made. Further, royal messengers were sent to the papal court, who secured an order that Thomas must consecrate the Abbot of St Augustine's without any act of submission, and reported on their return that the messengers of the archbishop continually slandered the king.

During these intrigues there was no obvious

and open rupture.   In April 1164, Thomas, with
ten bishops, and in the presence of the king,
consecrated the conventual church at Reading;
but when, in August of the same year, he
attempted to gain audience of the king, he was
refused.   It was probably at this time that he
made two attempts to leave the country secretly,
to lay his case personally before the pope; for
when an interview was at last granted (and it
seems to have been in September 1164), Henry
reproached him for trying to run away.

Immediately after this, the case of John, the
king's marshal, came to a head.   He had laid a
claim in the archbishop's court to a property
known as Mundham, parcel of the archiepiscopal
manor of Pagham, Sussex.   He was non-suited,
and appealed to the king, making oath that
justice had been denied him.   The archbishop,
summoned to answer this charge before the
king's court in Westminster, made no appearance,
but sent a plea of ill-health, and stated that the
case ought to be heard in his own court, from
which its removal had been secured by perjury.
Some of the archbishop's enemies rejoiced, for
they thought that at last his proud spirit was
broken, and that he would fail to attend the
great council at Northampton, to which he was
summoned for October 6.   The king intended
the whole proceeding to be humiliating to the
prelate, for instead of summoning him as had
always previously been the case, as one entitled
to an honoured place in the council, he sent the
summons by the Sheriff of Kent, as if for a
common criminal.   In no criminal guise, however, did Thomas mean to appear.   Remembering

that on a former occasion Henry had pronounced
Northampton too small for their two great
retinues, the archbishop engaged ample room
in advance, and approached the city with a
magnificent company of attendants and servants.
On nearing the gates he heard that the king
had placed his own retainers in the lodgings
provided for the archbishop's suite, and at once
sent an embassy to the king to say that unless
the premises were at once cleared, he and all his
company would return to Canterbury. The king,
seeing the blunder in his tactics, gave way, but
he had not the civility to leave his hawking to
attend the council at the time for which he had
called it ; and when the archbishop waited upon
the king he was refused admittance to his
presence. The council refused to accept the plea
that illness had prevented the archbishop's
attendance at the king's court in the matter of
John the marshal, and found that he was a
criminal "at the king's mercy," a sentence involv-
ing forfeiture of all his movable property. Then,
although no mention had been made of them in
the summons, many new charges were brought
by the king. First, the payment of £300 received
as warden of the castles of Eye and Berkhampstead was demanded. Thomas replied that
the money had been spent on repair of the castles
and of the Tower of London, but as no order
from the king was produced for such repairs,
the claim was supported by the court. Five
hundred marks spent by Thomas in the war of
Toulouse was claimed by the king as a loan ; a
similar sum, borrowed from a Jew for the same
purpose, was also claimed, though Thomas said

the king had promised to repay it. Next day, another sum of thirty thousand marks was claimed on account of all the revenues paid into the exchequer from vacant bishoprics and abbacies while Thomas was chancellor. The council supported the king, on the technical ground that Thomas did not produce orders and receipts for the expenditure of these moneys, though the defendant protested that he had spent every penny in the king's service and with his authority, that no mention of these charges had been made in the summons, and that at the close of his chancellorship he had received a full and regular discharge. He asked for delay that he might consult with the bishops, and the king swore that he would suffer no delay beyond the morrow.

Early next day there was a conference with the bishops, who almost all looked upon Thomas as a fallen man, and while some offered personal sympathy, none, save Henry of Winchester, gave any practical support. After the meeting, going into the great hall of the monastery at which he was lodged, Thomas missed the busy obsequious crowd of warriors and churchmen, knights and scholars who had previously thronged his court. With an instant perception of the dramatic possibilities, he sent his serving-men to bid poor folk attend him, which they did in great numbers, and were flattered when the worn, haggard, but still magnificent man told them how their prayers were his strong defence in the hour of his trial, when he was deserted by those whom he had long fed and clothed. The same day (Saturday, October 10), Thomas again appeared before the council, and offered to submit to a fine of two thousand marks in satisfaction of the alleged debt, but no definite conclusion was reached.

Sunday was devoted by the king to councils, while Thomas was confined to his rooms by illness, as also on the next day, when the king, thinking the malady a pretence, sent two earls to examine the patient. On Tuesday, the 13th, the bishops urged Thomas to resign the archbishopric and throw himself upon the king's mercy, thus averting grave dangers which threatened the Church and saving himself from charges of treason for breaking his feudal allegiance, and of perjury for violating the Constitutions which he had, however unwillingly, sealed at Clarendon. To which Thomas replied: "Our enemies are pressing upon us, and the whole world is against us: but my chief sorrow is that you who are the sons of my mother—the Church—do not take my part. Though I were to say nothing, all future ages would declare that you deserted me in the battle,—me, your father and archbishop, sinner though I am. For two whole days you sat as judges over me, and were a mote in my eye and a goad in my side—you who ought to have taken part with me against mine enemies. And I doubt not that you would sit as judges over me in criminal causes, as you have already done in civil matters, before this secular tribunal. But I now enjoin you all, in virtue of your obedience, and in peril of your orders, not to be present in any cause which may be moved against my person; and, to prevent you from doing so, I appeal to that refuge of the distressed, the Holy Roman See." And after further exhortations he concluded, " Be assured of one thing : though enemies press hard upon me ; though this frail body yield to their persecution, because all flesh is weak ; yet shall my spirit never yield, nor will I ever, by God's mercy, turn my back in flight, or basely desert the flock committed to my care."

Amongst the common people, rumour had been wildly flying for a couple of days. It was whispered that the king intended to put out the eyes, or cut out the tongue of the archbishop ; so that when he decided to personally say the mass on Tuesday, October 13, before proceeding to the council, the people thronged in and about the church. The archbishop wore his most sacred vestments, including the pallium, reserved for occasions of the utmost importance, and with his procession of priests and choristers entered the church. To the surprise of all, instead of approaching the high altar, the procession turned into the chapel of St Stephen, although it was not the day of that saint. A whisper went round that the selection of the altar of the first martyr meant that Thomas himself might be a martyr before the day was over. Sobs burst forth from the emotional people, the archbishop himself was moved to tears, and soon the whole crowded congregation shook with sobs and weeping. After a long pause the rich full voice of the archbishop was heard chanting the introit for St Stephen's day—" Princes also did sit and speak against me," and when he had gone through the whole service and turned to give the benediction, a hush fell over the kneeling mass of people, his figure was erect, and his face, showing no trace of his recent illness and dejection, was illumined with bright confidence.

Leaving the church in his magnificent robes, he proposed to walk forthwith to the castle and the council, but certain of his friends feared the king might consider such a course defiant, so he adopted the simpler dress of a canon regular. Doubtless he feared violence, for he hid a portion of the sacred wafer in his clothing, and bore his archiepiscopal cross, thereby placing himself in sanctuary. The enthusiasm of the crowd was great, and caused fear in the minds of the servants of the castle, so that as soon as Thomas and his immediate followers had entered, the gates were closed and the portcullis came thundering down. The peaceful bishops, thinking the king would regard the cross as a sign of distrust, tried to have it restored to its proper bearer, and Foliot, the Bishop of London, saying, "Good man, he always was a fool, and ever will be," tried to take it away by force.

The king did not enter the hall, but summoned the bishops and nobles, one by one, to an inner room, until Thomas was left alone with his two chaplains, Herbert of Bosham and William Fitzstephen, and a few guards. After a noisy discussion and clashing of arms which made the archbishop and his chaplains fear fatal violence, the king and his party entered the hall, and Thomas was asked whether he had, in violation of his oath of allegiance to the king, appealed to the pope. His reply was firm and temperate ; whereupon the nobles were enraged at the defiance of the king's authority, and some of the bishops, led by Roger of York, begged the

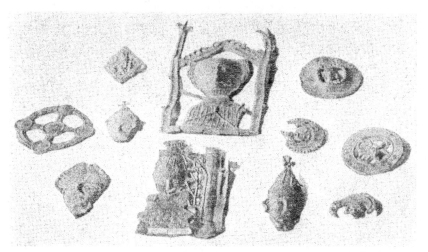

Some Pilgrims' Signs.

Slate Mould, for casting Pilgrims' Sign of Crucifixion (obverse), and Rings for suspending Signs, etc. (reverse).

PILGRIMS' SIGNS AND MOULDS, IN THE MUSEUM, CANTERBURY.

archbishop to yield, but only to be answered, "Get thee behind me, Satan."

Again the council retired to consult, then the bishops re-entered the hall, and with Hilary of Chichester as their spokesman, charged Thomas with inconsistency in having made them subscribe the "Constitutions," which involved fealty to the king, and now bidding them, on their allegiance to the Church, to support him in defying the king. He replied that all which took place at Clarendon promised loyalty, "except in matters touching the honour of the Church"; and finding him immovable, the bishops ranged themselves on the other side of the hall, as a sign of their failure. The nobles then came forth, headed by the Earl of Leicester, who sorrowfully addressed the archbishop, concluding with the words, "And now hear the judgment of the court." But the archbishop stopped him, denying the king's right of judgment, stating that the power of the Church is to that of the Crown as gold is to lead, reminding them that he had appealed to the pope, and charging the earl to obey God rather than man.

Then, bearing aloft his cross, and accompanied by his two faithful chaplains, Thomas strode majestically toward the door of the hall. At this ignoring of the king's authority there was a great outburst of jeers and execrations. Taunts and disgraceful epithets were hurled at the man whose power was broken, even by some who had been his friends and some whom he had fed, clothed, and raised to position. At each step that he took the tumult grew louder and fiercer. Some of the younger men picked up filth and refuse from amongst the rushes on the floor, and hurled them toward him, while others pushed and crowded in his way, frenzied with excitement, half ready to tear him to pieces, yet checked by his calm demeanour, his noble bearing, the memory of his old position and prowess, and the fear of offending against his sacred office. For a while he controlled his temper, until, as he neared the door he stumbled over a billet of fire-wood laid in the way, and almost fell to the ground, whereupon his persecutors burst into fresh taunts and peals of derisive laughter, and the foremost pressed nearer than before. The archbishop's patience could stand no more, and turning to bay he cried to a knight who called him traitor, "But for my sacred office I would make you rue that word"; at Ranulf de Broc he hurled a reminder that one of his relatives had been hanged; and the brother of the king, Earl Hamelin, he denounced as a lout and a bastard. Thus checking the few foremost enemies, he again turned to leave the room, and at about this point the order of the king that he should be allowed to depart peacefully, began to quieten the crowd.

From the gate of the castle, which had been locked against the crowd, the gate-keeper was missing, but the archbishop's horse-keeper opened the gate, in a way regarded by some of the chroniclers as miraculous.

Without the castle an immense concourse waited, saddened and angered by rumours that the archbishop had been murdered, and when he appeared there was an enormous ovation of cheers and enthusiasm, and he rode through a surging, rejoicing multitude, bearing aloft the cross with one hand, and blessing the alternately cheering and sobbing people with the other.

The rest of the pitiful story of the struggle need not be told at length, although it dragged over several years. After leaving the castle, Thomas asked for the royal safe-conduct, which the king refused, saying that he would consult the council on the morrow. There can be little question that he intended to force the archbishop into fleeing the country as an outlaw, without funds or influence; and to a large extent he was successful. Later in the day, a few nobles who professed to be still friendly to Thomas, informed him of a plot against his life, and that night, disguised, and with only three attendants he made his way into the fen country of Lincoln-shire. For eleven days he wandered, travelling by night, hiding by day, until on October 25, he reached Eastry, a couple of miles south-west of Sandwich, in Kent. On November 2, possibly spurred by hearing that an embassy from the king to the pope was sailing on that day from Dover, and by the fact that he had not received answer from the pope to his own appeal from Northampton, he embarked with his three companions in a small open boat, almost certainly from Sandwich, and landed at Gravelines, where he found lodging in a barn, and whence he wrote to the pope.

On November 4, he found shelter in a monastery near St Omer, and on the 6th and 7th was in St Omer itself, at the same time as the king's embassies to Louis of France, to the pope, and to the Count of Flanders.

About November 25, a great and imposing embassy from the king reached the court of the pope at Sens, and four days later arrived the archbishop with his paltry train of poor attendants.   Thomas laid before the pope the Constitutions of Clarendon, and his own pontifical ring, begging that he might be removed from the great office into which he had been thrust against his will, and where he felt that he had failed.   The pope bade him retain his archbishopric, pronounced six of the Constitutions to be separately acceptable, but the whole to be intolerable, and advised Thomas to retire to the Cistercian Abbey of Pontigny, in Burgundy, where he was hospitably entertained for two years.

At Christmas, Henry formally confiscated all the property of the See of Canterbury, and sent into exile all the relatives, servants, and known friends of the archbishop.   Possibly with a view to adding insult to injury, he made Ranulf de Broc custodian of the see, who took up his residence in the archbishop's palace at Saltwood Castle.   Meanwhile, as the pope was in difficulties, an exile from Rome, and opposed by a strongly-supported anti-pope, he did not feel able to help his archbishop as he probably would have liked to do ; but, in July 1165, he instructed Gilbert Foliot, Bishop of London, to associate himself with the Bishop of Hereford in admonishing the king *re* his relations with the archbishop.   This they did, but with no result, and the pope urged them to further efforts.   About October 14, 1165, Thomas himself wrote a long letter to the king, but with no result ; and, in April 1166, the pope felt called upon to move further in the matter. He addressed a letter to all the bishops, abbots, etc. (except the Bishop of York), appointing Thomas, Archbishop of Canterbury, as legate of all England, except the Bishopric of York. To Thomas he wrote authorising steps against all who had done violence to the property of the Church, but definitely refraining from dictating anything about the king's person. In May he instructed all the bishops suffragan of the See of Canterbury to compel restitution by all those who at the king's command had taken benefices previously held by the archbishop's nominees; the penalty of refusal to be anathema without appeal. And later in May he ordered the Archbishop of Rouen to teach the king more respect for the See of Rome, and better treatment of Thomas, failing which the king should be punished.

Thus supported, Thomas wrote two letters, pleading with the king, but received no answer. Then he threatened excommunication, but hearing that the king was seriously ill, contented himself with making his threat public, denouncing the Constitutions, and excommunicating seven of the king's councillors. Henry responded by threatening to expel all Cistercians from his dominions if the Order continued to shelter the archbishop, who therefore removed from Pontigny to the Benedictine Abbey of St Colombe, at Sens, which was under the special protection of the King of France. The king and the Anglican bishops under his influence appealed to the pope, and asked him to send legates to England to settle the dispute, but this was impossible, since he had already appointed Thomas his legate. The pope appointed "arbitrators," but neither party would submit to their arbitration ; and thus the negotiations dragged on until January 1169, when Thomas unexpectedly appeared before the king at Montmirail, abased himself and threw himself upon the king's mercy, excepting, however, matters touching "God's honour and my order," which meant that he still refused full assent to the Constitutions. Henry drove him away in anger, and he shortly thereafter excommunicated two disobedient bishops and fourteen usurpers of church lands, and announced that if Henry did not repent before February 2, 1170, the whole of England should be laid under interdict.

New attempts were made to patch up the matter, and both sides were urged to consent to personal reconciliation, without mention of the Constitutions ; and Thomas was induced to petition on November 18, 1169, for reinstatement of himself and his adherents in the king's favour and in enjoyment of all their rights and properties. To this Henry half-heartedly assented, but soon thereafter completed arrangements for his young son, Henry, to be crowned king by the Archbishop of York, the old rival of Thomas. Both Thomas and the pope forbade this as illegal, but the ceremony was performed on June 14, 1170 ; and almost immediately the king seems to have realised that his defiance of the Church had gone too far. He hurried back to France, met Thomas, said no word about the Constitutions, but promised full reparation to the archbishop and his adherents, and to be "guided by the archbishop's counsel" in the matter of reparation to the See of Canter-

bury for his defiance of its rights in the affair of
the coronation.

Meanwhile the offence of Roger of York had
been even greater than that of the king.   He had
defied the pope's direct prohibition, and it was
said that he had made a change, very offensive to
the pope, in the wording of the coronation oath, so
the pope suspended and very severely censured
the archbishop and all the bishops who had taken
part in the ceremony.   Thomas learnt that the
report *re* the oath was false, and begged the pope
to lessen the sentence ; and at the same time had
meetings with the king, at which it was agreed
that they should return to England together and
exchange the kiss of peace.   At the last moment
Henry pleaded inability to travel, and asked
Thomas to sail under the escort of John of
Oxford, one of his bitterest enemies ; but hearing
of a plot between the Archbishop of York, the
Bishops of London and Salisbury, and the Sheriff
of Kent, to intercept him on landing and to seize
any papal letters he might be carrying, Thomas
made his own arrangements for sailing, landed at
Sandwich on December 1, and proceeded to
Canterbury, where the people received him with
great joy and enthusiasm.   The king's officers
met him with a demand for the unconditional
absolution of the bishops who had been suspended,
and he agreed to absolve those of London and
Salisbury if they would swear to obey the pope.
This they refused to do, and, with Roger of York,
sailed to complain to the king.

Thomas essayed to visit his former pupil, the
young king, who now, although only fifteen years
of age, was keeping a court of his own.   On the

way he was met by messengers ordering him, in the young king's name, to go and perform his sacred ministry at Canterbury. There, however, day after day passed, until Christmas, without any appearance of the king for the reconciliation he had promised, and without any restitution of property or rights. In his own castle of Saltwood the de Brocs were firmly established, and insolently indifferent to his protests, and against them he heard many complaints from the tenants, neighbours, and poor folk. Even while he was on his way to visit the young king, Thomas heard that a vessel of French wines consigned to him at Canterbury had been seized at the port by Ranulf de Broc, who had beaten and killed some of the sailors, and imprisoned others in Pevensey Castle. A complaint to the young king secured an order for immediate redress, but the de Brocs were in nowise tamed—they saw clearly that Henry did not mean to support the archbishop, and that the peace between them was an unstable matter. Therefore they lay in wait to seize the archbishop, and failing in that intention, they hunted in his parks, carried away his dogs, beat his servants, robbed the pack-trains bringing food for his household, and, in derision, cut off the tail of one of his pack-horses. The leaders in these doings were Ranulf de Broc, his brother Robert, who had been a clerk and a Cistercian monk, but who had returned to a secular life, and their nephew John.

On Christmas Day, at high mass, the archbishop preached from the text, " Peace on earth to men of good will," and in the early part of the address, speaking of the troublous times, said there had already been one martyr Archbishop of

THE PILGRIMS' SNAIL.

Helix pomatia, *compared with the well-known* Helix aspersa *(two)*, Helix nemoralis, *and* Cyclostoma elegans *(two)*.

PILGRIMS' FLASKS, IN THE MUSEUM, CANTERBURY.

Canterbury, and there might soon be another. He broke into tears and sobs when he spoke of himself as being shortly about to leave the world, and the whole audience was deeply moved. Then, waxing vehement, he denounced those who misrepresented him to the king, and the bishops who had taken part in the illegal coronation. He excommunicated two vicars who had resisted his officers, and also the de Brocs for their outrages.

Henry's actual intentions, and the reasons for them, do not seem very clear. Probably he was frequently swayed to and fro, with much difficulty in finally deciding. The advisers of the young king evidently felt that the enormous popularity of the archbishop, wherever he went amongst the Anglo-Saxon people, threatened a possible rising against the Normans, for in ordering his return to Canterbury, they forbade him to linger in towns. Probably he was not so tactful as he might have been, for his progress back from London was slow; he received great crowds, gave confirmation to large numbers of children, and worked many miracles of healing. Of all this, however, Henry can have known little when he gave an order, on or about Christmas Day, for the personal arrest of the archbishop, naming three commissioners for the purpose, who sent to the young king at Winchester for a party of knights to effect the arrest, and set guards at both the English and the continental ports to prevent any possibility of escape.

Fate had not ordained, however, that these commissioners should make an arrest. Roger of York and the two excommunicated bishops had reached the king on December 26, and so had

E

messengers saying that Thomas was making triumphal progresses through the country, followed by an enthusiastic rabble, and by an armed force with which he besieged towns, and threatened to drive the young king from the land.   Henry was furious, and broke into uncontrollable rage.   " A fellow," he exclaimed, " who has eaten my bread has lifted up his heel against me!   A fellow who first broke into my court on a lame horse, with a cloak for a saddle, swaggers on my throne, while you, the companions of my fortune, calmly look on. Of the caitiffs who eat my bread, are there none to rid me of this turbulent priest?"   The words were spoken in great anger, but four of the knights, Reginald Fitzurse, William de Tracy, Richard Brito, and Hugh de Morville, took them as a command, and started forthwith for England, where they visited Saltwood, and took council with the de Brocs.

CHAPTER IV

THE MARTYRDOM

THOMAS had more than once been warned of
Norman assassins, and when the four knights
reached Saltwood late on December 28, he was
quickly advised by friends. His preparation to
meet the danger was by confession to his chaplain
and old tutor, Robert of Merton, after which he
received communion in the cathedral, and was
stripped and scourged in the chapter-house.
This kind of penance had been his custom ever
since he became archbishop. At three o'clock on
the 29th he dined as usual, then retired to his
private room and conversed with his friends and
followers until the knights were announced, when
he ordered them to be admitted, and continued his
own conversation, not seeming to notice them.
They were attended by an archer, and seated
themselves amongst the monks, on the floor, near
the archbishop, without any salutation. When he
saw them he looked for some time in silence, then
addressed Tracy, who did not reply. After a few
moments, Fitzurse, looking pityingly upon the
archbishop, muttered, "God help thee," whereupon Thomas crimsoned with anger at the tone
from such a man ; and the knights asked whether

he would hear the king's commands in private or before his attendants. John, of Salisbury, suggested that the clergy should retire, and they did so, but very soon Thomas recalled them to witness what should occur. The knights charged the archbishop with disloyalty to his recent compact with the king, and he replied that he believed he had done his full duty. They then said the king had ordered that he should go and do fealty to the young king, and swear to make amends for his treason ; and, naturally, he denied that he had ever been guilty of treason. Point after point was raised by the knights and answered by the archbishop ; until at length they fell into an ungovernable frenzy which was not unusual with Normans of the period, raging like madmen, jumping about, waving their arms, and tearing their gloves. The archbishop was partly infected, and with a blaze of his old-time war-spirit said he knew they had come to kill him, but cared not and feared them not, for he made God his shield, and having once run away from the country would flee no more. He reminded them that three of them had sworn fealty to him, and they angrily left the hall, followed by his last words of defiance.

His friend John of Salisbury protested that Thomas should have suffered the men in patience, and referred the matter to his council. Thomas was calmed, and they all gradually came to think that the knights' visit had been a mere drunken frolic. Meanwhile the knights armed (or adjusted and exposed the armour which had been hidden under their peaceful garb), and gathered the men they had brought from Saltwood Castle, and from the Abbey of St Augustine. They also, probably,

SALTWOOD CASTLE.

revised the arrangements they had made to prevent any rising of the people in favour of the archbishop, for the Mayor of Canterbury had been ordered in the king's name to publicly forbid any assistance to the archbishop, and he had probably set guards at the gates and in the principal streets of the city.

Tuesday had been a fateful day for Thomas, the day of his birth, of his flight from Northampton; of his exile from England; of his vision at Pontigny, warning him of martyrdom; and of his return from exile. Some of those around him drew his attention to these facts, when a cellarman of the priory, who had been talking with one of the soldiers of the knights' party, said that the archbishop would never see the evening of Tuesday. At this and other more definite warnings he only smiled sadly, reminding his friends that he had often said in France that he should not live into the next year, and that only two days remained of the present one. In the early morning he had spoken gloomily, in a way the attendants did not understand at the time, but remembered afterward, of the possibility of any one reaching Sandwich before daylight, and had added—"Well, let any one escape who wishes to do so." It is very difficult to explain the whole conduct of Thomas on this fatal day, but it is clear that he knew the danger to be serious. Probably his feelings included weariness and despair, a certain gratification at the thought of martyrdom, and at the prospect of rest after long, heart-breaking struggles, with flashes of the self-willed opposition roused in a strong man by the nearness of his enemies, contempt for the men who were now threatening him, and perhaps an underlying thought that in the last resort the sanctuary of the cathedral or the interference of the common people, who almost worshipped him, would stay the knights from the fatal extreme. Now one, now another of these feelings came uppermost, controlling the action of the moment.

The conduct of the knights was equally vacillating and contradictory. In the heat of their passion, roused by the king's fury, they had left the court with hearts full of murder. At Saltwood Castle, reinforced by de Broc, who was furious under his recent excommunication, and sitting as they did, amidst the theatrical surroundings of an absolutely darkened chamber, that they might not see each others' faces, they undoubtedly planned murder. In the hearing of some of their followers they must have mentioned that the archbishop must die, but their conduct is only consistent with the theory that none of them in his cooler moments believed the extreme step to be necessary. They expected the archbishop to yield to all the wishes of the king, and foresaw for themselves certain glory as the instruments in forcing this obedience.

The knights were not long in making their military preparations after their interview with the archbishop, and soon returned to the palace. The gloom of night must have fallen over Canterbury and its cathedral, for it was the end of December, and the dinner (not a hurried feast), which began at three o'clock, had been followed by time for at least some conversation between Thomas and his followers, for the scene with the knights, and for their arming. When they returned to the palace they found the doors closed and barred, and their hammering with sword-hilts brought no response. They did not knock long, however, for they were probably guided by William Fitz Nigel, the archbishop's seneschal, who had left his service only that very afternoon, and had, in fact, met the knights and turned back to introduce them, on their first appearance. In any case, guided by some one who knew the palace, they went through the orchard to where one of the windows was being replaced, and where the builders' scaffolding stood. Here they probably found those "hatchets and axes" which are mentioned in the contemporary accounts as having been part of their armament, and with which they quickly hewed down the boarding placed by the builders over their opening in the wall. The knights thus gained the inner courtyard, from which the servants scattered in all directions, "like sheep before wolves," some of them running into the room to bid their master flee to the church. "But he, mindful of his promise that he would not flee from these mere murderers of the body, refused to fly. The monks pressed him, urging that it was unseemly to absent himself from vespers, which were just then being sung in the church. Still he remained unmoved, deliberately resolved to await in a less sacred place that blessed consummation which he had sought with many sighs and prayers: lest reverence for the sacred building might arrest the purpose of the impious and defraud the Saint himself of the desire of his heart. For he is reported to have said in the hearing of many, after his return from exile, 'Ye have here one true Saint and Martyr, Elphegus, beloved of God. The divine compassion will provide for you another, and without delay.' But when neither reason nor entreaty could persuade him to seek refuge in the church, he was seized by the monks, who pulled, carried, and pushed him, in spite of his opposition, and appeals to them to desist."

So they came near the cellarer's door to the monks' cloisters, the enemy seeming close on their heels. One or more who ran in advance had opened the door, where (apparently) they expected great difficulty with the bolt or bolts, so much so that some of the accounts speak of it as a miraculous opening. After entering the cloister, some wished to fasten the door, but the archbishop would not allow it. Noticing that his cross-bearer lagged behind, he ordered the crucifix to be brought forward, and made some hasty attempt to organise a formal procession. "He walked on slowly, last of all, driving the rest before him, as sheep before a good shepherd. For the love of God had so cast out fear that neither in gesture nor step could it be noticed. It was as far from his outward appearance as from the inner stronghold of his soul. Once he cast a glance over his right shoulder, perhaps to see whether the king's men pressed closely, perhaps to see that none barred the door."

Along the north and the east cloisters the party passed, and even in that short journey the archbishop had three struggles with himself and with his monks; his care for them urging them on, his contempt for the knights, his great natural courage, and his resolve to die a martyr,

THE TRANSEPT OF THE MARTYRDOM, CANTERBURY.

urging him to meet his enemies without the church. Twice in the cloisters he refused to go further, and as the chapter-house door was reached, he turned into that grand but unconsecrated room, determined to await his foes. But the monks, by force and by persuasion, brought him to the door in the south-east corner of the cloisters, leading into the north transept.

Meanwhile, without the palace and the cathedral, rumour was busy. Crowds of people had collected, and rent the air with cries and lamentations for the archbishop who had been, or was to be, cruelly butchered. The brethren in the cathedral, undisturbed by the tumult without, were chanting the vesper service, when two servants rushed into the choir, with faces full of fear. The brethren hurriedly broke up their service, and the story that the archbishop, was slain rapidly spread amongst them. Some ran for hiding-places or for the doors, a few tried to resume the service, and some, going to the cloister door, met the archbishop, who was welcomed by one with the words—" Enter, father, enter ; abide with us, that if need be, we may together suffer and be glorified. We have been as dead through your absence, let your presence console us."

The moment the archbishop entered the cathedral, Fitzurse, with drawn sword, appeared at the cellarer's door, at the far corner of the cloister. Turning back, he called to his comrades, " This way! King's men! King's men!" and in a few moments he was joined by the other knights, who proceeded along the west and south sides of the cloisters. Meanwhile the monks had drawn

Thomas into the transept, and without waiting
for all those who were with him in the cloister,
closed and began to barricade the door. This
the archbishop hindered, saying, "Make not a
fortress of the house of God; by suffering, rather
than by fighting, we shall triumph over the
enemy"; then as the door was thrown open, he
drew the foremost with his own hands, crying,
"Come in, come in with all speed." Again there
was just time to close the door in the face of
the knights, and some essayed to do so. Again
Thomas faced about, saying, "What do these
folk fear?" and when they answered, "The armed
men," he replied, "I am going forth to meet
them. Let all come into the Church of God who
wish. God's will be done." Again his friends
pressed around him, trying to force him to the
high altar, as the place of greatest sanctity and
safety, while some urged him to hide or defend
himself in the crypt, or in one of the many upper
passages. They forced him up a few steps toward
the choir, but he again shook himself loose,
bidding them go finish their vespers; and as they
hesitated, wavered, or fled, he stepped back to
meet the knights, who, with Robert de Broc,
now strode through the door, crying, "Where is
Thomas Becket, traitor to king and country?"
To this there was no answer; then Reginald
Fitzurse cried, "Where is the archbishop?" to
which Thomas replied: "Here; no traitor, but
archbishop. Reginald, if thou seekest the archbishop, thou hast found him." Then, turning
to the larger party of the knights, he asked,
"What will ye?" Whereupon some cried, "Thy
death," and others — or perhaps some of his

friends, cried, "Flee, flee," and he mildly answered, "I am ready to suffer in the name of Him who redeemed me; far be it from me to flee, or to move one step from the straight path of righteousness. In the name of God, touch not one of these."

Trying to remove him from the church there was much hustling for a few moments, one struck him with the flat of a sword, calling upon him to flee. Fitzurse seized him by the mantle, and others tried to thrust him on to the shoulders of William de Tracy, who stooped to raise him upon his back. At this rough handling, the archbishop's anger flared up. For a moment he simply resisted, and was helped by one of his sturdy followers (probably Edward Grim), who placed one arm around his master and the other around the pillar in the centre of the transept. Then, gathering his great strength, Thomas shook himself free of friend and foe alike, throwing Fitzurse from him with a violence that made him stagger, and crying, "Back! pander. Touch me not, you owe me fealty. You and your fellows are mad, to come thus, armed, into holy church." Furious at the rebuff, Fitzurse cried, "I owe no fealty against my loyalty to my lord the king. Strike! strike!" and raising his sword, rushed at the archbishop. As the blow fell, Grim interposed his cloaked arm, which partly turned the sword aside, but such was the force of the stroke that after almost severing the protecting arm, it glanced along the left side of the archbishop's head, wounding both head and shoulder, and tearing through the many garments on his arm. Though dazed by the shock, Thomas bent his

head, clasped and raised his hands, and in a few
words commended himself and the Church to God
and the saints. Grim, who had been dashed to
the ground, crept a few feet to the nearest altar.
A second blow (almost certainly from William de
Tracy) fell on the head of the archbishop, and a
third, on the same spot, caused him to sink on
his knees, his hands, still clasped, falling before
him, and his head gradually bending forward
until he lay flat on his face. As he fell, he
murmured some words, faintly heard by the
wounded Grim, who reports them as : "For the
name of Jesus, and the guarding of the Church,
I am ready to embrace death." As he lay prostrate, Richard le Brito struck a great blow, which
completely severed the top of the skull, and struck
the pavement with such violence as to break
his sword. Hugh of Horsea (sometimes called
Mauclerc) chaplain of Ranulf de Broc, who had
joined the others as they entered the cathedral,
was taunted with having struck no blow. He
placed his foot on the shoulders of the corpse,
thrust the point of his sword into the great
wound and scattered the brains upon the floor,
saying, "The traitor is dead; he will rise no
more. Let us go."

They turned to the door, where Hugh de
Morville, the only knight who struck no blow,
had been holding back a crowd of townsfolk who
had pressed after the knights; and with their
war-cry of, "King's men! King's men!" rushed
back through the cloisters. One man, who ven-
tured to lament the murder, was wounded by
them; then under the guidance of Robert de
Broc, they ransacked the archbishop's palace,

seizing money, valuable vessels, costly raiment, and the splendid horses from the stables for themselves and followers, and taking many papal bulls, charters and other documents, which Ranulf de Broc afterward forwarded to the king.

Then, in the darkness of the mid-winter night, mounted on their stolen steeds and laden with plunder, the knights started for their dark ride over the long fifteen miles of the Roman Stone Street, back to Saltwood Castle.

Little they recked of the actual murder, for they were men of blood and war, and they believed they had served and pleased the king; but they could hardly fail, in that age when the sanctity of the Church was so strongly regarded, to be conscience-stricken by the thought of their sacrilege.

Robert de Broc was left in charge of the plundered palace, and we shall return to his doings anon.

When the knights reached Saltwood Castle, they talked over their exploit, and each boasted of his part in the murder; but evidently they were uneasy and fearful of the vengeance of the Church, for next day they fled from Saltwood to South Malling, a manor of the archbishop's near Lewes —a ride of forty miles. Here they threw their weapons and armour upon a great table in the hall, which after supper "started back and threw its burden to the ground. The servants replaced the arms, but a second, still louder crash was heard, and the things were found to have been thrown still further off. Soldiers and servants sought in vain for the cause of this action, until

one of the knights suggested that the table was
refusing to bear sacrilegious weapons." Whatever may have been the truth of this story, it was
commonly believed, and the table was shown a
couple of centuries later. That conscience, or
fear of the Church was working, is shown by the
flight from South Malling to Knaresborough, in
Yorkshire, the property of Hugh de Morville,
who was justice itinerant of Northumberland and
Cumberland, forester of Cumberland, a great
land-owner in the North, and altogether the most
important member of the murderous band. From
this point the knights' careers are not entirely
certain, although many pieces of record and
evidence, laboriously collated and compared, show
us that the popular traditions associating them
with miraculous disease, disastrous wanderings
and death (in the Holy Land, in Mechlin, etc.),
under dramatic circumstances, are quite unre-
liable. For a time they were under a cloud, but
within a couple of years of the murder they were
fully reinstated at court, and some of them
quickly rose to important position, while all seem
to have been fairly prosperous. As a matter of
fact, the enemies of Thomas both in church and
in court, were in the ascendant, and although
there was a great display of homage for Thomas
the marytr, this was for a long time largely confined to the poorer people, and had no effect upon
the opponents of Thomas the politician. The
Church exacted penance for sacrilege, but had
no power to punish for the murder; since the
very principle for which Thomas had so stoutly
contended, prevented the trial of the murderer of
a priest by any but a clerical court, and the

greatest punishment in the hands of such a court was excommunication.

Not only as regards the murderers themselves, but also as regards the curse upon, and the rapid extinction of their families, tradition is at fault. The actual fact is that most of them established prosperous, influential, and even titled families, some of which can be traced to this day.

CHAPTER V

As the archbishop fell prostrate, almost the last of the churchmen fled to the high altar for sanctuary, or to other parts of the cathedral for hiding. But as the knights passed away, and the wondering, horrified crowd of townspeople began to press into the transept, the servants and the brethren soon gathered, cleared and closed the cathedral, and then probably assembled under Odo the prior to consult as to what should be done. Meanwhile, Osbert, the archbishop's chamberlain, brought candles to set on the altar in St Benedict's Chapel, near the body. He saw the terrible wound, where the top of the skull hung by a piece of skin, and, tearing his own shirt, bound up the head. Then the monks returned from their hasty conference, saw the body lying face downward, with the hands clasped above the head as if in prostrate prayer, and with the brains and the blood mingling on the head and on the pavement—" the blood brightened from the brain, and the brain reddened by the blood, as if the rose and the lily were beautifully blended together." When they saw this, they burst into loud lamentations; but soon they turned the body

80

SOUTH AMBULATORY OF CRYPT, CANTERBURY CATHEDRAL.

Approaching Burial-place of St Thomas.

over, and when they saw the calm beauty of the
countenance, wreathed in a smile, the eyes closed
in peaceful sleep, a rich colour warm upon the
cheeks, and with no disfigurement save one thin
streak of blood running from the right temple
across the nose and the left cheek, their cries gave
place to wonder and admiration.   Beneath the
body they found an axe, which Fitzurse had
dropped when he drew his sword, and a hammer,
used in breaking into the palace, and near it were
the pieces of the sword of le Brito.   The scattered
brains and blood were collected into vessels, and
the body was reverently placed on a bier, to be
carried to the choir, and laid before the high altar.
Tongues were loosed, and while the monks decried
the sacrilege, they said comparatively little of the
murder, some going so far as to say that the
death was the natural result of obstinacy, while
another observed, " He wished to be king, and
more than king ; let him be king."   But as the
body was taken to the choir, these murmurs were
hushed.   While the townsfolk still stood and
wondered in the transept, the monks, in the
"glorious choir of Conrad," sat around the bier,
in the soft mellow light of the great candles that
had not been extinguished after the vespers, and
commented in hushed whispers, while Robert of
Merton told the private life and secret austerities
of their dead master.   The early schoolmaster,
intimate friend, and confessor of the archbishop
told them of haircloth and the monastic habit
hidden for years under the sumptuous robes of the
prelate, and of constant scourgings and self-
mortifications in secret by the man whom they had
despised as luxurious.   One of the complaints

F

against Thomas had been that he who was no monk had been made abbot of the monastery (which office was involved in the archbishopric), and as Robert gave them, piece by piece, the evidence of his true monasticism, and of the humility which had led him to accept taunt and reproach rather than display his self-mortifications, the wonder grew and the excitement of the monks increased. When, in proof of his statements the aged confessor moved the outer garments, and drew into sight the monk's habit and the hair-cloth shirt, the brethren could contain themselves no longer, but burst into shouts of joy, crowded and knelt around the corpse, kissing the cold hands and feet, and crying, "Saint Thomas! Saint Thomas!"

At this sound the common people crowded into the choir to gaze upon him who had been proclaimed a saint, and just about this time began what was to develop into the characteristic observance of the cult of St Thomas. It has been said that his brains and blood were gathered up. As the body was laid before the altar, vessels were placed below the bier to catch any drops of blood that might fall, and after the saintship was proclaimed, Arnold, the goldsmith of the abbey, took a vessel, with water and cloths, to wash up from the floor the last traces of blood remaining on the stones. Some of the citizens now, or earlier, dipped their fingers or pieces of cloth in the blood-spots, and one of these, dipping a portion of his shirt, afterward washed the blood into a little water which he gave to his paralytic wife, who was completely cured of her paralysis. Leaving miracles for the moment, however, we may return to the doings of the monks. Early on the morning after the murder, word was brought to them that Robert de Broc, who remained in charge of the palace, had sworn that the body should not be buried amongst archbishops, and had threatened to drag it from the cathedral, hang it on a gibbet, tear it with horses, cut it in pieces, or throw it in some pond or gutter to be eaten by swine or carrion birds. He had declared, " By the body of St Denis, if St Peter had so dealt with the king and I had been there, I would have driven my sword into his skull."

In fear of this fresh violence, the monks determined to bury the body quickly and secretly in the crypt. They closed the doors against the town folk, and, headed by the Abbot of Boxley and Richard the archbishop's chaplain (who became the next primate), proceeded to unrobe the body. The number of garments was astonishingly great, probably because of the wearer's chilly disposition, and as they were removed, surprise was expressed that he whom they had believed to be portly with high living, was really very spare. Wonder, too, was excited by finding the black, cowled habit of the Benedictines, and, under all, a hair shirt and drawers, of exceeding roughness, covered with linen outside, to prevent any chance of being seen, closely fitting to the flesh and swarming with vermin—"boiling over with them, like water in a simmering cauldron." Revolting as this appears, it was then regarded as the very extreme of saintly self-mortification ; and to a man of the refinement and fastidious taste of Thomas, it

must have been an especially severe penance.
At the sight the monks first looked at one
another in silent amazement, then bursting into
mingled laughter and tears in their half-hysterical
joy at finding such a saint, they said to each
other, "See how true a monk he was, and we
knew it not." Then, deeming that he was more
truly cleansed by self-mortification than he could
be by washing with water, and dreading lest de
Broc might interrupt if they delayed, they washed
not the corpse. Leaving the hair garments,
linen shirt, and hose, and Benedictine habit, they
placed over him, as he had wished, the magnificent vestments in which he had been consecrated
archbishop. To these they added his official
robes and insignia ;—tunic, dalmatic, chasuble
and pall, gloves, rings, and sandals, the sacred
chalice and the pastoral staff; and laid the body
in a tomb of marble, which they buried in the
crypt behind the shrine of the Blessed Virgin.
Though many alterations have been made in the
crypt, which then contained many altars, shrines,
and chapels, the spot may still be seen, under
what is now the chapel of the Trinity, at the east
end of the cathedral; and behind the very
beautiful chapel of Our Lady of the Undercroft.

The remains of blood and brain were placed
outside the grave, the crypt with its many
chapels and altars was closed, and no funeral
service was rendered, because of the desecration
of the church. In the cathedral itself were all
the signs of deepest mourning, not for the
murdered man, but for the insult offered to God.
No mass was sung, no bells were rung, the flagstones were taken from the floor, and hangings

from the walls, the altars were stripped and the crucifixes covered from sight.   In this state the place remained for nearly a year, until on December 21, 1171, on the day of St Thomas the Apostle (with the sanction of the pope's legates), it was re-consecrated, with a mass celebrated and a sermon preached by Bartholomew, Bishop of Exeter.   During all this time the services, without music, were conducted in the unconsecrated chapter-house.

Almost immediately, if not on the very day of the burial, miracles began to be reported, and whatever may be the explanation given by modern scepticism, modern science, or modern faith, to account for the wonders, this, at least, is historically clear—that the stories of the earlier wondrous works were not invented or even encouraged by the monks ; and that the cult grew by force of the gratitude of those who believed they were healed, and who overcame great difficulties and dangers, to show their thankfulness.

When early reports of miracles came to the monks, they kept them secret, and mentioned them only in the chapter-house, probably partly because many retained something of their old jealousy against Thomas, and certainly largely because all were afraid of de Broc and his rude men-at-arms, dwelling in the palace.   The king, the nobles, and knights, the principal bishops and higher clergy frowned upon and disputed the stories of marvellous cures.   The Archbishop of York (the old enemy, Roger Pont l'Evêque) declared, when supporting the government's endeavour to suppress the miracles, that Thomas,

like Pharaoh, had perished in his pride. The de
Brocs with their following kept all the roads and
near bridges leading into Canterbury, and
guarded the gates of the city and the doors of
the hospices, with men who were charged to
intimidate, and, if necessary, to arrest any who
spoke of the miracles or praised the martyr. But
the matter became common talk, for the
enthusiasm of those who had lost their ailments
could not be suppressed. When deterred from
speaking openly, they only talked the more
amongst their neighbours and friends, and when
attempts were made to throw doubt or discredit
on the miracles, they replied somewhat after the
fashion of the man healed at the Pool of Siloam:
"Whether he be a sinner, I know not: one
thing I know, that, whereas I was blind, now
I see."

As one by one, and afterward in larger
companies, the people came to give thanks at
the tomb of the martyr, and to offer candles and
gifts of money, the monks were obliged to
appoint one of their number to sit at the tomb
and receive the offerings; and they early
appointed Benedict, one of their number, to
record the most interesting of the reported
miracles, and to sift the evidence, because the
de Brocs and their party were searching for
proofs of fraud to use against the monks.
Benedict was careful, and very obviously honest,
methodical, and sceptical of inexact evidence.
He gives particulars of the diseases, many of
them of nervous origin, admits that some of the
cures were imperfect at first and only gradually
became complete, while others were temporary

in their effects ; and tells of one perfect cure, made with what was believed to be the " Water of St Thomas," though really the liquid was a fraud.

Benedict begins his account by the story of three visions of the martyr seen by himself, and relates the first miracle as having occurred to the wife of a knight in Sussex. She was blind and infirm, and when she heard of the murder, three days after it happened, she hailed Thomas as a saint, and cried, " St Thomas, precious martyr of Christ, I devote myself to thee. If thou wilt restore the blessing of my lost sight and health, I will visit thy resting-place to pay vows and offerings." Immediately she received her sight, and in six days her strength was restored. She delayed her pilgrimage and the infirmity returned worse than before, but on making a second vow, she recovered at once, and, with husband and household, repaired to Canterbury to give thanks.

We do not know exactly when Benedict began to write his record, but Edward Grim, relating the miracle above detailed, says that it, and several other miracles were kept quiet for a time, as though they were not believed, until the very multitude of marvellous acts broke down the opposition of the impious. Benedict may have begun recording immediately, though the accounts were not published. Easter of 1171 saw a special wealth of miraculous cases, which was repeated at the same time in the next year, when Benedict became so overwhelmed with the work of recording that another brother, William, was called in to help. He had not the systematic mind of Benedict, and finding that even the two of them could not deal with the whole, he frankly says that he selected only those cases which were most fully authenticated, most interesting or most instructive, "following the truth, and not the order; for what came early or what came late there is neither leisure to attend to, nor does it make much difference." Some of William's narratives are of the same cases as dealt with by Benedict. In certain instances they are evidently only independent condensations of notes or evidence taken for Benedict's account, but in other instances they are the result of later investigation and the examination of additional witnesses; at times throwing interesting light upon the earlier accounts.

The earliest reported miracles were, naturally, from Canterbury, the neighbouring country, and London. Even from the first the careful Benedict seems to have made selection, though he wrote all down in the order in which he heard of them, for he does not give the story of the paralytic wife of the Canterbury citizen, which is given by Edward Grim as the earliest miracle. At first, most of the cases were of folk in humble position and the number of men and of women was about equal, but as the total number of wonders increased, the recorders gave less attention to healing of poor folk and of women, probably because they were so much more numerous, and, therefore, relatively less interesting than cases of men in position.

The second miracle recorded by Benedict was at Gloucester, on the fifth day after the martyrdom, when Huelina, a London girl of sixteen, was cured of a periodical swelling of the head which had occurred since she was five years old.

IN THE CRYPT OF CANTERBURY CATHEDRAL.

Original Place of Burial of St Thomas.

The next day a knight in Berkshire, one William Belet, was cured of a great pain and swelling of the left arm, which had kept him bedridden for three months; and on the next day (January 4) a poor, blind, Canterbury woman borrowed a rag that had been dipped in the martyr's blood, touched her eyes and instantly received her sight.   On January 5, William de Capella, of London, a priest who had lost his speech through paralysis, came to the monks saying that a vision had appeared to him, and thrice to one of his clerical friends, saying that if he would visit Canterbury he should be healed.   The monks gave him blood of the martyr, mingled with water, and he permanently regained his speech and resumed his sacred office.   The only other case recorded before Lent, is of Stephen, a knight of Hoyland, who was cured of an obsession which had haunted him for thirty years.

During Lent, 1171, William Patrick, servant, of Warbleton, was cured by vision of maddening pain in the jaw; Robert, son of a knight of Surrey, bedridden by liver disease for eleven weeks after ineffective treatment by London physicians, was cured by appeal to St Thomas; Alditha of Worth, near Sandwich, was saved from death in childbirth by touching with a handkerchief the martyr had blessed; Ulviva, principal of a leper hospital, witnessed the miraculous multiplication of some of the saint's blood in a wooden vessel; William of Bourne found that some of the blood, given to an unworthy pardoner, broke the pyx in which it was placed, and disappeared; the same William saved a child's life by wrapping it in St Thomas's pall;

the son of a Canterbury citizen regained his speech through drinking some of the blood-tinctured water, as commanded in a vision ; and Goditha, wife of Matthew, of Canterbury, afflicted with horribly swollen legs, was secretly carried to the tomb by two neighbours and touched with the tinctured water.   She at once began to amend, and continued improving daily until her full strength was regained.

Many more great acts, says Benedict, were done before Easter, but they were "small and almost to be despised" compared with those that came after.

Very soon it came to be recognised that the saint worked miracles in a few principal ways, viz. : — First, by virtue of a garment which he had touched or of water tinctured with his blood : Second, in answer to vows of pilgrimage or gift : Third, by unsought vision.   The blood and brains gathered on the first evening were mixed with water, and this was diluted again and again, so that it sufficed to supply a tiny phial or ampulla to each of the hundreds of thousands of pilgrims who flocked to the shrine in succeeding centuries.   These ampullæ became the special token of Canterbury pilgrims, just as the palm denoted one returning from the Holy Land, or the cockle-shell a votary from the shrine of St James of Compostella.   Vows of gift gradually took the general form of a promise of a candle of the length of the sufferer, or in some rare cases of wealthy people, of the weight of the sufferer : and it became recognised that many invalids began to amend, and some completely recovered from the moment when they were "measured for St Thomas." The vision is said to have helped many who knew nothing of the appearance of the saint until their description of his face, with the blood-mark from the right temple to the left cheek, caused the vision to be identified.

On Easter Day, 1171, a crowd of Canterbury people claimed admittance to the crypt, to which hitherto, people had only been admitted singly and in secret. They had heard of a man who claimed to have been possessed of a dumb devil for five years, who had wallowed and foamed on the floor, and thereafter received his speech and composure as promised by two figures seen in a dream. The townsfolk accused the monks of hiding the talent entrusted to them, envying the martyr his glory, and robbing the sick of the blessing of health. Many were admitted, two or three were cured, and on the following Friday the monks decided to open the crypt freely, whereafter the monks had to tend and comfort "sick folk lying in pain all about the church," and "the scene of the Pool of Bethesda was being continually renewed, great and wonderful miracles were of daily occurrence."

People of all conditions reported cures of almost all possible kinds of disease and injury; in some cases the saint gave a painless death to those in great suffering; in two instances he told the suppliants they should not recover, and gave his reasons; a girl falling down a deep well, was saved by the miraculous creation of a stout beam from wall to wall;—and so on, in almost endless variety. Even the dead were raised to life. How, then, could one wonder that in spite of the king and the Archbishop of York, and the party of de Broc, pilgrims wishing for healing, or anxious to give thanks and candles and gifts became every day more numerous.

Religious pilgrimages were no new thing. Herodotus tells us that 700,000 pilgrims was no uncommon number to take part in the annual festival at the shrine of Bubastes, in ancient Egypt; Charlemagne, at his council at Chalons-sur-Soane, in A.D. 813, protested against and attempted to restrain pilgrimages, as interfering with ordinary callings and unsettling the people. Even at the time of the death of Thomas, England was full of shrines, relics, roods, and other places of pilgrimage, all with more or less repute for miracles; for the Christian pilgrimages had begun about the fourth century and were popular all through Saxon times. Those who could not visit Rome, Compostella, or the Holy Land, had choice of many home shrines. To mention only a few, there were St Cuthbert, Durham; St William, York; St William-the-Less, Norwich; St Hugh, Lincoln; St Erkenwald, London; St Wulstan, Worcester; St Swithun, St Valentine, St Judoc, and others, Winchester; St Edmund, Bury; Saints Etheldreda and Withburga, Ely; St Thomas, Hereford; St Frideswide, Oxford; St Werburgh, Chester; St Wilfrid, Ripon; St Richard, Chichester; St Osmund, Salisbury; and St Paulinus, Rochester. In fact, every cathedral and many churches had a shrine of more or less importance. Amongst those of most note stood those of Our Lady of Walsingham, second only to St Thomas of Canterbury in the whole history of pilgrim-popularity, and of the Virgin, at Lynn, at Canterbury and at Westminster.   Westminster also had the relics of Edward the Confessor; Chester and Bromeholm had pieces of the true cross; St Paul's, London, had a great and famous rood in the churchyard; Wilsden and Bexley had noted statues of the virgin, and many village churches had their object of pilgrimage;—as the statue of Our Lady of Chatham, the holy rood of Gillingham, and the many altars and chapels at Faversham—all these on the pilgrims' road from London to Canterbury.

To give any fair idea of the number of relics, works of art, and what we should now call "curiosities," kept in monasteries and other religious houses and exhibited to the curious and pious, would take far more space than can here be spared; but Boxley Abbey (on the pilgrims' way from Winchester to Canterbury) rejoiced in two "subtelties," which were severely condemned by the examiners under Henry VIII., and this may be taken as a fair example of the others. Relics of saints, bones, and clothing, wonder-working statues and pictures and tombs, were scattered all over the country, and all were the subjects of pilgrims' visits and devotion.

It is not surprising, then, that when the miracles of St Thomas began to be noised abroad, the suffering and the unfortunate—even those who had already tried many shrines without success — should flock to the new fount of healing.

On the very night of the murder some of the monks had left Canterbury to lay the facts before the pope, and his legates were sent, many months later, to investigate the murder, but there

was then no thought of canonisation.   In the
next year, however, as the fame of the miracles
spread, the pope sent a legation to test the truth
of the stories, and they returned to Rome bearing
a tunic stained with the martyr's blood, a piece
of the pavement, and some part of the scattered
brain, of which portions are still preserved in the
reliquary of Santa Maria Maggiore.   As a result
of this enquiry, the pope wrote letters authorising
the canonisation of the martyr, and a council met
at Westminster to accept and confirm the suggestion.   The formal canonisation took place on
Ash Wednesday, February 21, 1173, and the
date of the martyrdom, December 29, was made
the feast of St Thomas of Canterbury.

As the popularity of the shrine and the value
of the offerings increased, the king, who could not
prevail to suppress the pilgrimages, insisted on
receiving half the gifts ; but soon the pressure of
public feeling overwhelmed even his power ; he
bowed to the storm and became a most devout
pilgrim.

The king was at Argenton, in southern
Normandy, when the news of the murder reached
him.   His grief equalled his previous fury.   He
put on sackcloth and ashes, declared before God
that he had had no part in the tragedy, and
remained alone in his private apartment for three
days, taking no food save milk of almonds, which
was used in extreme fasts.   For five weeks longer
he remained in solitude, refusing to do any public
business, and at the end of that time sent an
influential embassy to Rome, to submit himself
and his kingdom to the sentence of the pope, and
to prevent, if it might be, the excommunication

and interdict for which the King of France and important leaders of the Church were clamouring. For a long time the pope would not even receive the king's embassy, but at last he did so, and contented himself with excommunicating the murderers. Henry still felt uncertain, so crossed to England, refused to see any one who bore closed letters, and had the ports and coast guarded to prevent the delivery of any bull of excommunication or interdict.

From all parts of the Continent, however, and from many faithful friends in England, Henry heard how his connection with the murder was viewed by the people. Every little misfortune that befel him was attributed to divine wrath, and he soon began to think a further penance was necessary. On May 16, he went to Normandy to meet the pope's legates, on the 19th there was a great council at the Cathedral of Avranches, and on Sunday, the 21st, he swore on the Gospels that he had not ordered or wished the murder, but that as he feared his fury had suggested it and as he could not execute the murderers, he was ready to make satisfaction. He swore to obey the pope, to restore all property of the See of Canterbury, to renounce the Constitutions of Clarendon, to support 200 soldiers for the Templars, and, if ordered, to go on pilgrimage to Rome or Compostella, or on a three years' crusade to the Holy Land, or against the Moors in Spain. The young king swore to carry out all that his father had promised, and reconciliation with the Church was considered complete.

Still the affairs of both king and kingdom grew darker and darker, until, in the spring of

1174 the case seemed well-nigh desperate. The king was at Bonneville-sur-Touques in Normandy, fighting against his rebellious son, Richard, when the Bishop-elect of Winchester arrived there on Saturday, July 6* (old Midsummer Day), confirming urgent messages already sent from England, and adding fresh details of rebellion in Yorkshire, in the eastern counties and in the Midlands, with invasion of the kingdom by the Scots, and threatened invasion from Flanders in support of Prince Henry. The importance of the crisis was so evident to the Normans surrounding the king that one of them is reported to have exclaimed: "The next thing the English will send over to fetch the king will be the Tower of London itself." Prompt in this, as in other emergencies, Henry immediately decided upon the one dramatic step that would strongly affect the imaginations of his people, a pilgrimage to the shrine of the miracle-working saint who was supposed to have brought the troubles upon the country. Starting at once, with his queen, members of his family, and several important prisoners, he reached Barfleur early on the morning of July 8, and at once set sail in spite of threatened storm. As the gale rose during the voyage, Henry advanced toward the prow of the vessel, and with eyes raised to heaven prayed in a distinct voice, "If what I have in my mind be for the peace of my clergy and my people, if God have determined to restore such peace by my

* Accounts disagree as to this date. Eyton, usually most accurate, gives it as June 24; possibly because it is recorded as Midsummer Day; but the later date seems more probable.

ST DUNSTAN'S CHURCH, CANTERBURY.

First Stone of the Penance of Henry II.

arrival, then may He in His mercy bring me safe into port ; but if He have resolved still further to scourge my kingdom in His wrath, may it never be given to me again to set my foot on land." The storm blew over, and the party safely landed at Southampton on the same day as they left Barfleur (another account fixes the landing on the morning of July 10). Deferring all business save the sending of his prisoners to various safe custodies, and presumably leaving the ladies and the younger members of his party in Southampton or Winchester, Henry started on the morning of the 9th and rode steadily toward Canterbury, eating only bread and water, and avoiding the principal towns.

On Friday, July 12, after riding through the night, he saw in the early morning sunlight the towers of the cathedral, and of the other churches of Canterbury. At the sight he dismounted, and proceeded on foot, through the deep mire of a road puddled by recent heavy rain until the church of St Dunstan was reached, where he threw off his silken robes and his boots, and donned (unless he had been wearing them throughout the journey) a penitential horse-hair shirt, covered by a shirt of woollen, with a great cloak thrown over all, against the heavy rain. The bells of the city had commenced ringing as the royal pilgrim approached the gates, and crowds thronged the streets, noting that as the king trod the stones of the city, his steps were marked with blood. At the porch of the cathedral he knelt until he was raised and conducted into the cathedral. In the transept of the martyrdom he again knelt, kissed the stones on which Thomas had

G

fallen, and confessed to one of the dignitaries. In the crypt, at the tomb of the martyr he knelt and prayed for a long time, sobbing, groaning, and weeping bitterly; after which Gilbert Foliot, the old opponent of Thomas announced the king's penitence, promising that he would restore all rights and properties of the Church, and give forty marks yearly for candles to be kept constantly burning at the martyr's tomb. The king confirmed the bishop's promises, and received absolution, and the kiss of reconciliation from the Prior of Canterbury. Then, bowing so that his head and shoulders were within the martyr's tomb, clad only in hair-shirt and a linen cover, the king received five strokes with a rod from each bishop and abbot, and three from each of the eighty monks. Bruised and exhausted, temporarily broken in spirit, as well as in body, the royal penitent resumed his cloak and was then left all night, fasting, on the bare floor of the crypt. Next morning he attended early mass, visited all the shrines and altars of the cathedral, drank at the martyr's well, took a tiny phial of the blood-tinctured water, and returned to London.

Such a striking demonstration of the power of the dead saint over the living mighty monarch, made a profound impression; but its effect was soon emphasised and enforced even upon the king himself. On his arrival in London, his health broke down as a result of the mental and physical strain; but within a week he heard that on the very day of the completion of his penance the King of Scots had been taken prisoner at Richmond in Yorkshire, and soon after, that the

Flemish fleet had been driven back on the same day.

The demonstration was complete. No more could the martyr-saint be resisted. The king rose in haste from his bed of sickness, thanking God and St Thomas. William de Tracy determined at once to give to the saint his manor of Daccomb, in Devonshire; which is still the property of the cathedral. And that another actor in the demonstration was deeply affected is shown by the fact that William the Lion, King of Scots, signalised his release from captivity by founding the Abbey of Aberbrothock to the glory of God and of St Thomas of Canterbury.

CHAPTER VI

BEFORE the martyrdom of St Thomas, the
abbey and burial-place of St Augustine, who
re-established the Church of England, was a
more important foundation than the Priory of
Christ Church, even though the latter was
headed by the primate. This was largely
because, following the precedent set on the
death of St Augustine, the great men of the
Church, including the very archbishops who were
personally interested in Christ Church, were laid
after their deaths in what must be recognised as
the rival sanctuary. And in an age when relic-
worship and pilgrimages were developing into an
enormously popular, well-organised craze, the
possession of relics was the one thing tending
most strongly to the prosperity of a place of
worship. So strong was the feeling of proprietor-
ship in the breasts of the Augustinians that when
Cuthbert, the archbishop, wished to break
through the old rule, he had to take the most
extraordinary precautions. He prepared a
document leaving his body to his own church,
and in perfect secrecy secured the support of the

pope and the king. Then, as his end drew near (in 759) he gave this last will and testament to his monks, ordering them to bury him secretly in the cathedral, and not to announce his death or toll the bell until he had been buried three days. When the death was known, the abbot claimed the body, but was checked by the archbishop's will, approved by pope and king. In 765, when the next archbishop, Bregwine, died, the Abbot of St Augustine's tried to seize his body by force of arms, but his party was beaten off, and thereafter, the rule with regard to burial of the archbishops was that they should rest in their own cathedral. From this act of Cuthbert the reliquary of Christ Church began to grow, and at the time of the murder of St Thomas, it had the remains of St Alphege, considered the most important by Thomas himself, with those of St Anselm, St Dunstan, and Lanfranc, the first archbishop under the Normans, as well as a long line of Saxon bishops. Still, St Augustine's claimed the greater importance, and only the tremendous furore caused by the miracles of St Thomas enabled the cathedral to take the premier position.

Even the fact that St Thomas so undoubtedly belonged to the church in which he was martyred did not check the desire of the rival house, for it is recorded in their own archives that they gave no less a bribe than the abbacy of St Augustine's to the keeper of the altar of the martyrdom, for bringing over to them the detached piece of the skull, for which he was responsible. This sort of theft was not at all unusual, for when another monk of Christ Church was made Abbot of

Peterborough in 1176, he stole and took away the flagstones of the transept of the martyrdom surrounding the one on which Thomas actually fell. From these he made two altars. Other reliquaries claimed (or even still claim) that they have parts of the martyr's body, which seems to indicate that they bought fraudulent relics, believing them to be stolen. Thus, the church of St Thomas of Canterbury in Verona had a tooth and part of the skull; at Mons and at Florence are still parts of the arms; and both arms were at one time shown in an English nunnery in Lisbon. Vestments worn by the saint, which most probably are quite genuine, are still preserved in Bourbourg, St Omer, and Douay; and other relics were long kept in Carlisle Cathedral, St Albans Abbey, and at Derby, Warwick, Glastonbury, Bury St Edmunds, Peterborough, Windsor, Chester, Alnwick, the Temple Church, London, and elsewhere.

We have seen how the outburst of miraculous power had attracted attention, breaking down the resistance, first of the de Brocs and their rough soldiery, and afterward of the church and the king.

The canonisation in 1173 gave the seal of the approval of the Church to a cult which had begun amongst the common people, and the king's penance, accompanied by the miraculous defeats of his principal enemies on the same day, gave an enormous testimonial and advertisement to the powers of the new saint.

Even before this, he had been recognised on the Continent in church dedications, and after it the number of churches, chapels, chantries, shrines, windows, statues, frescoes, etc., dedicated to St Thomas of Canterbury was almost past belief. The most important and interesting of these was the Abbey of Aberbrothock (Arbroath) founded in 1178 by William the Lion, King of Scots, on his return from the captivity which began on the day when King Henry did his penance and made peace with St Thomas. The Church of St Thomas at Acre, built in gratitude for success given in crusading, is another notable instance. The chapel at the southern end of London Bridge was dedicated to St Thomas the Martyr, and a very handsome chapel of St Thomas of Acre was built on the site where he had been born (now the hall of the Mercers' Company).

Dean Stanley says that to the popularity of this saint we may trace the frequency with which old and important bells were named Thomas, Great Tom, etc., and the fact that in England, Thomas is still the most largely used Christian name, with the single exception of John. The same writer tells that the vacant niche in the north front of Lambeth Palace contained a statue of St Thomas, to which, for centuries, all passing boatmen doffed their caps.

All through the country there are still traces of the cult. We have made some attempt at a census of the chapels, holy wells, etc., still associated or known to have been connected with the name of St Thomas, but have been forced by the very magnitude of the mass of material to abandon the task. A few of the remains will be mentioned later in this chapter: meanwhile, we may mention the very significant fact that a cursory search through the Clergy List gives some thirty-seven churches as still bearing their dedication to St Thomas of Canterbury, in spite of the tremendous rigour with which the cult was suppressed by Henry VIII. And of the hundreds of churches now dedicated to St Thomas the Apostle, it is probable that almost all were originally St Thomas the Martyr.

The growth of the cult was momentarily checked, but eventually encouraged and strengthened by a fire which broke out in Canterbury Cathedral in September 1174, and destroyed the choir. The monks and citizens alike were staggered by the disaster, but soon they prepared to build a new choir on a grander scale, and the money came largely from the offerings of pilgrims. The architect was William of Sens, who had been at work on the cathedral of his own city when Thomas lived there in exile. Before he completed the work he was disabled by an accident, and another William, an Englishman, finished the restoration, designing the part surrounding the shrine. Everything that lavish expenditure of money, time, and skill could do to render the church more magnificent, more imposing, more worthy of the priceless presence it was to enshrine, was ungrudgingly done. Noble stonework, beautiful glass, sumptuous painting and gilding, and priceless work of the goldsmith and jeweller were considered none too good, and at length a glorious shrine, surrounded by magnificent pillars, minor reliquaries and altars, and overlooked by a watching-chamber, where relays of devout men were waking day and night to guard

THE SITE OF THE SHRINE OF ST THOMAS, CANTERBURY CATHEDRAL.

against fire or sacrilege, stood ready for the remains which had lain so long in the crypt below.

The work was finished in 1220, when Langton, who was notable amongst churchmen for dividing the Bible into chapters, and amongst laymen as a leader in securing the Magna Carta from King John, was archbishop. Henry III., still a boy, was at last firmly established on the throne. It was fifty years from the murder, and was a leap-year (which was taken as an omen of abundant day of blessing). July 7, the day chosen for the translation of the relics, fell on a Tuesday, the important day all through the life of Thomas. Two years' notice of the great event had been given in all parts of Britain and of the Continent, by proclamation of the archbishop. At abbeys, monasteries, etc., along the roads, and especially at the many abbeys and manors of the archbishop himself, almost unlimited food and necessaries had been provided for the immense multitude that was expected. All the way from London to Canterbury, there was store of food for man and horse, free to all who cared to ask for it; and at many more distant points, and points on other roads, similar provision was made. At every gate of Canterbury, at four licensed cellars, and at four other places in the city, wine was supplied, without charge, to all who liked to ask for it, for days before the great ceremony, and every citizen who could squeeze a guest into a corner anywhere, had a guest or more billeted upon him.

In the evening of July 6, the archbishop, with the monks and their prior, went to the crypt, where they sang psalms and hymns, and joined in prayer until midnight. As the solemn hour struck, some of the brethren removed the stones that covered the tomb, and saw the remains which had been deposited, with tears and trembling, fifty years before. Four specially saintly priests took out the remains, the head was kissed by all present, then the head and the other remains were separately deposited in strong chests and carried to a guarded vault. On the 7th, a great and a grand company entered the cathedral, led by the boy king, and proceeded to the crypt. The pope's legate, the primate of France, the Lord High Justiciar of England, and four of the greatest nobles of the land shared with Langton the honour of carrying the sainted relics to their resting-place in the new and glorious shrine; and everything that could contribute to an imposing ceremony was present at the high mass by which the translation was celebrated, and which established the 7th of July as one of the great church festivals, the Feast of the Translation of St Thomas the Martyr.

Rich and poor, noble and lowly, from "every shire's end of England," and from many a foreign city, pressed in their thousands to the great event; and it is said that not less than 100,000 persons journeyed to Canterbury on the occasion. So great was the expense of their entertainment that the debt was not cleared until the time of Edmund of Abingdon, archbishop from 1234 to 1240.

Before this time, although the pilgrims had been very numerous, there had been no special time of pilgrimage, save that those who could defy the rigours of winter and the exceeding badness of the roads, tried to reach Canterbury about the anniversary of the martyrdom. Now, although there was still a great and a growing stream of pilgrims all through the spring, summer, and autumn months, the feast of the translation became the great occasion of the whole year; and so numerous did the pilgrims become that fairs were arranged for their especial benefit at places along the route, and at suitable times, to catch them going to or coming from the shrine. Some of these fairs still remain, and at least one of them maintains a great vogue in spite of the fact that there is practically no population around its site, and buyers and sellers alike have to travel some miles to take part.

The jubilees and centenaries saw unusually great pilgrimages, until 1520.—Before the centenary of 1570 the reforming zeal of the Eighth Henry had dealt with the whole cult of St Thomas, as will be shown in Chapter XIV.; and pilgrims came no more.

Of the more celebrated pilgrims it is almost unnecessary to say anything. Kings and queens, nobles of every rank, and churchmen of high degree, came from many continental countries as well as from all parts of our own land. Many gave priceless gems or great store of gold and silver to the shrine, following the example of Louis VII. of France, who gave a great jewel known as "The Regale of France," and said to have been a ruby (other accounts, carbuncle, and diamond) as large as a hen's egg.

To give a general idea of the doings of the mediæval pilgrims and of other wayfaring people of the time, we may take a few imaginary scenes in the pilgrimage of a couple of husbandmen, from their home in Hampshire. Each incident related will be from a thoroughly authenticated record of the time, the power of fiction doing no more than change its scene to the road in which we are now interested and to connect it with our own particular travellers.

William, or Will of Wonston, is a tenant farmer, plodding, industrious, and thrifty, whose wife has been a true helpmeet in the work of the farm and in the rearing of a sturdy family. His curly brown locks are tinging with grey beside the temples and over the ears, his shoulders have the stoop, and his feet have the heavy awkward tread that comes from a lifetime's tramping over farm land in heavy boots. But his eye is keen, his arm is quick and strong, his fingers are almost as handy as those of a seaman, and his clumsy walk can be steadily kept up for a whole long summer's day. His son, Alfred, is known as Alf of Micheldever, from the place of his present dwelling, just as his father's name is that of the village whence he came. The two places are only three miles apart, and the extent of William's emigration when he took the bold step of leaving his parental roof, is typical of the cautious movements of the country folk of his day. William has travelled somewhat, for he goes to Winchester at least once or twice every year, and he has been in Romsey, more than twenty miles away. But he has never travelled without a good errand, and for general information, finds it easier and cheaper to take it from chapman and drovers and others who pass his

very door than to go afield for it. Alfred has
seen even less of the world than has his father,
but he is a tall, straight, well-grown fellow of
twenty-two, no fool, though his horizon has been
limited. The pilgrimage on which they are
bound has long been planned, and has been
discussed not only with the relatives for several
miles around, but also with the good parish
priest, who says that such a journey, prayerfully
undertaken, is good for both body and soul.
William and his wife have many a time, in trouble
and distress, called upon the blessed St Thomas,
and they have ever found the trouble quickly
abated, the distress relieved ere long. Jankyn,
the cobbler, who thinks too much and prays too
little, reminds them that sometimes when they
have called upon St Thomas their prayers have
not been answered as they wished—but they say,
" Who knows that we were not justly punished
for our want of faith?" William argues that
if the saint has helped them so much when they
only vowed gifts of wax tapers or other poor
offerings, there is a necessity to show real thanks
by pilgrimage and personal worship; and, he
adds, "will not the blessed Saint the more
cheerfully aid us after that we have knelt at his
very shrine, and kissed the spot where barbarous
men slew him—in God's great wisdom—for our
good?" This year, the family is well grown, so
that the work of the farm can spare the father
and eldest son for a few weeks; the hay has been
harvested, the other crops are well forward, St
Swithun's day has been beautifully fine, and so,
the good man asks, why not see something of
men and places and things, open the mind with

travel, and shake off some of the stiffness that comes of over-constant work.

Neither father nor son cares much for horse-back riding : the horses are needed on the farm ; and along most of the way to Canterbury two sturdy legs can get over more ground in a day than four, so our pilgrims decide to start afoot.

Each has a wallet to contain the very few necessaries of the time, which principally consist of three pairs of hosen for each, with needles and wool for darning. One comb suffices well for two heads and beards, they sleep in their clothing ; and if they should need to wash a shirt they can always find a brook or pool, and wait until the garment dries in the sunshine, on a bush. The wallet has plenty of room for food for a couple of days ; and our pilgrims will buy a supply of bread and cheese, and cold cooked meat ; with spring onions for green food, about once in two days or so. They also carry a small box of pilgrim-salve, a mixture of good hogs' lard and isinglass, for chafed feet ; and another box of a salve for stings, bites, or festering wounds, which is made of goose-grease, resin, and tar. Of this sovereign remedy the good mother says that the goose-grease softens and soothes, the resin draws out the venom, the tar heals. Around each neck there are two cords or lanyards, one carrying a sheath-knife with a blade of six or seven inches, the other supporting a pilgrim's bottle, of earthenware, with four earthenware loops, two on each side, so that the cord passes through these loops and under the bottom of the bottle. These flasks can be filled with water or ale as opportunity offers, for our travellers mean to eat and drink by the wayside rather than in unknown inns and alestakes.

Their clothing is well-worn homespun, the wool so curly and kinky, so well twisted and close woven that it will turn the rain of most all day showers, except, perhaps just where it beats on the shoulders ; while for extra bad weather and for sleeping (indoors or out) each man carries a great cape, of no particular shape, but reaching to the knees, and a good nine feet in circumference.

Our pilgrims do not carry the usual staves, for they are both good quarter-staff men and prefer their own quarter-staves, short compared with the pilgrim's general sort, and unshod with iron. With their quarter-staves they are a match for any men except archers. Even a swordsman, unless unusually clever with his weapon, cannot beat the stout man with the ashen staff, who really knows its play. The ordinary pilgrimstaves are six or seven feet long, shod with a heavy iron ferrule, and generally with a sharp iron prod at the end. They are ugly weapons of offence, when swung around the head ; they are useful, spearwise, for keeping off vicious dogs, and their length makes them handy as jumping poles when crossing certain soft places, but they are poor weapons if a man once closes with the bearer, and are very little good for defence.

The good parish priest of the quaint little octagonal church of Micheldever has announced to his flock, that after early mass on Monday he will pronounce the blessing on scrips and staves for the pilgrims who are going on a long journey to the shrine of the blessed martyr, and his congregation on that morning is unusually large, and more than ordinarily earnest and attentive. It is the 18th of July, and the day of their local saint, the weather-controlling Swithun, was the 15th. The reverend father goes through the beautiful simple form of the old Sarum Missal; raising his hand in blessing, as he says :—

"The Lord be with you,"

and the people respond,—

"And with thy spirit."

He then says,—

"Let us pray."

"O Lord Jesu Christ, who of Thy unspeakable mercy, at the bidding of the Father, and by the co-operation of the Holy Spirit, wast willing to come down from heaven, and to seek the sheep that was lost by the deceit of the Evil One, and to carry him back on Thine own shoulders to the flock of the Heavenly Land; and didst command the sons of Mother Church by prayer to ask, by holy living to seek, and by knocking to persevere; that so they may the more speedily find the reward of saving life; we humbly beseech Thee that Thou wouldest be pleased to bless ✠ this scrip and ✠ staff (✠ at these places he makes the sign of the cross over the scrip and the staff lying upon the altar), that whosoever for love of Thy Name, shall seek to bear the same by his side, to hang it at his neck, or to carry it in his hands, and so on his pilgrimage to seek the aid of the saints, with the accompaniment of humble

WINCHESTER CATHEDRAL, REMAINS OF THE CHAPTER-HOUSE.

prayer, being protected by the guardianship of Thy right hand, may be found worthy to attain unto the joy of the everlasting vision; through Thee, O Saviour of the World, who, with the Father and the Holy Spirit, liveth and reigneth, ever one God, world without end.   Amen."

At this, all the kneeling worshippers said, "Amen," and devoutly crossed themselves, and the priest, taking each man's scrip and staff separately, and sprinkling each with holy water, hung the one around the neck and placed the other in the right hand of its owner, saying :—

"Take this scrip to be worn as the badge and habit of thy pilgrimage:

"And this staff to be thy strength and stay in the toil and travail of thy pilgrimage, that thou mayest be able to overcome all the hosts of the Evil One, and to reach in safety the shrine of the Blessed Saint Thomas of Canterbury, and the shrines of other saints whither thou desirest to go; and having dutifully completed thy course, mayest come again to thine own people with thanksgiving."

As there were only two pilgrims, the address was made separately to each; had there been many, the wording would have been plural, and addressed to the whole company.   After a final benediction the congregation dispersed; each one crossing himself with holy water as he passed through the porch.   In the churchyard there was much thronging to say farewell, almost all the neighbours kissed the pilgrims, and hung about them as if loth to let them adventure on so dangerous a journey.   William's wife and children went some miles along the way, giving parting

H

injunctions about eating and drinking enough and sleeping warmly, while the father and elder brother repeated and re-repeated their instructions about the work of the farm.

The whole journey of the first day, to Winchester, was only some eight miles, along a piece of the straight well-made Roman road from Winchester to Silchester, now a part of the high road to Basingstoke, but there was no hurry; the pilgrims sat long in the heat of the day to discuss some especially delicate mutton pasty and some home-made pomage or cider with which their flasks had been filled, After eating, they lay long in the grass looking up into the branches of a shady tree, and watching the myriad patches of sky that danced between the outer leaves. Their words were very few—until they came to Headbourne Worthy Church, where William took his son to the west end to see the great rood which then hung on the outer wall, and for the protection of which the church was afterward lengthened westwardly. There they knelt to ask a blessing on their journey at the first shrine they had met. Along the remaining mile and a half they stepped more briskly, past the beautiful abbey of Hyde, commenting upon the long roof and powerful squat tower of the cathedral, and talking of the September fair which William had more than once attended, on St Giles' Hill, east of the city—perhaps the greatest fair in all England. They did not linger long to admire the city gates, or the market cross, or the cathedral, but pressed on to the ancient hospital of St Cross, where then, as now, a dole of bread and ale was offered to every wayfarer. They took it with

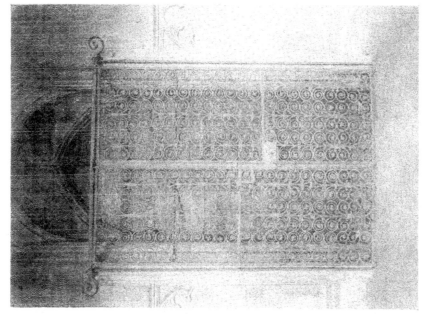

PILGRIMS' BARRIER, FORMERLY AT TOP OF SOUTH
TRANSEPT STEPS, WINCHESTER CATHEDRAL.

PILGRIMS' ENTRANCE, WEST WALL OF NORTH
TRANSEPT, WINCHESTER CATHEDRAL.

relish, for St Cross has always had a good bakery and brewhouse; then they went within, to talk for an hour with one of the brethren of the Noble Poverty whom William had known in younger days. Many hostelries and rest-houses were available, and they went to see the great Guesten-hall in the cathedral precincts where food and lodging were provided for pilgrims to the shrine of St Swithun, before going to spend the night with a relative. Next morning they were early afoot, viewing with wonder the palace of Wolvesey, the great school founded by William of Wykeham, the castle, the gates of the city, and God-begot House, a hospice for strangers and pilgrims which still remains intact near the market cross. They saw with surprise the whole of the Wykehamite boys run at great speed, with bare heads and flying gowns up to the top of St Catherine's Hill (one of the regulations of the founder), and come down laughing and breathless, to strip and plunge into the crystal-clear waters of the Itchen.

After matins in the cathedral, all pilgrims who wished to see the shrine of St Swithun were admitted by a small door, specially cut for this purpose (now walled up) in the west wall of the north transept, and they were marshalled through a part of the great fane by some of the brethren, who explained the relics, but only allowed them to touch or to kiss the caskets in which they were enshrined. They passed around behind the choir and to the top of the steps leading into the south transept, but they were not allowed to go into the south transept, nave, or choir, because the monks knew that many pilgrims were diseased and verminous, and kept their own part of the church free from contagion. The beautiful iron gates which blocked them at this point are preserved in the north-west corner of the nave. The bones of many kings and queens, many sainted men and women were (and still are) in the tombs and mortuary chests, and although the brother who showed the relics gabbled his information in a way that could scarce be understood, some of the more learned pilgrims explained to the others. After being allowed to gaze upon the high altar and the great rood, and to make their offerings, the pilgrims were dismissed through the door by which they entered, and William and his son took their way toward their homeward road, to where, just without the city, stood Hyde Abbey. Here a ring at the porter's bell secured their admission, and a brother showed them the head of the martyred St Valentine, given to the monks in 1041 by the devout dowager Queen Emma, the remains of their own one-time abbot and now canonised saint, Grimbald, and the remains of St Josse or Judoc, brought to this country by good Christians fleeing to Winchester from the persecutions of the Danes. The marvellous silver shrine excited their wonder, as did the great silver rood given by King Cnut. They trod with hushed footsteps near the tomb of the great Saxon king and lawgiver, Alfred, and when their chance remarks showed the brother that they claimed Saxon blood, he told them how their abbot at the time of the Norman Conquest had been Elfwy, brother of Earl Godwin, and that when Harold went to meet the Norman, Elfwy, with twelve brawny monks and a score of stout

Hampshire men-at-arms had followed him, and almost every man had fallen on the fatal field of Senlac. After exhausting all these wonders, our pilgrims went to hear a mass in the church of St Bartholomew, opposite the abbey gate, for here, as in the Minster, the common pilgrims were not allowed to join in the monks' service.

The monks' walk, through the beautiful rich meadows of Hyde, past the monks' bailiff's house, which still remains as Abbot's Barton farm, with a tiny oratory as part of its building, led them again to Headbourne Worthy, and the highway. The church, already mentioned, is said to have been founded by St Wilfred, and is in one of several farm-villages, or Worthies, granted to the Priory of St Swithun by Egbert, in 825.

Through Kingsworthy, Abbotsworthy, and Martyrsworthy, through Itchen Abbas and Itchen Stoke, all beautifully situated in the vale of Itchen, and each with its beautiful little church, they came to New Alresford, another of the little towns given (with its neighbour, Old Alresford), to the Priory of St Swithun by one of the Saxon kings. The new town had been rebuilt by Bishop Lucy in the days of King John, and had been rechristened New Market; but the old people liked the old name, and it is Alresford to this day. Our pilgrims looked at the great pool made by Bishop Lucy when he rendered the Itchen navigable from here to Winchester, and provided the pool to keep the water deep in times of drought; and they marvelled at the great number of wild water-fowl to be seen on the mere. All these villages were busy and prosperous. Alresford itself was a great cloth-weaving town, and

had good tanneries, which brought hides from all
parts of the county and shipped the leather by
the bishop's navigation to the great St Giles'
fair. The churches were all of Saxon origin,
but almost every one had been restored or enlarged in early Norman days. All were open,
and all had some object of interest : wall paintings
that told their stories to even those who could
not read ; crucifixes and figures of saints, and in
many cases shrines and altars where the candles
were ever burning. Through Bishop's Sutton
the road was the same as the present highway
to Alton and London ; but two miles beyond, the
pilgrims took a branch to the right. At Bishop's
Sutton there was a manor-house of the Bishop
of Winchester, where many pilgrims, rich and
poor, found food and shelter ; but our friends
William and Alfred were yet young in their
pilgrimage, and were chary of asking for or
accepting any form of charity. So they pushed
on to Ropley, with a fine large old church, that
stood up brilliantly on its hill-top as the western
sun fell full upon it, and which gave them a most
impressive view, silhouetted blackly against a
brilliant evening sky, as they looked back toward
it on leaving. About a mile beyond this village
came a steep rise, between deep chalky banks
clad with shrubs and flowers, with overhanging
trees that deepened the evening shade until it
seemed almost like night ; but on emerging at the
top into a blaze of sunset glory, they turned into
a field on the left, and saw below them, stretching
mile after mile toward the sinking sun, the
glorious, well-tended, fertile Itchen valley. As
they drank in the beauty of the prospect, a wider

landscape than the young man had ever seen before, they gave thanks to God for having made the world so fair, and to St Swithun for keeping the weather so fine. The beautiful calm of his day had been their final inducement to undertake the pilgrimage.

As the sun sank below the plain they remembered that nights were chill, and hurried on to reach a wayside house where a travelling tinker had told them they could find rest. The tinker had laughed at the idea of abiding in any house on a warm night in July, and had told them the rule of the summer road, which was to sleep during the heat of the day, work (if you were a working man) morning and eve, and travel at night when it was cool enough to make walking a pleasure. But William had a fancy for a roof overhead.

When they were shown to their bed, Alfred wondered why the straw was shaken loose, and eight or nine inches deep, in a frame of boards, instead of being in a cloth case as they had it at home. His father explained that with beds in ticks or cases it was very difficult to keep them free from vermin when used by all sorts of travellers, whereas, when the straw was loose the vermin dropped through to the floor, and next day the straw could be well shaken out and the floor swept. When he examined the straw, however, he expressed fear that they would have a troubled night, unless the bedding *had* been very well shaken and swept beneath, for this was oaten straw. Many travellers thought that oat and barley straws bred fleas, but he believed the real trouble was that they had rough stalks, up which the insects could crawl to the sleeper, while wheat straw, the only sort that should be used for beds, was too smooth for insects to cling to. To our travellers' sorrow these fears proved only too well founded, and being used to clean sleeping at home, they passed a restless night. When light came first peeping through the little windows, William suggested to his son that they should arise. Let us to the nearest water and there "undress and wash our legs and rub them well for the love of the fleas, for there is a peck of them in the dust under this trashy oaten straw. Hi! they bite me so, and do me great harm, I have scratched my shoulders until the blood flows." [1]

A wash and a rub down, after well shaking and searching their clothing, made them much more comfortable, and they broke their fast with thankfulness beside a little stream, rejoicing in the glorious sunshine, the song of birds, and the ripening glow upon the grain. They talked over what the tinker had said of travelling at night, and decided that they would sleep no more in small wayside hostelries unless they should have much rain, and thanks to good St Swithun, they had little fear of that.

The road was almost deserted, for they were in a part only traversed by pilgrims from Winchester to Alton; they had not yet come to the road from Portsmouth or the way from the West and Western Midlands. Moreover, the great annual stream of pilgrims had passed here a month agone for the festival of the Translation, and though that was now some fortnight past, the

[1] This, like the rest of the incidents in this chapter, is based on actual records of the time.

CHURCHES ON THE WINCHESTER PILGRIMS' WAY.

Headbourne Worthy.   Kings Worthy.
Itchen Abbas.   Bishop's Sutton.
Ropley.   East Tisted (and Vicarage).

return stream had not yet met them. As they lay, after their morning meal, however, they were hailed by a travelling doctor, accompanied by a stout youth, who bore a great pack, and was hung around with such a series of musical instruments that he looked like the carrier for a whole band of music. These greeted our travellers, whom they had seen at the inn, and the doctor, with many Latin-like oaths and phrases began to abuse the uncleanliness of the bedding. He and his youth had suffered little, for they were seasoned travellers, and anointed themselves with repellent unguents, some of which he pressed upon our two pilgrims, "not for vile coin, but for love of pilgrimage and fellowship, and the blessed Saint." With cautions against trusting any wayfarer ringing in their ears, they refused the offer, without offence, and William ere long showed the doctor their own two remedies; whereat he pronounced the pilgrim-salve a harmless lewd unguent, void of any active property : while the other ointment he declared to be crude but in some sense effective, and bearable on strong skins.

Learning that they meant to lie there awhile longer, the doctor unfastened some part of his pack, and taking new bread, brought from his last resting-place, he crumbled it, mixed it with certain medicaments, and proceeded to make a great stock of pills. These were rolled by the youth, and the doctor made them up in tiny "screws" of paper, which he neatly laid, head-and-point in a tray. As he worked, he talked, for he said he ever needed company, and the roads were more deserted than he ever remembered. Moreover, the forest tract around Alton was much infested with robbers, in spite of the fact that the wardens of St Giles' fair in Winchester kept five mounted sergeants-at-arms there all the year round for the protection of merchants and chapmen from London, and he thought the simple pilgrims would be the better of the protection of a man of learning like himself.

Anon they resumed their way, through charming lanes and beautiful woodlands, stopping for a few moments at certain wayside cottages for the doctor to prescribe for an ailing infant or to leave a "rheumatic ointment" for an old grandmother. Along the south side of Rotherfield park they went, and as they turned into the Portsmouth road, three or four travellers were visible—first signs of a busy throng. As they reached East Tisted, the doctor's companion laid down his pack in the midst of the village, and went to a cottage to borrow a bench for his master to stand upon. Meanwhile, the learned man spread a gorgeous carpet of blue with a red border, and the centre space worked with a florid orange sun, a yellow moon, white stars, and many hieroglyphics. On this he ranged his boxes and trays, then, donning a long rusty cloak (once black) and a tall conical hat, and piecing together a jointed wand, he mounted the bench. The youth had retired for a few moments behind a hedge, and reappeared as a gorgeous spectacle. He wore a crimson coat with great golden buttons; on his head was a spangled cap, set with three bells, between his knees were strapped a pair of cymbals; at his back, sticking out like a wing between his shoulders, was a great tabor, like an enlarged tambourine, which he beat with a drumstick attached to his left elbow; across his chest was a set of Pan-pipes, such as are now used by the orchestra of Punch and Judy, and in his left hand he bore a triangle, which he twanged with a key held in the right. Blowing a merry tune on the pipes, and working a booming, clanging, jingling, jangling accompaniment on the other instruments, the gorgeous youth walked up and down before his master until almost the whole population of the village had gathered; and many wayfarers had stopped on the edge of the crowd.

The doctor began with a deprecation of his vulgar musician, who was but as the poor bell of a church to call men to a great feast of knowledge. Then he denied any pretence to be a mere travelling quack or herbalist: he made no pretence to cure all diseases with one nostrum, but had different remedies for different complaints. Dealing first with the packets of herbs, he said, "Draw near, give ear, take off your caps and hoods, and look at the herbs I show you. My Lady of Mercy, whose servant I am, sends me to your land, and because she loves the poor as well as the rich, she bids me sell to the poor for a penny—the rich lord to pay five pounds for the same priceless remedies. You will not eat these herbs, for they are so strong and bitter that if the greatest horse or ox in this land should have upon his tongue a piece of the size of a pea, he should straightway die a horrible death. You will steep them for three days in a quart of good white wine; if you have no white, take red, if you have no red, take cider or vinegar; if you have none of these, take good honest water; for many a man hath a well at his door who hath not casks in his cellar. After three days, drink a thirteenth part on each of thirteen mornings, fasting, and you will be cured of all your ills."

Then he similarly recommended his sovereign balm for wounds, an ointment for rheumatism, elixirs for children teething, and finished with an exordium on the pills :—

"I do not say my pills will cure all ills, but who can be cured will be cured; what pills can do, my pills will do. They will not raise the dead, but they will save you from dying; and my pills only cure *one* thing—they cure a bad stummick. If you have that tired, sleepy feeling at bedtime; that wish to lie longer when you ought to arise; that drowsiness in the heat of the day; that weariness after working; put it down to a bad stummick, and my pills will cure a bad stummick.

"If your babies are fretful and cross; if your young men refuse to obey you; if your maidens peek and pine; or if your husbands grumble that the meal be not served; put it down to a bad stummick, and my pills will cure a bad stummick.

"If you have aches or pains in the arms or legs; aches or pains in the back or belly; aches or pains in the sides or shoulders; aches or pains in the head or throat; put it down to a bad stummick, and my pills will cure a bad stummick."

There was much more to the same effect, which we need not repeat, and our pilgrims did not stay to hear it all, though they thought the doctor a mighty fine man. They went into the church to hear eleven o'clock mass, after which they found the doctor ready for the journey, sitting in the centre of some dozen or fourteen wayfarers, to whom he was showing the thin rapier cunningly hidden in one section of his wand, and explaining how he would deal with the robbers, should any appear while they were passing through the dreaded Alice Holt Wood.

A mile beyond East Tisted they reached Pilgrim House, where they halted for refreshment, and three miles more brought them to Chawton, with a beautiful old church which the devout pilgrims much admired, while the other wayfarers clustered around the doctor to hear his nomony again. This time he had arranged for several of them to lead the buying, and to have their money returned when they left the village, and by this means the sales at Chawton were greatly encouraged. William and Alfred, meanwhile, were especially interested in the fine rood screen, which still remains there, with its beautifully carved crucifixion.

At Alton, a thriving brewing town, the direct road from Alresford joined that which our pilgrims had taken, and many travellers were about. The doctor made a great harvest in the evening, and tried to induce some of his companions to wait over another day, but as they would not, he arranged to journey with William and Alfred, as being stout, honest, simpleminded folk; and the next morning, while they went to early mass in the large handsome church, he bought new drugs from an apothecary in the town, and made up a new stock of his remedies.

Here was no difficulty in finding good, clean accommodation; and the travellers paid no more than they had done on the previous night. A halfpenny each was charged for their beds. If they had been riding, they would have paid a penny each for the bedding and food of their horses, and then no charge would have been made for themselves.

Before leaving Alton they looked at a large pond from which ran the river Wey, along whose valley they were to travel for some twenty miles. At Holybourne the church attracted William and Alf, while the village green formed a sale-ground for the doctor, and this arrangement, which suited both parties, was kept up so long as they went together.

At Froyle, as their flasks were empty, they halted at an ale-stake, of which there was one at every cross-roads, and also about every half-mile along the highway. In many cases they were mere huts, with a brewing-shed at the back. Some of them were kept by feeble old women, who made but a poor pittance by selling ale alone; others were prosperous places, where cakes, bread, cheese, cold cooked meat, smoked fish, and other necessaries could be bought, and some of these did a business rivalling that of the inns, though they had no sleeping accommodation for man or horse. They took their name from the stake or staff projecting well into the road from the front of each, and terminating in a wisp of brushwood, bound like a birch broom. This was known as the bush, and gave rise to the proverb that "good wine needs no bush."

Many a good position for an ale-stake was also a good stand for a begging hermit, and since reaching the Portsmouth road at Tisted, they had seen two or three hermitages, squalid huts or tiny decent cottages, but each with the holy man on his little bench at the door, cowled, bearing book or crucifix or palmer's staff, and with a shell for the offerings of the pious. As the road became busier, all these signs of wayside life became more numerous.

The four or five miles beyond Froyle was the dangerous part of the road, and Alf remarked to his father that although the doctor carried his rapier drawn, he fell back some distance behind the others whenever a thick clump of trees grew close to the wayside. Across the Wey they could see the dangerous Alice Holt, stretching for miles, and known to shelter many outlaws ; but they saw nothing worse than two or three honest wayfarers, and by the time they passed Bentley they had forgotten their fears, the doctor was merrily chatting and occasionally bursting into song. He was indeed a good companion. A mile or more beyond Bentley they were climbing a short hill, shaded by well-grown trees, when they suddenly heard cries for help, mingled with quick exclamations, curses, and the sound of blows. They rushed forward, and saw a party of merchants beset by three well-armed horsemen. Some of the merchants' servants were trying to lead away their laden pack-horses, while their masters and a stout serving-man armed with a pike, attempted to check the robbers. At the sight, the doctor's varlet gave a great shout, dropped his pack, and whirling his iron-shod pilgrim's staff around his head, rushed into the fray ; Alfred followed with his quarter-staff, and William brought up the rear as quickly as his stiffened limbs allowed. For a moment the horsemen were daunted, but seeing that they had only to deal with footmen, they renewed their attack. The merchants' man received a sword-cut on the head, the doctor's youth was ridden down and trampled, but not before he had stunned one of the horsemen, and Alfred was knocked senseless by a blow which would have killed him but for the defence of his quarter-staff. Then, the efforts made by the servants to rescue the pack-horses proved their undoing, for the fore-most of the robbers pursued them, and terrorised them into driving where he would. The other robber revived his stunned companion, while the merchants were doing the same for those who had come to their assistance. Soon the three robbers took charge of the pack-train, sending the servants back ; and as they disappeared along the road, the doctor came into view from some safe place, explaining that he had been gathering herbs for the benefit of the sorely-wounded pikeman.

A council of war was quickly held ; the merchants said they were travelling to Winchester market with valuable spices and mercery. They despatched their servants in little groups to seek for the sergeants-at-arms, while Alfred, recovered from his stupor, and with the big bruise on his head dressed by the doctor, agreed to follow the robbers to where

ST CATHERINE'S (PILGRIMS' CHAPEL), GUILDFORD.

With unique Arrangement of North and South Doors on two Storeys.

A GRASS-GROWN PIECE OF THE PILGRIMS' WAY.

The Approach to St Martha's, Guildford.

they should stop for the night, then to return to the road and await the party. He had not far to go, for the robbers were met by a larger band, of eight men, and all of them went to a neighbouring priory, where they claimed the usual hospitality as "king's men who had ridden far." The porter scanned them through his grated wicket but did not admit them, and the abbess, after looking them over, refused to open the door. So they broke open the barred door of the tithe-barn, made themselves and their horses comfortable for the night, and divided their plunder.

When Alfred returned to his party he found that they had discovered the sergeants-at-arms, together with the bailiff of Alton and an armed knight and his squire. They were somewhat staggered when they heard of the augmentation of the party, but determined to approach the priory as quietly as possible, camp not far away, and attack the robbers as soon as they started in the morning. The merchants and their serving-men had been armed with bill-hooks and forks from a neighbouring farm, from which the farmer and one of his men came, armed with flails, so that they had a superiority in numbers, though not in weapons.

Early next morning the robbers, who had eaten nothing all night, started toward Farnham. As soon as they were fairly on the way, an onslaught was made upon them, but they were fighting men, well mounted, and they fought desperately, dispersing the mob that came against them, and wounding many. The

I

attackers, on their part, were no cowards, and soon the knight struck down one of the leaders ; Alfred, wild with the pain of his bruised head, singled out the man who had given him the blow, and first disabling his horse by great strokes with his quarter-staff on the hamstrings, forced his foe to the ground and before long laid him senseless. A flail-blow brought down a third, and another was unhorsed by one of the sergeants-at-arms. Several others were wounded, and when they saw reinforcements coming in the shape of a small body of serving-men from the priory, all who could sit their horses, rode off toward Farnham. In the sheriff's party were scarce enough mounted men to make it safe to pursue, so they contented themselves with restoring the merchants' horses and goods, beheading the four miscreants who remained in their hands, and setting off toward Alton. The doctor and our pilgrims were content to have no more fighting, so took their way, as first arranged, toward Farnham, keeping a sharp lookout lest they should stumble upon the robbers encamped. It was well they did so, for they had not gone far along the road ere they saw clouds of dust, and had only fairly withdrawn amongst some trees, when a large party, including several of their foes, galloped past toward Alton. It was not difficult to guess their errand, and in a couple of hours the party came back, leading the merchants' pack-horses. Very slowly the pilgrims followed them toward Farnham. As they approached that town, they hid again, sending the doctor's youth to reconnoitre, when he found four mounted men of the robber party on guard at the entrance to the town.[1]

Needless to say, our little pilgrim band lay in hiding until night, then made a circuit of Farnham, without any attempt to see the old church or the great castle and palace of the Bishop of Winchester, or even to sell pills and potions in the market-place.

Some four miles beyond Farnham, our party was reassured by the approach of a large party of well-mounted wealthy pilgrims, and learned from some of their servants that they had come that morning from Waverley Abbey and were riding to the Abbey of Newark, along the Hog's Back, a narrow ridge giving wide views over great fertile stretches both to north and south. Our own pilgrims were keeping to "the" Pilgrims' Way, along the southern side of the Hog's Back, so they left the mounted company at Whitewaysend and bore to the right to the village of Seale, where they gave thanks for their preservation from peril; and even the doctor, though he had carefully avoided any of the fighting, for once joined them in the church and missed a chance of making sales. Past the priory and the old church of Puttenham they hurried, but could not pass the beautiful little church of Compton, with its noble chalk pillars, its several altar-tombs, its cell with an ancient and holy anchorite, and its unique arrangement

---

[1] This series of fights actually occurred in 1342. The robbers were men of high position, including several knights. The towns were Lichfield (Alton) and Stafford (Farnham), and when the robbed merchants went to Stafford (the county town) for justice, they found the gates of the city in possession of the robbers, who again defeated them and drove them back to Lichfield.

of a chapel above the chancel and opening into it. Here they lingered long, breathing the sweet strong breath of the great cedar-trees that line the churchyard. Then resuming their Pilgrims' Way at the point where are the late Mr G. F. Watts' home and public picture-gallery, they wound along for three miles through beautifully timbered land, until, just after passing Brabœuf Manor they emerged on the Godalming road, at the very foot of the mound on which St Catherine's Chapel is placed, though hidden from their view by a screen of trees. From here the doctor went toward Guildford, for it was Saturday, one of the market-days, and good for business.

William and Alfred climbed to the beautiful little chapel, and were astonished at the curious method for allowing pilgrim crowds to see the relics, without tramping over the floor of the chapel or mixing with the worshippers if it were service-time. In addition to the west door, and ordinary doors in the centres of north and south walls, doors had been made, high up, in the central window-places of the side walls. They were approached by wooden steps. A lay brother, who was sitting on a little bench commanding a view of the ascent, led the pilgrims to the south side, up the steps, and through the upper door on to a platform built across the chapel, from the sides of which the relics were supported in beautifully painted shrines and caskets, so that the whole floor-space of the chapel was left clear for other purposes. After viewing the relics, the pilgrims went down to the ferry at the foot of St Catherine's Hill, to look

"THE PILGRIMS' CHURCH," COMPTON, SURREY.

With unique Arrangement of open Chapel over Chancel.

at the peaceful little river Wey, then went forward to a hostelry of which the doctor had told them in Guildford. Here they had intended to stay until the Monday morning only, but as the doctor was anxious to make some sales on Tuesday, the second market-day, they agreed to wait until Wednesday morning. There were three parish churches : St Nicholas at the bridge-head, with the Loseley Chapel and the very fine new altar-tomb of the late rector, Arnold Brocas ; St Mary, a very large church with two chapels, many altars, and the most elaborate stonework and tracery they had seen outside Winchester ; and Trinity, locally known, from its position, as the high church. The bridge, much more impor-tant than any they had seen ; and the strong Saxon castle, built upon a fortress-mound of still earlier date, and altered and strengthened by the Normans, proved great wonders. Early on the Sunday they went to the chapel of St Marta and All Martyrs, on the summit of a hill three miles east of Guildford, a place of peculiar interest because it served for pilgrims only, and had no local population of worshippers. Some folk said that this building had been originally begun in the valley below, and that each day's work had been carried up the hill by fairies ; but the doctor laughed at such tales, and said the church had been built in times of war and trouble, when the people, for safety, lived on the hill-top, and that gradually, as the land became settled and safe, the folk moved to the fertile plains below, and eventually forgot that there had ever been a village on the hill.

In Guildford there were far more pilgrims and

other wayfarers than at any other point on the road, for the way from the west of England by Basingstoke and the great roads from Portsmouth and Chichester had joined their track. Moreover, the great return tide from the Feast of the Translation began to meet them, so that now the way was busy enough. It was strictly a Pilgrims' Way, with no made road-bed : generally open, but sometimes fenced with a high hawthorn hedge on the lower side, and leading along the side of the Downs as near a level as might be. On the Wednesday our party left Guildford by the Pewley Hill path, which gave them a good view of the Chantry Wood, through which the main Pilgrims' Way ran ; of St Marta's Chapel on its height, which was probably first a high place of Baal ; and of the Tything Farm, where dwelt the ministers of St Marta's. Their path lay over Albury Downs, and to the little village of Albury with its fine old church (now in Albury Park), near which they joined the chief Way. Through Shere and Gomshall, Wotton and Westcott Heath, they reached Dorking, a good market town.

The next day's tramp, to Merstham, crossing the river Mole at Burford Bridge, which still has its Way Pool, then bending back along the side of Box Hill, Betchworth Hills, Buckland Hills, Colley Hill, above Reigate and through Gatton, was only a short journey, with few incidents. The little church at Gatton was interesting, and the church of Merstham, with its south wall covered with frescoes of the life of St Thomas, detained them a long time.

The next day's walk was alongside Quarry

Hangers, Arthur's Seat, Gravelly Hill, above Godstone, past Marden Castle, near Flinthouse Farm and Limpsfield Lodge to Titsey, where the church, no longer existing, gave them a pause. Past Pilgrim's Lodge Farm and along the hillside high above Westerham, by Pilgrim House, and in almost a straight line to Chevening, where they turned aside about a quarter of a mile to visit the church ; but only stayed a short time there, as they were pressing toward Otford.

This little village, standing where two or three clear streamlets join the little river Darenth, was then much more important than it is now. The castle, now partly ruin and partly farm-building, was then a seat of the Archbishops of Canterbury, and had been a favourite abode of the sainted Thomas. Here all might see the great well or pool (it still exists) which he had drawn from the too dry earth by a stroke of his staff, and in its healing waters our pilgrims bathed before they slept. Here, too, it was said that no nightingale ever sang, because when one had interrupted the saint's devotions, he enjoined that it and all its tribe should thenceforth be silent in that place. The church was dedicated to St Bartholomew, whose special virtue was that a woman who was expecting to become a mother, might secure either male or female offspring by bringing to the saint a young cockerel or a pullet as the case might be, and offering it with suitable prayers.

Good plain lodgment was found in the buildings of the castle, and next morning the pilgrims were early afoot for Kemsing, where the image of the Saxon saint, Editha, was powerful in the preservation of grain from all blast, blight, mildew, or other disaster. Hearing much of this at Otford, William bought a peck of wheat, and Alfred a peck of oats, which they carried to the priest of Kemsing, who took from each bag a handful to lay upon the altar of the Saint. After the proper form of prayer and blessing, he sprinkled each handful with holy water, then gave it back to the bringer to be mingled amongst the seed-corn of the next sowing. The bulk of the offering was retained for the use of the church ; and the pilgrims, each stuffing his hallowed grain into a stocking, stowed it in a corner of his wallet. About five miles from Otford lay Wrotham, with a church of great size and magnificence, adjoining the remains of another great palace of the archbishops, a large part of which had been pulled down about 1355 by Simon Islip, who used the material for building his palace at Maidstone. A story connected with the palace was that of the vision of Richard of Dover, the successor of Thomas, who, in 1184, saw a vision by his bedside, which said, "Who art thou? Thou art he that hast scattered the goods of the Church, therefore shalt thou be scattered." The next morning he set out on a journey to Rochester, already planned, but was struck with "horrour and a chill cold," that he alighted at Halling and died the next day. The church was, and is still, rich in brasses and ornaments ; and has an unusual processional passage under the tower.

The way of most pilgrims from Wrotham was by the path still known as the Pilgrims' Way, along the side of the Down, above Trotterscliffe,

WROTHAM : CHURCH AND PART OF ARCHBISHOPS' PALACE.

above Birling, famous for the " Birling drink," sure cure for the bite of a mad dog ; and so to Halling and across the Medway.   But many took the lower road, through West Malling, to Maidstone.   The Kentish capital was a town of great importance and interest, with its great church and college of All Saints, its archbishop's palace, with one of the finest tithe-barns in the world ; its castle, its ancient bridge, and last, but by no means least, the Hospice for Pilgrims, built in 1261 by Archbishop Boniface, and dedicated to SS. Peter, Paul, and Thomas the Martyr.   At Malling, on the way thither, the pilgrims stayed to visit the abbey, a nunnery of the Benedictine order, founded in Saxon times, as well as the church and the Norman castle.

The Sunday quietly spent in Maidstone, and along the banks of the beautiful Medway, prepared the travellers for one of the most interesting sights of their whole journey ; and as our husbandmen were not willing to wait with the doctor until after his harvest at the Tuesday's market, they left him and his youth and started early for Boxley Abbey, some two miles out of Maidstone. Here, before entering the abbey proper, they heard mass in the little chapel of St Andrew (now two cottages), after which they went to see the abbey buildings.   A brother showed them the great dining-rooms and dormitories, the commonroom for pilgrims, the brewhouses and bakehouses (now a great barn and cowshed), and at last took them to the church to see the two great wonders of which the fame had gone into all lands.   The first of these was a rood or crucifix, said to have been made by an English carpenter during imprisonment in France, of such "exquisite arte and excellencie," that it surpassed all other roods, for "straunge motion, variety of gesture, and nimbleness of joints." On his liberation the carpenter was bringing his masterpiece to sell in London, but as he passed through Rochester, his horse broke away, and, leaving its master far behind, ran until it reached Boxley, where it kicked with its heels at the door of the church. When the door was opened, the horse walked in, and would not be removed by the monks, nor by his master, who eventually traced the runaway, until the monks had purchased the rood, whereafter the horse went away quietly enough. The rood had this peculiar quality, that if a pilgrim brought a gift of value insufficient for his position, it frowned and looked horrible, if he gave a fair sum, its features relaxed, while if the gift were as much as he could really afford, the eyes and lips, and limbs moved, and the smile was heavenly.

The other wonder was a small stone image of St Rumbald, which every visitor was expected to try to lift before he was allowed to see the Rood of Grace. If he were guilty of any unrepented sin, or if a woman were unchaste, the little figure could not be lifted; but if their consciences were clear, they lifted it very easily. In case of failure, they were not to see or offer to the rood until they had confessed to, and had been shriven by, one of the monks, after which they could always easily perform the test of Rumbald.

The Pilgrims' Way lay about a mile above the abbey, and skirted along the slope of the Downs, as it had done through Surrey and the west of Kent, with glorious views of the Garden

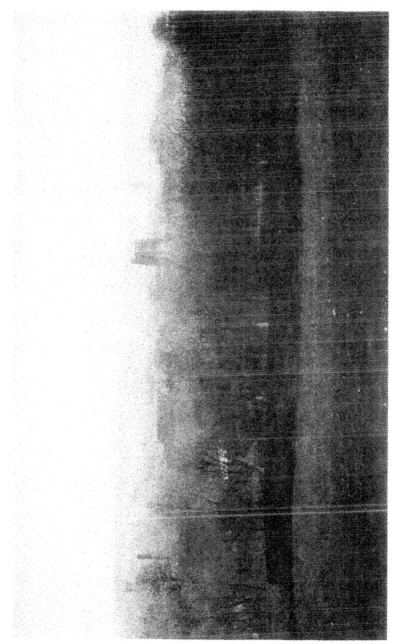

MAIDSTONE, FROM THE SOUTH-WEST.

of England.   They passed the ruins of Thornham
Castle, said to have been built by a Saxon
named Godard, and near the churches of Thornham, Hollingbourne, Harrietsham, and Lenham,
at each of which they called, yet reached Charing
in good time to see the palace, one of the oldest
residences of the Archbishops of Canterbury ; and
the church, which contained the block on which
John the Baptist had been beheaded.   After
supper they walked to the top of Charing Hill, to
see the glorious prospect, the wide vale stretching
away to south and east and west, and the distant
hill-line crowned by a fortress-like church tower.
And, sitting there as the sun declined, remembering that next day they ought to reach Canterbury,
they recalled to each other the wonders they had
seen, and the adventures they had met since
leaving home.

They had several times seen men carrying a
javelin in the right hand, and a letter or wallet in
the left, hurrying along the road, and the doctor
had told them that these were messengers,
employed by the king or some great man.   They
travelled further and faster than any horse could
do on the rough roads of those times—one of them
would make the journey from Canterbury to Winchester in two long summer days, and most of
them would carry a missive for any one for a
consideration, if it did not hinder his regular work.
So that night they got a kindly monk to write a
letter to the carrier from Winchester to Micheldever, asking him to tell their family (none of
whom could read) of their safe arrival nearly at
the end of their journey ; and next morning they
met a messenger who for twelve pence was willing

to carry the missive. That day they passed the churches of Westwell, Eastwell, and Boughton Court; within sight of Godmersham, past Chilham, and through Bigberry Wood to Harbledown, where they joined the road from London, saw the relics at the leper hospital, and entered Canterbury by the same way as the penitent Henry II. and Chaucer's pilgrims.

CHAPTER VII

GEOFFREY CHAUCER AND HIS WORKS

IT seems necessary to a proper understanding of the cult of St Thomas, and of the characters of the pilgrims and pilgrimages to his shrine, that we should know something of the history of the poet of the pilgrimages.

Geoffrey Chaucer was born, most probably, in or about 1340, and in a house in Thames Street, London, which he owned after his father's death. His paternal grandfather, Robert le Chaucer, was appointed a collector of the duties upon wines in the Port of London, in 1310. John, the poet's father, inherited Robert's property (left in trust), and when he was between twelve and fourteen years old, in December 1324, he was kidnapped and an attempt made to marry him by force to Joan de Westhale. He was rescued by his stepfather, who took action against the kidnappers and had them fined £250, an enormous sum in those days, and one they were unable to pay. As a result they sent pleas to parliament, including one in 1328, which stated that John Chaucer was alive, at large, and still unmarried. The importance of this lies in disproving the long-accepted statement that Geoffrey Chaucer was born in 1328. John Chaucer married Agnes, a niece of Hamo de Compton, at some date of which we have no trace, and she survived him; so that unless he married more than once, she was the poet's mother.

In 1356 a certain Geoffrey Chaucer, almost undoubtedly the one in whom we are interested, was a page in the household of Elizabeth de Burgh, Countess of Ulster, and wife of Prince Lionel of Antwerp, third son of Edward III., and it is perhaps well to remember that on September 19, of this year, the Black Prince fought the great battle of Poitiers; the news of which would strongly stir every young Englishman. Until 1359, at least, Chaucer remained in the same service, and in 1359 he became a soldier, probably in the service of Prince Lionel, who then accompanied his father to the invasion of France. Meanwhile, at Christmas 1357, the Countess of Ulster was at Hatfield, in Yorkshire, a favourite seat of the Plantagenet kings, and the place where Prince William of Hatfield, the second son of Edward III., had been born. The visit of the countess was a long one, and during this Christmastide she entertained John of Gaunt, who was afterward to be a true friend to Geoffrey Chaucer, and who, probably, first made his acquaintance at this time. This Yorkshire visit has an important bearing upon some of the works doubtfully ascribed to Chaucer, and declared by certain critics to be the work of some other man, because they contain a few north-country forms of words and grammar.

In the French Campaign of 1359-60, Chaucer was taken prisoner while serving before "Retters," a town which can not be identified with certainty. He was ransomed on March 1, 1360, when the king "contributed" £16 toward the ransom. About this time, probably on his return from the war, he became a member of the king's household; and in 1367 the king granted him, "for past and future services," an annual sum of twenty marks for life. He was then a yeoman of the king's chamber, and sometime before the end of 1368 he was promoted to be an esquire of the lesser degree.

Chaucer was probably married in 1366 (or earlier) to Philippa, one of the maids of the queen's chamber, for, on September 12, 1366, a pension of ten marks a year for life was granted to Philippa Chaucer; and this was drawn in 1374, and in some later years by Geoffrey Chaucer her husband. It has been suggested that this maiden was probably Philippa Roet, daughter of a knightly family, and sister of Katherine Roet, who became the third wife of John of Gaunt. If this is so, probably Geoffrey was the father of Thomas Chaucer (died 1434), who was member of several parliaments, was Speaker of the House more than once, and was chief butler to Richard II. and succeeding kings. This Chaucer changed his own arms, late in life, for those of Roet, which are shown on his tomb, and there are many pieces of evidence which connect him with Geoffrey. Thus the probabilities *re* Philippa Roet strengthen the connection with Thomas, and the strong probabilities *re* Thomas strengthen the Philippa Roet claim, but neither can be said to be established with absolute certainty.

In 1369, Chaucer was again in France, fighting in that disastrous war of pestilence and pillage, brightened by no great feat of arms, which lost for England so much of her continental possessions, and caused the lingering death of the gallant Black Prince. The next year he was abroad on the royal business, and a protection was given for his property against creditors until Michaelmas 1370. He was certainly in England in October of that year, when he drew his pension, and this was drawn by him, personally, in the next two years. These matters are mentioned, not for their importance, but to show the materials on which the story of the poet's life is based.

On November 12, 1372, Chaucer was appointed, with two citizens of Genoa, to negotiate an arrangement with the duke and merchants of Genoa for their traders to settle in some English port: and by November 22, 1373, the pension roll tells us that he was back in England.

On St George's Day, 1374, the king granted to Chaucer a pitcher of wine per day for life; this was compounded in money in 1377, and in 1378 exchanged for a second pension of twenty marks a year. In May 1374 he leased from the City Corporation the dwelling-house above Aldgate; in June he was made controller of the Customs of the Port of London for Wools and Hides; agreeing to be constantly in attendance and to keep the accounts with his own hand; and in the same month he and his wife received grant of

GEOFFREY CHAUCER.

Reproduced from Harl. MS. (Occleve's "De regimina Principum").

£10 a year pension from John of Gaunt, for good services rendered.

In 1375 he was given the guardianship of the estates of two minors—offices of profit—and in the next year the king made him a grant of over £70, the value of some wool forfeited for non-payment of duty. Late in 1376 he was on a secret mission with Sir John Burley ; early in 1377 he went on secret service to Flanders with Sir Thomas Percy, and late in the same year he was in France, probably in connection with the peace treaty then in negotiation.

In June 1377, Edward III. died, but Chaucer continued to be employed by the court. Early in 1378 he was probably with the party negoti-ating a marriage between Richard II. and the French princess, and in June of the same year he went with Sir Edward Berkeley on a mission to the Lord of Milan ; almost certainly returning about the end of January 1379. In 1380, 1381, and 1382, Chaucer and his wife must have been closely in touch with the household of John of Gaunt, for on the New Year's Day of each of these years the lady received a silver-gilt cup and cover from John of Gaunt.

In 1381 the same John of Gaunt paid over £50 for the novitiate fees of an Elizabeth Chaucer in the Abbey of Barking. Whether this was a daughter of Geoffrey, we do not know ; but we do know something of a little son, Lowys (Louis or Lewis), for whom, ten years later, he wrote a lesson-book, a *Treatise on the Astrolabe*.

In May 1382, Chaucer received a new controllership of customs, with permission to do the work by deputy ; and early in 1385 a

K

similar permission was given for his old controllership of wool and hides. To the parliament of 1386 he was called, as one of the two
knights of the shire, for Kent. In October of
that year, he gave evidence on behalf of Lord
Scrope in a case dealing with the heraldic
bearings of that nobleman, in the record of
which it is said that the witness was "forty
years old and upward," and that he stated he
had borne arms for twenty-seven years.

At this time the affairs of the king began to
be troublous, and Chaucer suffered in the
temporary eclipse of the royalist party. He
gave up his house on the Gate in October, and
lost both his controllerships in or before
December of the same year. After midsummer
in 1387, his wife probably died, for there is no
later record of the payment of her pension; and
in May 1388, he assigned both his own pensions
to one John Scalby, thus suggesting that he was
in financial difficulties and mortgaged his expecta-
tions. In May 1389, the king dismissed the
councillors who had been in the ascendant, John
of Gaunt returned to England and to influence,
and Chaucer was made a Clerk of the Works for
the palace of Westminster, the Tower of London,
and other royal properties. In 1390, he was
employed on other practical works, at St George's
Chapel, Windsor, and the tilt-yard in Smithfield;
and was made a commissioner for the repair of
roads and river-banks between Greenwich and
Woolwich.

Chaucer was evidently entrusted with royal
moneys to a considerable extent, for, twice in
one day (September 6, 1390) he was robbed by

the same gang of highwaymen, once at Westminster, and once at Hatcham in Surrey, some three miles from London Bridge. He lost his horse and other property, as well as £20 belonging to the king, and it is satisfactory to know that a writ of January 6, 1391, forgave him the repayment of the money, and that most of the members of the gang were taken and hanged.

In June and July 1391, he resigned or was removed from his clerkships of works, but for (at least) a couple of years longer he continued as commissioner of roads and river-banks. In 1391, too, he was engaged upon a work which was very truly a labour of love, the writing of an astrolabe for his little ten-year-old Louis, then under the tuition of Strode, of Merton Cellege, Oxford. It begins :—" Lyte Lowys, my son, I perceive well by certain evidences thine ability to learn sciences touching numbers and proportions ; and as well consider I thy busy prayer in special to learn the *Treatise on the Astrolabe*. Then for as much as a philosopher saith, 'he wrappeth him in his friend, that condescendeth to the rightful prayers of his friend,' therefore have I given thee a sufficient astrolabe as for our horizon compounded after the latitude of Oxenforde. . . . This treatise will I shew thee under full light rules and naked words in English, for Latin canst (knowest) thou yet but small, my little son. . . . And Lowys, if so be that I shew thee in my light English as true conclusions touching this matter, and not only as true but as many and as subtle conclusions as be shewed in Latin in any common treatise of the astrolabe, konne me the more thank. And pray God save the king that is lord of this language, and all that him faith beareth and obeyeth, everiche (each) in his degree, the more and the less."

Soon after this the poet must have been in financial difficulties, and a poem remains, addressed to Henry Scogan, his friend, his disciple in poetry, and a courtier, as from one "as dull as dead, forgot in solitary wilderness" (Greenwich) to one "who kneelest at the streamès head of grace, of all honour, and worthiness"; and it is supposed possible that a new pension of £20 a year for life, granted to Chaucer in 1394, was a result of this appeal. For some years he took subsidies in advance of his pension (once, as little as six shillings and eightpence) and in 1398 he was being sued for a debt of £14, and secured royal letters of protection against his pursuers. In October he begged some more support, "for the sake of God and as a work of Charity," and Richard granted him an annual tun of wine. Exactly a year later, when Richard was deposed and Henry IV. upon the throne, the new king granted him an additional pension of forty marks a year, with the result that he took a house in the garden of St Mary's Chapel, Westminster, for a term of fifty-three years, "if he shall live so long," from December 24, 1399. This peculiar term of years means nothing more than that what was granted was really a lease for life, in which it was felt necessary to insert a definite term of years; and probably the exact number was coterminous with the lease of some adjoining property. Nothing further is known, certainly, of the poet's life, save that he drew instalments of his pensions during 1400. On October 25 he died, and was buried in St Benet's Chapel, Westminster Abbey: where later poets have been grouped around him until the old name of the chapel has been superseded by the familiar title of "The Poets' Corner." Though so little is really known of Geoffrey Chaucer (a host of "facts" in the older biographies are uncertain or untrue), the few things we do know fit in well with his works. There is an undoubted period of French influence, a period of Italian influence, and a period of native, unaided genius; accounted for by the wars and diplomacy in France; the embassies to Italy; and the period of controllerships and commissionerships in England. Professsor Ten Brink, one of the keenest critics of Chaucer's text, places his principal works in these periods as follows:—1. French influence and originals (before 1372):—*The Romaunt of the Rose; The Book of the Duchess; The Second Nun's Tale;* and part of *The Monk's Tale.* 2. Italian influence (1373-1384):—*The Clerk of Oxford's Tale; Palamon and Arcite; Complaint to his Lady; Complaint to Pity; Complaint of Mars; The Parson's Tale; The Man of Law's Tale; Troilus and Cressida; The Parliament of Fowls;* and *The House of Fame.* 3. Native genius(1384-   ):—*The Legend of Good Women;* several of *The Canterbury Tales; The Treatise on the Astrolabe; The Complaint of Venus; The Envoy to Scogan;* and *The Envoy to Bukton.*

An infinite amount of discussion has surged around the question of the real authorship of various works attributed to Chaucer, but their consideration is beyond the scope of the present book. Some of the strongest and most careful criticism is based on the use or neglect of the various dialects of English, of which the three great divisions in Chaucer's time were Northern, Midland (including London ; and through London affecting Kent), and Southern. Chaucer's authorship is strongly questioned because certain works contain a few northern words and phrases : yet this seems strange, in view of his visit to Hatfield in Yorkshire, at a time when his mind was particularly impressionable, and of the fact that he makes the Clerks of Cambridge, in the Reeve's Tale speak the northern dialect. May we not rather see in the frequency of Yorkshire forms an evidence of early work, and in the occurrence of forms peculiar to the Kentish branch of the southern speech a suggestion of the later period ?

The great gifts of Chaucer to the English tongue and nation, are two. First, from the popular point of view, is the invaluable historical and social record given mainly in the *Canterbury Tales*. Second, and infinitely greater in real importance, is his influence on fixing and establishing the English language, by his work as the first, and, for a long time, the only author who used that tongue for writing which was great and classical, yet popular in the extreme. Poetically, Chaucer is marked by many strong characteristics. His keen observation and love of nature are illustrated at every turn, even more strongly by his similes and casual allusions than by his studied descriptions—fine though the latter undoubtedly are.

His aloofness, which allowed him to see without personal bias, made him an excellent interpreter of the moods and feelings of men and

TOMB OF GEOFFREY CHAUCER, WESTMINSTER ABBEY.

women :—he is as true in his picture of the gat-toothed Wife of Bath, as in those of the "very perfect, gentle knight," or the Poor Parson of a Town. His great dramatic power is constantly shown, but nowhere more strongly than in the characterisation of the Canterbury pilgrims :—each typical of a well-marked and important class, yet each clearly individualised in the brief space given by the prologue and links. For examples of his pathos, one may refer to the death of Arcite, in the Knight's Tale, or the lament of Constance in the Man of Law's ; sublimity of description is found in the vision in the Temple of Mars in the Knight's Tale ; and for description of womanly grace, what can be better than the picture of an English girl, which begins :—

> "I saw her dance so comelily,
>   Carol and sing so sweetély,
>   Laughé and play so womanly."

In the present volume, only a portion of the *Canterbury Tales* can be dealt with, but on the general subject of Chaucer's works we may well quote James Russell Lowell : "One of the world's three or four best story-tellers, he was also one of the best versifiers that have ever made English to trip and sing with a gaiety that seems careless, but where every foot beats time to the time of the thought."

CHAPTER VIII

CHAUCER'S PILGRIMS : MEN OF THE WORLD

GREAT as were the many gifts of Geoffrey Chaucer to English literature, none of them can compare with the wonderful storehouse of the *Canterbury Tales*, and especially their prologue, links, and incidental references to the pilgrims. Full of pictures, freely yet firmly and crisply drawn by a keen observer, they show us the men and women of the time, sketching both their doings and their modes of thought in an inimitable style. Thus they form the essential material of which history is made, and they come to us unsophisticated, from one writing of his own times.

This book is not the place in which to dissect or elaborately comment upon the works of Chaucer, and no one can obtain their full value save by an intimate acquaintance with the works themselves ; yet it may be profitable to deal briefly with the characters of the pilgrims and with the tales they told, in the hope of inducing many who have not made a study of Chaucer, to do so. In "modernising" the English, no attempt has been made to translate or to paraphrase. The spelling has been wholly or partially modernised wherever it seemed advan-

PILGRIMAGE TO CANTERBURY.

(From the Etching by Louis Schiavonetti and James Heath; after the Painting by Thomas Stothard.)

1. The Miller.
2. „ Host.
3. „ Doctor of Physic.
4. „ Merchant.
5. „ Sergeant-at-Law.
6. The Franklin.
7. „ Knight.
8. „ Reve.
9. „ Squire.
10. „ Squire's Yeoman.
11. The Ploughman.
12. „ Poor Parson.
13. „ Nun's Priest.
14. „ Second Nun.
15. „ Prioress.

PILGRIMAGE TO CANTERBURY.

(From the Tableau by Lewis Sicouell and James Heath, after the Painting by Thomas Stothard.)

15. The Prioress.
16. " Squire.
17. " Manciple.
18. " Clerk of Oxenford.
19. " Chaucer.

20. The Wife of Bath.
21. " Pardoner.
22. " Summoner.
23. " Monk.
24. " Friar.

25. The Goldsmith.
26. " Weaver.
27. " Haberdasher.
28. " Dyer.
29. " Tapiser.

30. The Cook.

tageous to do so, and where the rhyme or rhythm could not suffer as a result. In only a *very* few cases has a word been changed, where an absolute synonym was available; and for the

CHAUCER
(*From the Ellesmere MS.*).

rest, foot-notes have been given to such words as are likely to be difficulties to any reader. Accents to mark syllables which were accentuated in the fourteenth century, but which usually are not so to-day, have been sparingly used, and in a few monosyllables which require such a long pronunciation as to be practically dissylables, the vowel has been doubled, accentuating the second one. This usually occurs at the beginnings of lines. In preparing this version, the excellent text of the Globe Edition has been almost entirely relied upon.

First amongst the pilgrims we naturally place Chaucer himself, and it is to be regretted that we have not the same material for his portrait as we have in the case of his companions. Still, he has given us a few glimpses of the character in which he wished to appear. He was a lover of his fellows, a born gossip, who tells us :—

> " And shortly, when the sunné was to rest,
> So had I spoken with them everyone,
> That I was of their fellowship anon."

He was modest and unobtrusive, keeping near enough to hear the tales of the other pilgrims, but not forcing himself forward. The host did not know him, but at the close of the tale of the Prioress called him :—

> " What man art thou ?
> Thou lookest as thou wouldest find a hare ;
> For ever upon the ground I see thee stare.
> Approaché near, and look up merrily.
> Now 'war[1] you, sirs, and let this man have place ;
> He in the waist is shaped as well as I ;
> This were a poppet[2] in an arm t'embrace
> For any woman, small and fair of face.
> He seemeth elfish by his countenance,
> For unto no wight doth he dalliance."

[1] beware   [or children
[2] puppet, or doll ; used as a term of endearment, especially to babies

This description seems contradictory, for the reference to the waist infers that he was a burly man, as was the host; and the description of such a man as a "poppet" might be intended satirically. Yet "small and fair of face," and "elfish," imply an under-sized, delicately-built person, and such a shape would agree with the character which meekly accepted the host's judgment that his story was drasty (rubbishy) and a mere wasting of the time. An incidental reference in the prologue to the Parson's Tale shows that Chaucer, the pilgrim (and presumably Chaucer, the man), was in the habit of regarding himself as a gnomon of six feet in height when he wanted to tell the time :—

> " Four of the clock it was then, as I guess
> For eéleven foot, a little more or less,
> My shadow was at thilké [1] time, as there
> Of such feet as my lengthé parted were
> In six feet equal of proportioun."

Though the host was a very different man, there can be no doubt that as a character he was just after Chaucer's own heart. His description is given later, in introducing the tales of the first day. His good-humour, mirth and jollity kept the party of pilgrims constantly amused and entertained, his tact smoothed over the differences that arose by the way, and his fine presence and bold speech prevented any one disputing his decisions. If he was rough and coarse, from our point of view, it was in keeping with the coarseness of the day; he was generous and sympathetic by nature, and, moreover, was "wise and well

[1] that

y-taught." There is some reason to believe that he was drawn from life, for the name, Harry Bailey, is found in records of the time. As his character is well developed in the links between the tales (see later chapters), there is no need to elaborate it here.

The knight was another character evidently loved by Chaucer. Of him he says :—

> " A knight there was and that a worthy man,
> That fro the tymé that he first began
> To riden out, he lovéd chivalry,
> Truth and honoúr, freedom and courtesy.
> Full worthy was he in his lordés werre,[1]
> And thereto had he riden, no man ferre,[2]
> As well in Christendom as in heathenesse,[3]
> And ever honoured for his worthiness.
> At Alisaundre[4] he was when it was won ;
> Full ofté time he had the board begun[5]
> Aboven allé natións in Pruce,[6]
> In Lettow[7] had he reyséd[8] and in Ruce[9]
> No Christian man so oft of his degree.
> In Gernade[10] at the siege eke had he be
> Of Algezir,[11] and riden in Belmarye.[12]
> At Lyeys[13] was he, and at Satalye,[14]
> When they were won ; and in the Greaté Sea[15]
> At many a noble armee[16] had he be.
> At mortal battles had he been fifteen,
> And foughten for our faith in Tramysene.
> In listés thriés,[17] and ay slain his foe.
> This ilké[18] worthy knight had been also
> Sometimé with the lord of Palatye[19]
> Agayn[20] another heathen in Turkye ;[21]
> And evermore he had a sovereign prize.
> And though that he were worthy, he was wise,

[1] war
[2] further
[3] heathen lands
[4] Alexandria, captured in 1356
[5] sat at the head of the table
[6] Prussia
[7] Lithuania
[8] raided
[9] Russia
[10] Granada
[11] Algeçiras, 1344
[12] ? Palmyra
[13] Lyeys, Armenia
[14] Attalia, 1352
[15] Mediterranean
[16] warlike expedition
[17] thrice
[18] same
[19] A state in Asia Minor
[20] against
[21] Turkey

And of his port [1] as meek as is a maid.
He never yet no villany ne said,
In all his life, unto no manner wight [2]
He was a very perfect, gentle knight.
But for to tellen you of his array
His horse was good, but he ne was not gay ;

THE KNIGHT
(*From the Ellesmere MS.*).

Of fustian he weared a gypon [3]
Aáll besmóthered with his habergeon [4]
For he was late y-come from his voyáge
And wenté for to do his pilgrimáge."

[1] demeanour
[2] no manner wight—no kind of person

[3] jupon, a short vest
[4] coat of mail

If we accept 1387 as the date of Chaucer's tales, the knight must have been a well-seasoned warrior, for we are told that he was at the siege of Algeçiras when it fell to Alfonso XI. after an investment of twenty months, in 1344, and yet at the time of the pilgrimage he was "late y-come from his voyage." The fighting in Russia and Lithuania may well have been earlier, though it is difficult to fix exact dates to the military enterprises named, for the countries were in an almost constant state of warfare. The Teutonic knights, with whom he "full often had the board begun," were a powerful militant order, founded in the Holy Land, and reorganised in 1190 after the siege of Acre. They obeyed the Augustinian rule, and as especial secular objects had the tending of sick and wounded pilgrims and war against pagans. Very possibly the fact that St Thomas of Canterbury had been taken as the patron saint of Acre caused Chaucer to connect this pilgrim knight with the body founded in that city. The Teutonic knights conquered Poland in 1220, to turn it from heathendom to Christianity, and between 1230 and 1240 they captured Prussia, for the same purpose. In 1309 their headquarters were moved to Marienburg, and their most prosperous period was from 1351-82 when they ruled over lands extending from the banks of the Oder in the east, to the Gulf of Finland in the west, and were more influential than any monarch in the politics of Europe. The people of the conquered countries were frequently in revolt, hence our knight would have ample chance of fighting in Lithuania, Poland, and Russia. Satalye (Adalia or Attalia), the capital

of Pamphylia, had been taken from the Turks by
the Venetians in 1307, from them by the Mongols,
a little later, and regained for Christianity by the
Genoese in 1352.   The capture of Alexandria in
1356 was another incident of the interminable
wars between Christian and paynim, which, since
the crusades in the Holy Land had broken down,
enlisted the services of the knights-errant.   When
we realise that during the very time when
Chaucer's knight was warring in Spain and in the
East, the English kings were in glorious war
with France (battle of Creçy 1346, Poitiers 1356),
it is plain that Chaucer definitely chose an errant
knight of the Cross as his type of chivalry.   Like
other knights of the time, when the purity of
chivalry was much decayed, he regarded fighting
as partly a matter of business, and cheerfully took
his "sovereign prize" when plunder was divided.

His character, as a "very gentle, perfect
knight," is well maintained in his tale and in the
few other references to him.

> "With him there was his son, a young squiér
> A lover and a lusty bacheler
> With lockés crulle[1] as they were laid in press.
> Of twenty year of age he was, I guess.
> Of his statúre he was of even length
> And wonderly delyvere[2] and great of strength
> And he had been some time in chyvachie,[3]
> In Flanders, in Artois and Picardy,
> And borne him well, as of so little space,
> In hope to standen in his lady's grace.
> Embrouded[4] was he, as it were a mead
> All full of fresshé flowerés white and reede ;[5]
> Singing he was, or fluting, all the day ;
> He was as fresh as is the month of May.

[1] curling
[2] active
[3] active service
[4] embroidered (i.e. his garments)
[5] red

Short was his gown, with sleevés long and wide ;
Well could he sit on horse and fairé ride ;
He couldé songés make and well endite,
Joust eke, and dance, and well pourtray and write.
So hot he lovéd that by nightertale [1]
He slept no more than doth a nightingale.
Courteous he was, lowly and servysable [2]
And carved before his father at the table."

The young squire, though prone to a little personal vanity, will be seen to be one of those

THE SQUIRE
(*From the Ellesmere MS.*).

obedient (serviceable), handy young men who did so much for the comfort, and even the success, of the knight who travelled in simple style. Chaucer tells us that in riding with one yeoman only, the

[1] night   [2] obedient

THE CLOISTERS, CANTERBURY.

Cellarers' Door.
Door to Transept of Martyrdom.

Door to Monks' Dormitory.
West Cloister: Knights' Route.

knight consulted his own taste ; and we see that the squire's training had been in the house of some knight other than his father, for his active service had been in places unmentioned in the knight's list.

> " A yeoman had he and servánts namo[1]
> At that time, for him listé[2] ridé[3] so ;
> And he was clad in coat and hood of green.
> A sheaf of pocock[4] arrows, bright and keen,
> Under his belt he bare full thriftily—
> Well could he dress his tackle yeomanly ;
> His arrows droopéd not with feathers low—
> And in his hand he bare a mighty bow.
> A nut-head[5] had he with a brown viságe.
> Of woodcraft well koude[6] he all the uságe.
> Upon his arm he bore a gay bracér,[7]
> And by his side a sword and bokeler[8]
> And on that other side a gay daggére,
> Harnesséd[9] well and sharp as point of spear ;
> A Christopher[10] on his breast of silver sheen ;
> A horn he bore, the baldrick was of green.
> A forster[11] was he, soothly as I guess."

The Yeoman requires little comment, but the next lay character opens several glimpses into the conditions of the country.

> " A Merchant was there with a forkéd beard,
> In mottéley,[12] and high on horse he sat ;
> Upon his head a Flandrish[13] beaver hat ;
> His bootés claspéd fair and fetisly ;[14]
> His reasons he spake full solempnély,[15]
> Sowning[16] alway th'encrees[17] of his winning.
> He would the sea were kept for anything
> Betwixé Middelburgh and Oréwelle.
> Well could he in exchaungé[18] sheeldés[19] sell.

[1] no more	[8] buckler	[13] of Flanders
[2] chose	[9] furnished	[14] neatly
[3] to ride	[10] a sacred image of St	[15] impressively
[4] peacock	Christopher ; worn	[16] tending
[5] close-cropped head	as an amulet	[17] the increase
[6] knew	[11] forester	[18] exchange
[7] arm-guard	[12] motley clothing	[19] French crown pieces

This worthy man full well his wit [1] bisette,[2]
There wisté [3] no wight [4] that he was in debt,
So estatly [5] was he of governaunce [6]
With his bargáins and with his chevyssaunce [7]
For sothe [8] he was a worthy man withal
But sooth [8] to say, I noot [9] how men him call."

It was the habit of merchants to go on pilgrimage simply to avoid their creditors, while some particular "bad time" blew over or some

THE MERCHANT
(*From the Ellesmere MS.*).

venture came to maturity, and Chaucer, with a touch of his sly humour, carefully avoids telling us whether his present merchant's journey was for this purpose. He does not say that he was wealthy, or free from debt, but says that he kept folk from knowing he was in debt, if it were so. His Flandrish hat suggests that he traded to

[1] knowledge
[2] utilised
[3] knew
[4] person
[5] substantial
[6] management
[7] obtaining credit
[8] truth
[9] know not

Flanders—many merchants bought their goods abroad, and chartered a ship in which they returned home with them; and the selling of French crown pieces at a profit on the exchange, also fits with the idea of his travelling. The keeping of the sea betwixt Middleburg and the mouth of the river Orwell was important to many merchants, for pirates abounded and constant complaints were being made to the crown, with the result that at times the king gave the custody of the narrow seas to the merchants themselves. In this connection the "Shipman" may well be introduced.

> " A Shipman was there wonynge fer [1] by west ;
> For aught I woot [2] he was of Dartémouth.
> He rode upon a rouncy [3] as he couthe,[4]
> Iín a gown of falding [5] to the knee
> A dagger hanging on a lace had he
> About his neck under his arm adown.
> The hooté [6] sunne had made his hue all brown ;
> And certainly he was a good felawe.[7]
> Full many a draught of wine had he y-draw [8]
> Fro Bordeaux-ward while that the chapman [9] sleep
> Of nicé consciénce took he no keep.
> If that he fought, and had the higher hand ;
> By water he sent 'em home to every land.[10]
> But of his craft to reckon well his tides,
> His stremés [11] and his dangers him beside
> His harbourage and his moon, his lode-menage [12]
> There was none such from Hullé to Carthage.
> Hardy he was, and wise to undertake [13]
> With many a tempest had his beard been shake ;
> He knew well all the havens as they were,
> From Jutland to the Cape of Finisterre,
> And every creek in Brittany and Spain.
> His barge y-clepéd [14] was the Maudélayne."

[1] hailing from far	[6] hot	[11] currents
[2] know	[7] fellow	[12] cargo-stowing
[3] farm horse	[8] drawn	[13] speculate in merchandise
[4] could	[9] trader	
[5] frieze or "dreadnaught"	[10] threw the conquered overboard	[14] called

He was, for aught Chaucer knew, a man of Dartmouth, then one of our principal ports, and one from which a considerable passenger traffic was done in pilgrims from the west and midlands to St James of Compostella. His ship was called the *Maudeleyne* (or *Magdelene*); and curiously enough, we have records of an actual ship of that name, registered at Dartmouth,

THE SHIPMAN
(*From the Ellesmere MS.*).

whose master in 1379 was George Cowntree; and in 1392 was Peter Risshenden. He was in the habit of stealing wine from the casks of Bordeaux, even while the chapman or merchant was aboard—but while he slept; and if he was victorious in fight he "sent his prisoners home by water," or in true piratical style made them "walk the plank" and drown themselves. All sailors were fighting men, and as the royal navy consisted simply of merchant ships commandeered from time to time, this was very necessary. The various countries were constantly veering about, between peace, open warfare, and half-respected treaty truces, and even when the lands were nominally at peace, the retaliatory laws of trade were constantly altering. Thus, at one time it was forbidden to buy foreign goods for English money (all must be "truck" or barter), and everything was done to encourage the import of silver-ware, gold-ware, and bullion. At another time the reverse policy applied, and no foreign money was to be accepted here. Truly the merchant who dealt in "sheeldes" must needs be a wise man to watch the laws and to profit by the exchanges. With such constant changes, when there was not open war there was fiscal warfare, and the man who put to sea without adequate means of defence was looked upon as a fool who deserved to be robbed by a seaman of any other nation; just as the man wrecked upon a dangerous coast was killed by the inhabitants lest he should claim the salvage of his own ship and cargo. Even the great Venetian fleet which sailed to England and Flanders once a year carried thirty bow-men on every vessel.

The seaman rode upon a "rouncy," or farm horse, evidently one he had hired from a livery-man; and probably such a creature was imposed upon him as being most suitable for one who could not ride very well. Why he joined the pilgrims we know not, but probably he had often carried such travellers between England and the Continent. He would know well the international laws or rules for governing pilgrims; such as, that if any man killed a fellow-traveller, he should be bound to the corpse and thrown into the sea, or if on land, should be bound to, and buried alive with the corpse. Any one who used a knife to the effusion of blood should lose one hand; or who struck with the hand only, drawing no blood, should be ducked three times in the sea. The pilgrim who abused, insulted, or slandered another was to be fined one ounce of silver for each offence; and a robber convicted of theft was to have his head shaved, boiling pitch poured thereon, the feathers of a pillow shaken over him, and to be put ashore at the first port where the ship touched. Truly strange penalties to be inflicted by the honest ship captain who stole wine for his own use "while that the chapman sleep."

A pilgrim who travelled a little later than Chaucer's day (1434), has given a touching account of the crowding, the sea-sickness, the smells, and the rough handling and chaff of the sailors, from which the pilgrims suffered. He says :—

> " Men may leave all gamys
> That sailen to Saint Jamys
> For many a man it gramys [1]
>   When they begin to sail.
> For when they have take the sea
> At Sandwich or at Winchelsea
> At Bristow, or where that it be
>   Their hearts begin to fail."

[1] grieves

The captain, like the common seamen, chaffed his pilgrim passengers, crying in their hearing :—

> "Haul the bow line! vere the sheet!
> Cook, make ready anon our meat,
> Our pilgrims have no lust[1] to eat
> I pray God give them rest.
>
> .   .   .   .   .
>
> This meané while the pilgrims lie
> And have their bowlés fast them by,"

while others,

> "Laid their bookés on their knee,
> And read so long they might not see :
> 'Alas! my head will cleave in three.'"

Returning from the Shipman to the lay character following the Merchant in Chaucer's own arrangement, we find :—

> " A Sergeant of the Lawé, ware and wise,
> That often haddé been at the Parvys,[2]
> There was also, full rich of excellence.
> Discreet he was, and of great reverence ;
> He seeméd such, his wordés were so wise.
> Justice he was full often in Assize,
> By patent and by plain commissioún ;
> For his sciénce and for his high renown.
> Of fees and robés had he many one ;
> So great a purchaser was nowhere known.
> All was fee simple to him in effect,
> His purchasing mighté not be infect.[3]
> Nowhere so busy a man as he there nas[4]
> And yet he seeméd busier than he was.
> In termés had he case(s) and doomés all[5]
> That from the time of King William were fall ;[6]

[1] wish
[2] parvis, church porch : at the porch of St Paul's lawyers met to consult
[3] attacked (successfully)
[4] was not
[5] judgments
[6] befallen, occurred

Ther-to[1] he could endite and make a thing,
There couldé no wight pinch[2] at his writing ;
And every statute knew he plain by rote.
He rode but homely in a medley coat,
Girt with a ceint[3] of silk, with barrés smale ;
Of his array tell I no longer tale."

The Sergeant of Law was a man of great importance, a judge itinerant, and one who on his investiture was obliged to give a feast extending over seven days and costing a

THE SERGEANT-AT-LAW
(*From the Ellesmere MS.*).

minimum of £400. Yet this Sergeant evidently kept up his general practice. At the Parvis or great west porch of St Paul's he met clients and juniors for consultation after the closing of the courts at noon ; he was a great conveyancer (or "purchaser"), capable of drawing an unassailable

[1] moreover   [2] cavil   [3] cincture, belt

CHAPEL OF "OUR LADY OF THE UNDERCROFT," IN THE CRYPT, CANTERBURY CATHEDRAL.

Behind this was the Tomb of S¹ Thomas the Martyr.

deed ; and he knew the laws and the cases which had established precedents for the previous three hundred years, from the reign of William the Conqueror. Yet he did not scorn the company of the modest pilgrims, nor did he wear any "silk hood, or pelure[1] on his cloak," as was part of his official costume, but "rode but homely in a medley coat." Even more than in the case of the knight, the doctor, the merchant, and the monk, this mixing with a chance party of pilgrims shows how much a frank equality was practised amongst people of greatly different stations.

His immediate travelling companion was a man of good position, one of that class which has left us the moated granges and manor-houses, and fine country residences built around spacious court-yards. The sort of man who kept open house, with sport always afoot, neighbours and friends constantly coming and going, full pantries, butteries, and larders, and a constant profusion of vegetables, herbs, and fruit from the deeply-tilled walled garden, game from the chase, fish from the well-stocked ponds, and poultry from the deep-strawed barn-yard and the great dove-cote of brick or stone. The sort of man who presided at county meetings, tactfully arbitrated in local disputes, acted as judge or steward at the athletic contests, and led off the round dance when friends, tenantry, and servants thronged his hall at Christmastide.

> "A Frankéleyn was in his company.
> White was his beard as is a dayésyé,[2]
> Of his complexioún he was sanguíne,[3]
> Well loved he by the morrow[4] a sop in wine ;

[1] rich fur   [2] daisy   [3] ruddy   [4] in the morning

To liven in delight was ever his wone,[1]
For he was Epicurus' owené sone,
That held opinioun that in plain delight
Was verily felicity parfít.[2]
A householder, and that a great, was he :
Saint Julián[3] was he in his countree ;
His bread, his ale, was always after oon[4]
A better envinéd[5] man was nowhere noon.
Withouté baké meat was never his house,
Of fish and flesh, and that so plenteoús

THE FRANKLIN
(*From the Ellesmere MS.*).

It snowéd in his house of meat and drink.
Of allé dainties that men couldé think
After the sundry seasons of the year,
So changéd he his meat and his sopér[7]
Full many a fat partridge had he in mew[8]
And many a bream and many a luce[9] in stew[10]

[1] custom
[2] perfect
[3] saint of hospitality
[4] one quality, the best
[5] supplied with wine
[6] known
[7] drinks
[8] pens or cages
[9] pike
[10] fish-ponds

Woe was his cook but if [1] his saucé were
Poynaunt [2] and sharp and ready all his gear.
His table dormant [3] in his hall alway,
Stood ready covered all the longé day.
At sessioúns there was he lord and sire ;
Full ofté timé was he knight of the shire.
An anlaas,[4] and a gipser [5] all of silk,
Hung at his girdle, white as morning milk ;
A sheriff had he been, and a countour.[6]
Was nowhere such a noble vavasour." [7]

Perhaps to introduce more strikingly the differences in rank ; or possibly because no thought of incongruity occurred to him, Chaucer next introduces a group of five craftsmen, about whom a great deal might be said.

" A Haberdasher, and a Carpenter,
A Webbe,[8] a Dyer, and a Tapycer,[9]
And they were all clothed in one livery
Of a solémn and great fraternity ;
Full fresh and new their gear apikéd [10] was ;
Their knivés weré chaséd not with brass,
But all with silver, wrought full clean and weel,
Their girdles and their pouches every deel.[11]
Well seeméd each of them a fair burgeys [12]
To sitten in a Guild-hall, on a deys.[13]
Everich [14] for the wisdom that he kan [15]
Was shapely [16] for to be an alderman.
For cattle haddé they enough and rent [17]
And eke their wivés would it well assent ;
And ellés [18] certain weré they to blame.
It is full fair to be y-clept [19] Madame,
And goon [20] to vigilies [21] all before
And have a mantle royally y-bore."

[1] unless
[2] piquant
[3] lying or sleeping ; *i.e.* it was not removed from its trestles and set aside after meals, as was the general custom
[4] dagger on a lace or cord
[5] pouch
[6] accountant (in this case, probably an honorary auditor)
[7] landowner
[8] weaver
[9] tapestry worker
[10] trimmed
[11] every whit
[12] burgess
[13] dais
[14] each
[15] knew
[16] fitted
[17] income or profit
[18] else
[19] called
[20] go
[21] vigils

Probably these were not citizens of London, where they would have belonged to different guilds instead of to one "solemn and great fraternity"; and this idea is supported by the mention of their fitness to sit in guild-hall as aldermen. The great London Guilds, of which the weavers was the oldest, and the haberdashers the most important in Chaucer's day, confined themselves to the interests of their own crafts. They controlled the apprentice system, appointed bailiffs to overlook the goods made by their members, and to punish bad craftsmen; they forbade any working by candle-light, or on the great church festivals, as between Christmas Day and the day of Purification of the Blessed Virgin, and they condemned adulterated goods to be seized and burned, on the principle of the weavers' motto:—"Weave truth with trust." But there were other guilds, in smaller towns and cities, of which all good citizens could become members. A good example is the Guild of the Holy Cross, at Stratford-on-Avon, a town noted for weaving and glove-making. There, both men and women were eligible for membership, and the guild was helpful in all the affairs of life and death; both temporal and spiritual. It kept a chapel, with priests and choristers, baptised the infants, taught the children, held feasts for the fostering of brotherhood, appointed an ale-taster to prevent adulteration of bread and beer, made peace between those who quarrelled, reinstated a brother who suffered by fire or other disaster, maintained the aged poor, buried the dead, and said masses for their souls. It made the local laws, managed the local markets and fairs, and its officers were the most important townsmen ; so that their wives were naturally "called Madam," took precedence at the religious services, and had their "mantles royally y-bore" by the handsomest of their husbands' apprentices. In this connection we may well introduce the Wife of Bath, who also loved precedence in

THE WIFE OF BATH
(*From the Ellesmere MS.*).

church, but who secured it rather by her self-assertion and ill-temper than by acclaim of her fellow-citizens.

> "A good wife was there of besidé Bathe,
> But she was somewhat deaf, and that was scathe[1]
> Of cloth making she haddé such a haunt[2]
> She passéd them of Yprés and of Gaunt.

[1] unfortunate   [2] connection

In all the parish wife ne was there none
That to the offering before her shouldé goon ; [1]
And if there did, certain so wroth was she,
That she was out of allé charity.
Her coverchiefs full finé were of ground—[2]
I dursté swear they weyéden [3] ten pound—
That on a Sunday were upon her head.
Her hosen weren of fine scarlet red,
Full straight y-tied, and shoes full moist and new
Bold was her face, and fair, and red of hue.
She was a worthy woman all her life,
Husbands at churché door she hadaé five,
Withouten other company in youth—
But their-of needeth not to speak as nowthe—[4]
And thriés had she been at Jerusalem ;
She hadaé passéd many a strangé stream ;
At Rome she hadaé been and at Boloigne,[5]
In Galice at Saint James,[6] and at Coloigne,[7]
She koudé[8] much of wandering by the way.
Gat-toothéd[9] was she, soothly[10] for to say.
Upon an ambler easily she sat,
Y-wimpléd well, and on her head a hat
As broad as is a buckler or a targe ; [11]
A foot mantél about her hippés large,
And on her feet a pair of spurrés sharp.
In fellowship well could she laugh and carp ;
Of remedies of love she knew per chance,
For she koude [12] of that art the oldé dance.''

It will be noted that this worthy lady is described as of "beside" Bath, a dweller in some neighbouring village, which, perhaps, accounts for her success in securing precedence at church. The extent of her wanderings, combined with the fact that her cloth surpassed that of the noted

[1] go
[2] ingrained dye
[3] weighed
[4] now
[5] famous for an image of the Virgin
[6] of Compostella, in Galicia
[7] shrine of the three Kings of the East
[8] knew
[9] goat-toothed ; *i.e.* lascivious
[10] truly
[11] shield
[12] knew

foreign weavers, suggests that she was an organiser and director of labour rather than a working artificer, as were the weaver, dyer, tapiser, and others of the pilgrim band.

The reference to her five husbands "at church door," recalls a time when wedding services began outside the church, and Chaucer makes her state the fact in her prologue, where she suggests that she was first married at twelve years old :—

> " For, lordings, since I twelve year was of age ;—
> Husbands at churché door I have had five."

And although she was now a widow she was prepared to marry again, and made no secret of the fact :—

> " Welcome the sixté, when that ever he shall
>   .   .   .   .   .   .
> When mine husbánd is from the world y-gone,
> Some Christian man shall weddé me anon."

The character she gives herself is much worse than that given by Chaucer in the original prologue. She tells how three of her husbands were good, and rich, and old; they loved her dearly, wherefore she flouted them in every way :—

> " They had me given their land and their treasúre,
> Me needed not do longer diligence
> To win their love, or do them reverence ;
> They lovéd me so well, by God above,
> That I ne tolde [1] no deyntee [2] of their love !
> A wise womán will set her, ever in oon, [3]
> To get their lové there as she hath noon ; [4]

[1] accounted   [2] pleasure   [3] always   [4] none

> But since I had them wholly in my hand,
> And since they had me given all their land,
> What should I taken heed them for to please,
> But[1] it were for my profit and mine ease.
> I set them so a-worké by my fey
> That many a night they sungen 'well-away!'
> The bacon was not fetched for them I trow
> That some men have in Essex at Dunmow."

It is quite evident that she would be no fit competitor for the Dunmow flitch, given to married couples who have lived a year together without unpleasantness. In her advice to wives, to browbeat and deceive their husbands, she says—

> " For half so boldély can there no man
> Sweare and lyé as a woman can."

She worried her three old husbands into the grave while she was yet young.

> " My fourthé husband was a revelour[2]
> That is to say, he had a paramour
> And I was young and full of ragerye,[3]
> Stubborn and strong, and jolly as a pie.[4]
> Well could I dancé to a harpé smale,
> And sing, y-wis, as any nightingale,
> When I had drunk a daught of sweeté wine."

To revenge the unfaithfulness of this husband, she gave free rein to her mirth—

> " I made him of the samé wood a cross
> Not of my body in no foul manére,
> But certainly I madé folk such cheer,
> That in his owen grease I made him fry
> For anger and for very jealously.
> By God, on earth I was his purgatory
> For which I hope his soulé be in glory !

---

[1] unless   [2] reveller   [3] wantonness   [4] magpie

PILGRIMS' STAIRS TO SHRINE, NORTH SIDE OF CHOIR.

Chapel of St Andrew (old Reliquary) on left.

> He died when I came from Jerusalem
> And lith[1] y-grave[2] under the roodé beam
>
> .   .   .   .   .
>
> It nys[3] but waste to bury him preciously
> Let him fare well, God give his soulé rest,
> He is now in his grave and in his chest[4]!"

Her fifth husband, whom she had courted while her fourth still lived, and whom she loved, for very contrariety, because he loved her not, proved a tyrant. He bade her stay at home, telling her old Roman stories and Bible examples, and often quoting:

> " Whoso that buildeth his house all of sallows,[5]
> And pricketh[6] his blindé horse over the fallows,
> And suffereth his wife to go seeking hallows,[7]
> Is worthy to be hanged on the gallows."

She tore three leaves out of one of the books in which he was always reading these stories, and knocked him into the fire, whereupon he struck her on the head, causing her to faint, and eventually causing deafness. When she recovered from her swoon, she found him lamenting her supposed death, feigned to make up the quarrel, but bit him severely on the cheek;—after which they lived happily until his death.

This bold, handsome, gat-toothed, shameless woman is one of the strongest characters drawn by Chaucer. Resuming the tale of his other pilgrims, however, we meet the Cook:—

> " A cook they haddé with them for the nonce,
> To boil the chickens with the marrow-bones,
> And poudré-marchant[8] tart and galyngale[9]
> Well could he know a draught of London ale;

[1] lyeth
[2] buried
[3] is not
[4] coffin
[5] willows
[6] spurreth
[7] shrines
[8] a flavouring
[9] a sweet root

He couldé roast and seethe and boil and fry,
Maáken mortreux [1] and well bake a pie
But great harm was it, as it thoughté me
That on his shin a mormal [2] haddé he.
For blankmanger,[3] that made he with the best."

What little more we know of him, that he was a gross, vulgar, drunken boor, will be seen in the

THE COOK
(*From the Ellesmere MS.*).

chapters dealing with the tales. After him the Shipman is introduced, about whom something has been said, and next comes the Doctor of Physic :—

"With us there was a Doctor of Physíc;
In all this world ne was there none him like,
To speak of physic and of surgery ;
For he was grounded in astronomy.

[1] a stew   [2] a gangrenous wound   [3] blanc-mange

He kept his patiént a full great deal
In hourés[1] by his magic natureel.
Well could he fortunen[2] the ascendent
Of his imáges[3] for his patiént.
He knew the cause of every maladye,
Were it of heat, or cold, or moist, or dry
And where they engendered and of what humour ;
He was a very perfect practisour.[4]

THE DOCTOR OF PHYSIC
(*From the Ellesmere MS.*).

The cause y-known, and of his harm the root,
Anon he gave the sické man his boote.[5]
Full ready had he his apothecaries
To send him druggés and his lectuaries,[6]
For each of them made other for to win,
Their friendship was not newé to begin.

[1] astrological hours
[2] foretell
[3] astrological signs
[4] practitioner
[5] medicine
[6] medicated syrups and confections

Well knew he the olde Æsculapius
And Dioscorides and eke Rufus,
Old Hippocras, Haly and Galyen,
Serapion, Razis and Avycen,
Averrois, Damascene and Constantine
Bernard and Gatesden and Gilbertine.
Of his dieté measurable [1] was he
For it was of no superfluity,
But of great nourishing and digestible.
His study was but little on the Bible.
In sanguine [2] and in pers [3] he clad was all,
Linéd with taffeta and with sendal. [4]
And yet he was but easy of dispence, [5]
He kepté what he won in pestilénce.
For gold in physic is a cordial
Therefore he lovéd gold in special."

To go into all the vistas opened up by this description would take more space than can be spared. Suffice it to say that this mention of the pestilence and one or two other brief and quite casual references are all that Chaucer gives to the greatest and most striking events of his day, those great recurrences of " the plague," which in a short time had swept away half the population of the kingdom. In London alone, his own city, 50,000 people had been buried (more than half the population) during 1348-9 in the special plague cemetery opened in Spitalcroft, and there had been other terrible visitations in 1361 and 1369.

The next layman mentioned is a poor man, brother of the Poor Parson of a Town.

" With him there was a Plowman, was his brother,
That had y-laid of dung full many a fother [6]
A trué swynker [7] and a good was he,
Living in peace and perfect charity

| [1] moderate | [3] blue | [5] a small spender | [7] labourer |
| [2] red | [4] a fine silk cloth | [6] cartload | |

God loved he best with all his wholé heart,
At allé timés though him gamed[1] or smart,[2]
And then his neighébore right as himselve.
He wouldé thresh and thereto ditch and delve,
For Christés sake, for every pooré wight,
Withouten hire, if it lay in his might.
His tythés paidé he full fair and well,
Both of his proper swynk[3] and his cattel.
In a tabard he rode, upon a mare."

Like his brother the Parson, he is lovingly touched by Chaucer, and one of the very few who told no tale or whose tale has not been preserved. Every line shows him to be a simple, honest, unpretentious man.   Even the last word adds a finishing touch well in keeping with the sketch, for in those days none but a very poor man would ride a mare.

" The Miller was a stout carl for the nonce
Full big was he of brawn and eke of bones;
That provéd[4] well, for over-al, there he came[5]
At wrestling he would have away the ram.[6]
He was short-shouldered, broad, a thické knarre,[7]
There was no door he could not heave off harre,[8]
Or break it at a running of his head.
His beard, as any sow or fox, was red
And thereto[9] broad, as though it were a spade.
Upon the cope[10] right of his nose he had
A wart, and thereon stood a tuft of hairs,
Red as the bristles of a sowés ears ;
His nosé thirlés[11] blacké were and wide ;
A sword and buckler bare he by his side ;
His mouth as wide was as a great furneys,[12]
He was a janglere[13] and a goliardeys,[14]
And that was most of sin and harlotries.
Well could he stealen corn and tole thriés[15]

[1] was gay	[6] prize for the wrestling	[11] nostrils
[2] suffered	[7] gnarled	[12] furnace
[3] labour	[8] hinge	[13] singing minstrel
[4] had been tested	[9] moreover	[14] ribald jester
[5] wherever he came	[10] top	[15] thrice

And yet he had a thumb of gold pardee.
A white coat and a blue hood weared he.
A baggépipe well could he blow and soun,
And therewithal he brought us out of town."

The Miller is rough and rude; he tells his tale without request and in spite of the host's

THE MILLER
(*From the Ellesmere MS.*).

urging him to wait.   He admits that he is drunk —"I know it by my sound," but bids them blame the ale and not himself.

He quarrels with the Reve, as we shall see anon, and he is dishonest, with the proverbial heavy thumb to weigh his own toll of the grist, yet he is a good-natured boor who plays them out of town with his pipes.

The Reve, evidently intended from the first as a counter to the Miller, is, like him, a thief. By trade a carpenter, he has become the manager or bailiff to some great landowner; and as the saying goes in the north—"it's a poor bailiff who has a bad day when his lord has a good 'un." If he has not "a thumb of gold," he makes

THE REEVE
(*From the Ellesmere MS.*).

a profit here and there, and on the principle of "set a thief to catch a thief," he knows all the tricks and evasions of the underlings. His slim, starved physique contrasts with the brawny bulk of the Miller, and his wit supplies the place of force; yet he has not wit enough to restrain his temper and his tongue when he imagines the Miller is taunting him through his tale of a carpenter. This we shall see in a later chapter, meanwhile—Chaucer's picture of the Reve :—

" The Revé was a slender choleric man,
   His beard was shave as near as ever he can ;
   His hair was by his earés round y-shorn,
   His top was dockéd like a priest biforn,[1]
   Full longé were his leggés and full lean,
   Y-like a staff, there was no calf y-seen.
   Well could he keep a garner and a bin,
   There was no auditor could on him win.
   Well knew he by the drought and by the rain
   The yielding of his seed and of his grain.
   His lordés sheep, his neat,[2] his dayérye,[3]
   His swine, his hors,[4] his stoor,[5] and his poultrye,
   Was wholly in this Revés governing.
   And by his covenant gave the reckoning
   Since that his lord was twenty year of age ;
   There could no man bring him in arrearage.
   There nas [6] bailiff, nor herd, nor other hine,[7]
   That he ne knew his sleight [8] and his covyne ;[9]
   They were adread of him as of the death.
   His dwelling was full fair upon a heath,
   With greené trees y-shadowed was his place.
   He couldé better than his lord purcháse.
   Full rich he was a storéd privily,
   His lord could he pleasen subtilly
   To give and lend him of his owen good
   And have a thank and get a gown and hood.
   In youth he learned had a good myster,[10]
   He was a well good wright, a carpenter.
   This Revé sat upon a full good stot,[11]
   That was all pomely [12] grey and highté [13] Scot ;
   A long surcoat of pers [14] upon he hade,
   And by his side he bare a rusty blade.
   Of Norfolk was this Reve of which I tell,
   Beside a town men clepen [15] Baldeswell.
   Tuckéd he was as is a friar, about
   And ever he rode the hindmost of our rout."

[1] in front	[6] was not	[11] cob
[2] young cattle	[7] hind = farm labourer	[12] dapple
[3] dairy stock	[8] trickery	[13] named
[4] old plural = horses	[9] craft	[14] blue
[5] fatting cattle	[10] mystery ; *i.e.* handicraft	[15] call

"THE CHAIR OF ST AUGUSTINE," CANTERBURY CATHEDRAL.

In which the Archbishops are enthroned.

CHAPTER IX

CHAUCER'S PILGRIMS: MEN OF THE CHURCH

THE immense relative importance of the Church and the religious houses in the fourteenth century is very difficult to appreciate, unless one has made a special and a careful study of the subject. In Chaucer's company of thirty-one persons, we find no less than twelve attached to religion, and most of them occupying their full share of the attention of their companions and of the reader. In this, as in so many other cases, our author fairly reflects the conditions of the time; and if we add to the church-folk going on pilgrimage, those who received the pilgrims at the various "hallows" on their way, we shall gain some idea of how large loomed the Church, still; although in too many cases the faith of priests and people alike was undermined and rotten. Too many of the monks, bishops, priests, pardoners, and others were lost in dead formalism, replacing faith and earnestness by brilliant ritual and meaningless repetition, or had sunk into luxury, idleness, covetousness, and licentiousness. Too many of the people had lost all idea of God, and had replaced their religion by a selfish truckling and chaffering with the Lord or His saints, to heal their bodies, prosper their

185

business, or save their souls—for a small consideration. With others, the faith had become a sort of mumbo-jumbo superstition, a propitiation of the deity with presents; a dabbling in the excitement of holy conjuring-entertainments and wonder-workings. Yet there was faith in the land. There were true, devoted sons of the Church, and earnest, self-denying brothers of the

THE PRIORESS
(*From the Ellesmere MS.*).

people, and if they were less obtrusive than those who thrust with side and with shoulder for place and power, their lives were sweet and pure, helpful and inspiring. If we see less of them than of the baser breed, it is only in accordance with the observation, that "the evil that men do lives after them; the good, is oft interred with their bones."

The first of the "religious" introduced by Chaucer is the Prioress, a worthy woman, who evidently thought much of the rules of courtesy and manners. In her office as head of a priory of nuns she needed much judgment and discretion, firmness, sense of order, and capacity for management. The success of the house, the comfort and religious progress of the sisters, and the entertainment of strangers and pilgrims would largely depend upon her.

"There also was a nun, a prioress,
 That of her smiling was full simple and coy ;
 Her greatest oath was but by saint Eloy
 And she was clepéd[1] madame Eglantine.
 Full well she sung the sérvicé divine,
 Entunéd in her nose full seemély,
 And French she spake full fair and fetisly[2]
 After the school of Stratford-atté-Bow,
 For French of Paris was to her unknow.
 At meté well y-taught was she withal,
 She let no morsel from her lippés fall,
 Nor wet her fingers in her saucé deep.
 Well could she carry a morsel and well keep,
 Thaát no drop ne fell upon her breast.
 In courtesy was set full muchel her leste.[3]
 Her over-lippé wiped she so clean,
 That in her cup there was no ferthyng[4] seen
 Of greasé, when she drunken had her draught
 Full seemély after her meat she raughte,[5]
 And silkerly[6] she was of great disport[7]
 And full pleasánt and amiable of port,
 And painéd[8] her to counterfeité cheeré[9]
 Of Court, and be estately of mannere,
 And to be holden digne[10] of reverence.
 But for to speaken of her consciénce,
 She was so charitable and so pitous[11]
 She wouldé weep if that she saw a mouse
 Caught in a trap, if it were dead or bled.
 Of smallé houndés had she that she fed

[1] called
[2] gracefully
[3] her bent was strongly toward courtesy
[4] crumb or scrap
[5] reached
[6] certainly
[7] deportment
[8] took pains
[9] manners
[10] worthy
[11] sympathetic

With roasted flesh, or milk and wastel breed ;[1]
But sore wept she if one of them were dede,
Or if men smote it with a yerdé[2] smerte ;[3]
And all was consciénce and tender heart.
Full seemély her wimple pinchéd was ;
Her nose trelys,[4] her eyen[5] grey as glass,
Her mouth full small and there-to soft and red ;
But sikerly[6] she had a fair forehead :
It was almost a spanné broad I trow
For, hardily,[7] she was not undergrow.[8]
Full fetys[9] was her cloak as I was 'ware ;
Of small coral about her arm she bare
A pair of beades,[10] gauded all with green,
And thereto hung a brooch of gold full sheen,
On which there was first writ a crowned A,
And after *Amor Vincit omnia.*
Another nunnè with her haddé she
That was her Chapéleyne, and Priestés three."

In the description there are one or two puzzling points. It seems uncertain whether "entuned in her nose" was intended as a compliment or not ; but in view of the rest of the picture we may fairly safely say that the poet referred to some form of intoning which was considered particularly correct. French of Stratford-at-Bow, again, though often quoted in sarcastic sense, was probably the accent taught in the Benedictine nunnery of Stratford-at-Bow, and recognised as the most refined form in a country where French was still the court language. Her manners in eating were the best, in a time when forks were unknown, when sippits of bread were used for conveying sauce and gravy to the mouth, and when the highest refinement in a book of

[1] waste bread	[5] eyes	[8] under-sized
[2] stick	[6] certainly	[9] graceful
[3] smartly	[7] truly	[10] a rosary
[4] well-shaped		

courtesy was to instruct that in carving, one should

"Set never on fish nor flesh, beast nor fowl, truly
  More than two fingers and a thumb, for that is courtesy.
  Touch never with your right hand no manner meat surely."

THE SECOND NUN
(*From the Ellesmere MS.*).

Even her oath, "by saint Eloy," was a refinement, like the rest of her doings, and possibly it was not an oath at all, but rather an exclamation directed to her horse. For St Eloy is a patron of muleteers and horsemen, who urge their beasts and invoke their patron by the cry of Eloy! Eloy! The carter in the Friar's tale, when his horses clear the slough, cries to one of them, "I pray God save thee, and sainte

Loy." The attendant nun was in accordance with the rules, which forbade a prioress to go anywhere, or even to see a man in her own priory without the attendance of a nun, but the describing of this lady as a Chapeleyn is a puzzle.

THE NUN'S PRIEST
(*From the Ellesmere MS.*).

The Monk, a complete contrast, is drawn with just as much skill as is the modest, mincing Nun:—

"A Monk there was, a fair for the maistrie,
An outridér, that loved venerie :[1]
A manly man, to be an abbot able,
Full many a dainty horse had he in stable,
And when he rode men might his bridle hear
Gyýngling [2] in a whistling wind as clear,
And eke as loud, as doth the chapel bell,
There as this lord was keeper of the cell.
The rule of saint Maure [3] or of saint Beneit,[4]
Because that it was old and somewhat streit,[5]

[1] hunting   [2] jingling   [3] prior under St Benedict
[4] Benedict, founder of the Benedictines   [5] strict

This ilké Monk let oldé thingés pace [1]
And held aftér the newé world the space.
He gave not of [2] that text a pulléd [3] hen
That saith that hunters be not holy men,
Nor that a Monk when he is recchélees [4]
Is likened to a fish that is waterlees;

THE MONK
(*From the Ellesmere MS.*).

That is to say, a Monk out of his cloister.
But thilké [5] text held he not worth an oyster ;
And I said his opinion was good.
What [6] should he study and make himselven wood, [7]
Upon a book in cloister alway to poure,
Or swynken [8] with his handés and labóur,

[1] go
[2] cared not for
[3] strangled
[4] reckless :—but the meaning is
   not quite clear

[5] this same
[6] why
[7] mad
[8] toil

As Austyn[1] bids ? how shall the world be served ?
Let Austyn have his swynk[2] to him reserved.
Therefore he was a prikasour[3] aright ;
Greyhounds he had, as swift as fowl in flight ;
Of priking[4] and of hunting for the hare
Was all his lust,[5] for no cost would he spare.
I saw his sleeves y-purfiled[6] at the hand
With grys,[7] and that the finest of the land ;
And for to fast'n his hood under his chin
He had of gold y-wrought a full curious pin,
A love-knot in the greater end there was.
His head was bald that shone as any glass,
And eke his face as he had been anoint.
He was a lord full fat and in good point[8]
His eyén[9] stepe[10] and rolling in his head,
That steaméd as a furnace of a lead ;
His bootés supple, his horse in great estate.
Now certainly he was a fair preláte.
He was not pale, as a forpynéd[11] ghost :
A fat swan loved he best of any roast ;
His palfrey was as brown as is a berry."

This is the prototype of the " sporting parson,"
whose practice has always seemed somewhat
more lax than his preaching or profession, but
for whom the Englishman has an amused
toleration, if not actually a sneaking affection.
His ostentation in dress and living, which
brought the reproach of many sincere Christians,
was not by any means condoned by the Church,
for at council after council it was reproved. In
London in 1342, and in York in 1367, complaints
were made that many monks and bishops wore
clothing "fit rather for knights than for clerks,"
that they wore long beards, shamelessly short
tunics, and coats, " which did not come down to

---

[1] St Augustine
[2] toil
[3] spurrer of horses
[4] hard riding
[5] fancy
[6] edged
[7] grey fur
[8] well equipped
[9] eyes
[10] bright
[11] starved

THE GUESTEN HALL, WINCHESTER.

Where Pilgrims were lodged.

ENTRANCE TO THE ABBOT'S LODGING (NOW THE DEANERY), WINCHESTER.

Where Food was distributed to Pilgrims.

the middle of the legs, or even cover the knees ";
that they carried ornamented knives as large as
swords, finger-rings, expensive belts, purses and
bags, ornamented shoes and brilliant-coloured
chequered boots, and luxurious appointments
generally. Many sumptuary laws were laid
down, but monks who made light of the rule
of Austyn (St Augustine) probably took little
heed of the orders of a church council.

The reference to a fat swan recalls the fact
that our country had then great extent of marsh
and swamp land, and swans bred in countless
thousands. In Landseer's "Bolton Abbey in
the Olden Time," a swan is amongst the game
brought in by the forester, and in Stow, we find
an account of the provision for a dinner at the
investiture of a sergeant-at-law, which includes
twenty-five beeves, fifty veals (calves), a hundred
sheep, a hundred and twenty-five swine and
boars, and a hundred and seventy swans.

> " A Friar there was, a wanton and a merry
> A lymytour,[1] a full solempné[2] man,
> In all the orders four[3] is none that kan[4]
> So much of dalliance and of fair languáge ;
> He haddé made full many a marriáge
> Of youngé women at his owen cost :
> Unto his order he was a noble post,[5]
> Full well beloved and familier was he
> With franklins over all in his countree ;
> And eke with worthy women of the town,
> For he had power of confessioún,
> As said himself, moré than a curát,
> For of his order he was licenciat.
> Full sweetly heard he his confessioun
> And pleasant was his absolutioun

[1] limiter
[2] solemn ; in the sense of important
[3] the orders of Augustines, Carmelites, Dominicans, and Franciscans
[4] knows
[5] support

N

He was an easy man to give penánce
There as he wist [1] to have a good pittánce ;
For unto a poor order for to give
Is signé that a man is well y-shrive ; [2]
For if he gave, he dursté make avaunt [3]
He wisté [4] that a man was répentaunt :
For many a man so hard is of his heart
He may not weep although he soré smart,
Therefore instead of weeping and prayéres
Men might give silver to the pooré freres.

THE FRIAR
(*From the Ellesmere MS.*).

His tippet was ay farsed [5] full of knives
And pinnés for to given youngé wives ;
And certainly he had a merry note ;
Well could he sing and playen on a rote [6]
Of yeddings [7] he bare outrély [8] the pris [9]
His necké white was as the flower-de-lys,
Thereto [10] he strong was as a champioun.
He knew the taverns well in all the town
And every hostiler and tappestere [11]
Bet [12] than a lazar [13] or a beggestere ; [14]

[1] expected	[6] little harp	[11] tapster
[2] shriven—repented	[7] proverbs	[12] better
[3] boast	[8] utterly	[13] leper
[4] knew	[9] appreciation	[14] beggar
[5] stuffed (a cook's term)	[10] moreover	

For unto such a worthy man as he
Accorded not, as by his facultee,
To have with siké[1] lazars acquaintáunce ;
It is not honest, it may not avaunce[2]
Foór to dealen with no such poraille ;[3]
But all with rich and sellers of vitaille.[4]
And over all, ther as[5] profit should arise,
Courteous he was and lowly of servyse,[6]
There nas[7] no man nowhere so virtuous.
He was the besté beggar in his house,
For though a widow haddé not a sho,
So pleasant was his *In principio*,
Yet would he have a farthing ere he went :
His purchase was well better than his rent.
And rage he could, as it were right a whelp.
In lové-days[8] there could he muchel help,
For there he was not like a cloisterer
With threadbare cope,[9] as is a poor scholér,
But he was like a master, or a pope ;
Of double worsted was his semi-cope,[10]
That rounded as a bell out of the press.
Somewhat he lispéd for his wantonness,
To make his English sweet upon his tongue,
And in his harping, when that he had sung,
His eyen[11] twinkled in his head aright
As do the starrés on a frosty night.
This worthy lymytour[12] was clept[13] Huberd."

This character is less known to us in song and story than is the jovial monk, or even the friar who carefully stayed in his own religious establishment. The limiter was a travelling father confessor, whose ministrations were "limited" to a definite district, and who was attached to a religious house. He was supposed to beg for his friary, and Chaucer tells us what a good beggar

[1] such
[2] benefit
[3] poor folk
[4] victuals
[5] in cases where
[6] helpfulness
[7] was not
[8] days (and especially feasts) for making friends of those who had been at enmity
[9] cape
[10] short cape
[11] eyes
[12] limiter
[13] called

this one was. One line on this point is not clear, "his purchase was well better than his rent,"—which has been thought to mean that people gladly gave him money to go away, and thus to save the cost of entertaining him; or, alternatively, that the amount he collected was considerably more than he paid over to the brethren. As some of these limit-rounds were "farmed" or taken on contract by the limiters, the latter explanation is possible without any reflection on

THE SUMMONER
(*From the Ellesmere MS.*).

the friar's honesty. He was a man of the world, condoning sin, selling easy penance for good pittance, and is one of the many signs of the canker which had eaten to the heart of the Church, and which has done so in every religion in times of prosperity.

But if the Monk and the Friar represented luxury and laxity, what shall be said of the Summoner and the Pardoner, men of the worst

possible lives, who used the cloak of the Church
for doings which would not have been tolerated in
professed men of the world.

" A Summoner was there with us in that place,
That had a fire-red cherubynnés face,
For sawcefleem [1] he was, with eyen [2] narrow.
As hot he was, and lecherous, as a sparrow,
With scaléd [3] browés black, and piléd [4] beard
Of his visaáge children were afeard.
There nas [5] quick-silver, litharge nor brimstone,
Borax, ceruce, [6] nor oil of Tartar known,
Nor ointément that wouldé cleanse and bite,
That him might helpen of the whelkés white,
Nor of the knobbés sitting on his cheeks.
Well loved he garlick, onions and eke leeks,
And for to drinken strong wine, red as blood ;
Then would he speak, and cry as he were wood. [7]
And when that he well drunken had the wine,
Then would he speak no worde but Latyn.
A fewé termés had he, two or three,
That he had learnéd out of some decree,—
No wonder is, he heard it all the day,
And eke ye knowen well how that a jay
Can clepen *Watte* [8] as well as can the pope.
But whoso could in other thing him grope,
Then had he spent all his philosophy ;
Ay *questio quid juris* would he cry.
He was a gentle harlot and a kind ;
A better fellow shouldé men not find.
He wouldé suffer, for a quart of wine,
A good fellów to have his concubine
A twelve-month, and excuse him atté full ;
And privily a finch eke could he pull ; [9]
And if he found owher [10] a good felawe,
He wouldé teachen him to have no awe,
In such case, of the Archédeacon's curse,
But if a manne's soul were in his purse ;

[1] pimpled	[6] cerate—white lead
[2] eyes	[7] mad
[3] scabby	[8] shout Wat !
[4] close-cropped	[9] rob a simpleton
[5] was not	[10] anywhere

For in his purse he should y-punished be ;
' Purse is the Archédeacon's hell,' said he,
But well I wot[1] he liéd right indeed,
Of cursing ought each guilty man him dread,
For curse will slay,—right as assoiling[2] saveth ;
And also war[3] him of a *Significavit*[4]
In danger had he at his owén guise[5]
The youngé girlés[6] of the diocese,
He knew their counsel, and was all their reed[7]
A garland had he set upon his head,
As great as it were for an alé stake ;[8]
A buckler had he made him of a cake."

This drunken blackguard, with his garland of flowers above his pimply, fat face, with cheeks swelled like those of a "cherubynne" on a tombstone, was a minor officer of an archdeacon's court, appointed to deal with licentiousness, and serving himself at the cost of both court and offenders. By making himself familiar with the "finches" or greenhorns of his district, and acting as adviser to the silly girls (which in those days meant young men as well as young women), he put himself in the position to extort blackmail for failing to execute fictitious summonses ; and when the blackmail ceased, he would give a hint to some approver, on whose evidence the reckless youngsters would be summoned and punished. In the frailties of the clerics, who were vowed to celibate lives, these summoners found many chances for profit, and their methods are elaborated in the Friar's tale, which was rudely interrupted and bitterly resented by the Summoner in

[1] know
[2] absolution
[3] beware
[4] warrant for imprisonment of an excommunicated person
[5] manner
[6] young folk of both sexes
[7] adviser
[8] beer-house ; the garland was as large as the " bush " used as a sign.

the party.   The Friar tells us that the archdeacon punished fornication, witchcraft, baudery, defamation, adultery, absence from sacrament, usury, simony, and "many another manner crime"; he was hardest upon evil livers and those who paid less than their just tithes.

> " He had a summoner ready to his hand ;
> A slyer boy was none in Engéland ;
> For subtilly he had his espialle [1]
> That taughté him whéer him might avail.
>
> . . . though this summoner be wood [2] as a hare,
> To tell his harlotry I will not spare,
> For we be out of his correctión,
> They have of us no jurisdictión.
>
> This falsé thief, this summoner, quoth the Friar,
> Had always baudés ready to his hand,
> As any hawk to lure in Engéland,
> They told him all the secree [3] that they knew,
> For their acquaintance was not come of new ;
> They weren his approvers privily.
> He took himself a great profit thereby ;
> His master knew not always what he wan. [4]
> Withouten mandement, [5] a lewéd [6] man
> He coulldé somne, [7] on pain of Christé's curse
> And they were glad to fillé well his purse.
>
> He had eke wenches at his retinue [8]
> That whether that sir [9] Robert, or sir [9] Hugh,
> Or Jack, or Rauf, or whose that it were
> That lay by them, they told it in his ear.
> Thus was the wench and he of one assent,
> And he would fetch a feignéd mandément,
> And summon them to the chapter bothé two
> And pill [10] the man, and let the wenché go."

[1] spies
[2] mad
[3] private information
[4] won
[5] order
[6] ignorant
[7] summon
[8] retained by him
[9] sir, the title for a priest, not for a knight
[10] rob

He knew of more bribery and corruption than could be told in two years.

> "For in this world nys[1] doggé for the bow
> That can a hurt deer from a whole y-know
> Bet[2] than this summoner knew a sly lecchour[3]
> Or an avowtier[4] or a paramour."

The honest men in the Church did all in their power to check such men as these; but in an unlettered, loosely-organised society the subtle, unscrupulous man could long flourish without material hindrance; especially when the king and the Church were at variance as to their mutual spheres of jurisdiction, and when the archdeacons depended upon fines for a material part of their income. The people were too ignorant or too terrified to complain effectively, and the archdeacons were liable to think the officer who brought most cases and extorted most fines was worthy of praise,—without inquiring whether his private cases and bribes were in proportion to the cases in court. So the Summoner went his evil way with little check; and said to the devil, as in the Friar's tale :—

> "Now, brother . . . I you pray,
> Teach me, while that we riden by the way,—
>
> .   .   .   .   .   .
>
> Some subtléty, and tell me faithfully
> In my office how I may mosté win,
> And sparé not for consciénce nor sin,
> But as my brother tell me how do ye.
>   Now by my trothé, brother dear, said he (the fiend)
> As I shall tellen thee a faithful tale,
> My wages be full straighté and full smale ;[5]

[1] is not
[2] better
[3] gross sensualist
[4] adulterer
[5] small

PART OF ROOF OF GUESTEN HALL, WINCHESTER.

The Floor and the Brick Wall (both modern) divide the old single Hall into two Buildings of two Storeys.

My lord is hard to me, and dangerous,
Aánd mine office is full laborous ;
And therefore by extortións I live ;
Forsooth, I take all that men will me give,
Algate [1] by sleighté, or by violence.

.   .   .   .   .   .

Now certes, quoth this Summoner, so fare I ;
I sparé not to taken God it wot,[2]
But if [3] it be too heavy or too hot,
What I may get in conseil [4] privily ;
No manner consciénce of that have I ;
Nere [5] my extortión I might not liven
Nor of such japés [6] will I not be shriven."

From this professional reprover of sin, who
shows no surprise or horror when he finds he is
riding with a fiend from hell, let us turn to his
boon companion, a rascal even more degraded :
for while the Summoner resents the description
given of, and the opinions ascribed to his class,
the Pardoner glories in his shame and jests about
his deceptions. While the Summoner tells a
vulgar tale, the Pardoner tells a well-managed
story with an excellent moral, then shows his
insincerity by offering (for a consideration) to
show the very relics which he has confessed to be
rank frauds.

As these inseparables ride side by side, the
Pardoner sings a song of which all trace has been
lost, but which was probably a popular love-song
of the day ; and his thin goat's voice is accompanied by the deep bass burden of the Summoner.

"With him there rode a gentle Pardoner
Of Rouncevale, his friend and his compeer,
That straight was comen fro the court of Romé
Full loud he sung *Come hither, lové, to me !*

[1] in all ways	[3] unless	[5] were it not
[2] knows	[4] by deception	[6] cajoleries

This Summoner bare to him a stiff burdoun [1]
Was never trump of half so great a soun.
The Pardoner had hair as yellow as wax
But smooth it hung as doth a strike of flax ;
By ounces [2] hung his lockés that he had,
And therewith he his shoulders overspread.
But thin it lay, by colpons [3] one and one
But hood, for jollity, ne wered he none,
For it was trusséd up in his wallét
Him thought he rode all of the newé jet ; [4]

THE PARDONER
(*From the Ellesmere MS.*).

Dishevelled, save his cap, he rode all bare.
Such glaring eyen [5] had he as a hare,
A vernicle [6] had he sewed upon his cap ;
His wallet lay before him in his lap
Bret-full [7] of pardon, come from Rome all hot.
A voice he had as small as hath a goat ;

[1] burden or accompaniment
[2] shreds
[3] strips
[4] style
[5] eyes
[6] the " true image," a copy of the handkerchief of St Veronica, worn by pilgrims to her shrine
[7] full to bursting

No beard had he, nor never shouldé have,
As smooth it was as it were late y-shave ;
I trow he were a gelding or a mare.
But of his craft, from Berwick unto Ware
Ne was there such another Pardoner,
For in his male[1] he had a pillow-beer,[2]
Which that, he saidé, was our lady's veil ;
He said he had a gobbet[3] of the sail
That Sainté Peter had when that he went
Upon the sea, till Jesus Christ him hente.[4]
He had a cross of latten,[5] full of stones,
And in a glass he haddé piggés bones.
But with these relikés, when that he fond[6]
A pooré parson dwelling upon lond,[7]
Upon that day he got him more moneye
Than that the parson got in monthés tweye ;
And thus with feigned flattery and japes
He made the parson and the people his apes.
But, truély to tellen atté last,
He was in church a noble ecclesiast ;
Well could he read a lesson or a story,
But alderbest[8] he sung an Offertory ;
For well he wisté, when that song was sung,
He musté preach, and well affile[9] his tongue
To winné silver, as he full well could ;
Therefore he sung the merrierly and loud."

Rouncevale was probably the name of the fraternity to which the Pardoner belonged. There was a Rounceval Hall in Oxford, and a hospital of the Blessed Mary of Rounceval near Charing Cross, in London, probably both named from the church of Roncevailes near Pamplona in Spain, which was built in memory of one of Charlemagne's leaders, and attained a great vogue amongst pilgrims. The change in the relative importance of places is illustrated by the casual mention "from Berwick unto Ware,"

[1] pack
[2] pillow-case
[3] cutting
[4] caught
[5] sheet metal
[6] found
[7] land
[8] best of all
[9] smooth

showing that Ware was a notable last stage toward London, and was regarded as a sort of southern boundary of the Midlands.

The relics carried by this precious Pardoner were, alas! about on a par with too many of the fraudulent oddments sold by unscrupulous wonder-mongers to credulous or covetous priests and monks; and by them shown to still more credulous people. The attitude of reasonably well-educated men toward these frauds is shown by Chaucer's frank statement that the bones in the glass were those of a pig: and his cautious statement that the Pardoner "said" what the other relics were. The latten cross, studded with cut stones, and borne in full view, is the one thing unequivocally mentioned. The Pardoner is perfectly frank about his own methods and deceits, for in the prologue to his tale he tells us:

> "... in churches when I preach,
> I painé[1] me to have an hauteyn[2] speech,
> And ring it out as round as goeth a bell,
> For I kan[3] all by roté that I tell.
> My theme is always one, and ever was,—
> *Radix malorum est Cupiditas.*[4]
> First, I pronouncé whennés that I come,
> And then my bullés shew I, all and some;
> Our liegé lordés seal on my patente,
> That shew I first, my body to warrent,
> That no man be so bold, ne[5] priest, ne[5] clerk,
> Me to disturb of Christé's holy work;
> And, after that, then tell I forth my tales,
> Bullés of popés and of cardinales,
> Of patriarchs and bishoppés I shew,
> And in Latín I speak a wordés few

[1] take pains
[2] dignified
[3] know
[4] love of money is the root of evil
[5] nor

To saffron [1] with my predicatión
And for to stir them to devotión :
Then shew I forth my longé crystal stones
Y-crammed full of cloutés and of bones,—
Relics be they, as wenen [2] they each one ;
Then have I in latoun [3] a shoulder bone
Which that was of an holy Jewés sheep.

　　Good men, I say, take of my wordés keep,—
If that this bone be washed in any well,
If cow, or calf, or sheep, or oxé swell
That any worm hath eat, or worm y-stung,
Take water of that well and wash his tongue,
And it is whole anon ; and furthermore
Of pockés, and of scab, and every sore."

This water had many other valuable
properties for man and beast ; and he related
the virtues of a mitten :—

" He that his hand will put in this mittayn,
He shall have multiplying of his grain,
When he hath sowén, be it wheat or oats,
So that he offer pence, or ellés groats.

　　Good men and women, one thing I warn you,
If any wight [4] be in this churché now
That hath done sinné horrible, that he
Dare not for sin of it y-shriven be,
Or any woman, be she young or old,
That hath y-made her husband cuckéwold,[5]
Such folk shall have no power, ne no grace
To offer to my relics in this place ;
And whoso findeth him out of [6] such blame
They will come up and offer in Goddés name,
And I assoil them by authority
Which that by bull y-granted was to me.
By this gaud [7] have I wonné year by year,
A hundred marks since I was Pardoner
I preaché so as you have heard before,
And tell a hundred falsé japés more ;
Of avarice and of such cursedness

[1] tinge or flavour
[2] believe
[3] sheet metal ; doubtless a box
　　or case
[4] person
[5] committed adultery
[6] free from
[7] trick

Is all my preaching, for to make them free
To give their pence, and namely unto me ;
For mine intent is not but for to win,
And no thing for correctión of sin."

When people did not subscribe, after his plain statement that non-subscribers were self-confessed notorious sinners ; he held them up to public rebuke and scorn, mentioning no names, but giving hints and signs.

" Thus spit I out my venom under hue
Of holiness, to seem holy and true.
But shortly, mine intent I will devise,—
I preach of no thing but of coveityse ;[1]
Therefore my theme is yet and ever was
Radix malorum est Cupiditas.
Thus can I preach against that samé vice
Which that I use, and that is avarice ;
But though myself be guilty in that sin
Yet can I maken other folk to twin[2]
From avarice, and soré to repent ;
But that is not my principal intent
I preaché no thing but for coveityse.[3]

   .   .   .   .   .

For I will preach and beg in sundry lands ;
I will not do no labour with mine hands,
Nor maké baskettés and live thereby,
Because I will not beggen[4] idelly.[5]
I will none of the Apostles counterfeit,
I will have money, woollé,[6] cheese and wheat,
Al[7] were it given of the poorest page,
Or of the poorest widow in a villáge,
Al[7] should their children starvé for famíne.
Nay, I will drinké liquor of the vine,
And have a jolly wench in every town ;"

   .   .   .   .   .

Then, with the admission that "myself be a

[1] covetousness
[2] part
[3] covetousness
[4] beg
[5] idly
[6] wool
[7] though

full vicious man," he began a moral story after drinking a draught of corny ale.

At the conclusion of the tale he made an impassioned appeal to his hearers against covetousness, and whether from sheer impertinence or because it had become an irresistible habit to do so, promised them absolution—

> " So that you offer nobles, or sterlíngs,
>   Or ellés silver brooches, spoonés, rings.
>   Boweth[1] your heads under this holy bull !
>   Come up, ye wivés, offer of your wull ![2]
>   Your names I enter here in my roll anon ;
>   Into the bliss of heaven shall ye gon :[3]
>
>   .   .   .   .   .   .
>
> I have relikes and pardon in my male."[4]

That such a picture is no great exaggeration, we know from ample evidence. These pardoners and granters of indulgences, protected by bulls from the pope or some foreign religious house, wandered about the country, or from one land to another, without even the checks that were imposed on limiters and summoners. Taking up their trade from sheer greed of easy gain, these black sheep had sufficient education to enable them to secure credentials, and had then sufficient wit to keep themselves out of the clutches of the Church and the sheriff while they preyed upon the fears of the ignorant, the superstitious, and the simple religious folk.

The basis of the idea of pardons and indulgences was the Treasury of Merits, supposed to be formed by the merits of the Redeemer, the Virgin, saints, and holy people, possessed in

---

[1] bow   [2] will   [3] go   [4] wallet

excess of those needed for their own salvation. These merits formed a reservoir, which had long been drawn upon before its value was defined in a bull of Pope Clement VI. in 1350, when he explained that the superabundant merits had been formed into a treasury, "not one that is deposited in a strong room or buried in a field, but intended to be usefully distributed to the faithful, through the blessed Peter, keeper of Heaven's gate, and through his successors." There was "no fear of an absorption or diminution of this treasure, first because of the infinite merits of Christ, and again because the more numerous the people reclaimed through the use of its contents, the more it is augmented by the addition of their merits." The merits of this treasury were to be won by prayer and fasting, penance and psalm-singing; but those who could not say the necessary number of prayers were allowed, instead, to contribute to good works. Thus great funds were collected for the waging of war in Palestine, and elsewhere against the paynim, for building bridges, churches, and cathedrals, and for the support of the poor; and so far the system was good. But abuses crept in, and men like Chaucer's pardoners, wandering out of the jurisdiction of those who had given them their documents, or trading on forged or stolen bulls, gave account to no one, and brought immense discredit on the Church.

Pope Boniface IX. (1389-1404) recognised the scandal, and made it the subject of one of his pontifical letters to the Church, in which he says that these pardoners are sometimes secular priests and sometimes friars, but always very

GODBEGOT HOUSE, WINCHESTER.

Anciently a Pilgrims' Rest-house.

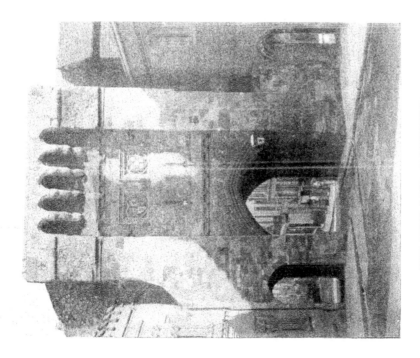

THE WEST GATE, WINCHESTER.

impudent. They dispense with all ecclesiastical license, and go from village to village, making speeches, showing relics, and selling pardon. The success of authorised pardoners causes self-seeking pardoners to issue from the school or the priory or from nothingness, greedy, true vagabonds, infesting the highways, caring for none, but impertinently plying their trade. They scruple not to loose on earth that which may be bound in heaven. They proclaim to the faithful and simple people their true or pretended authorisations, and in pursuit of hateful gain, sum up their impudence by claiming authorisations which are false or pretended. For a paltry money payment they throw the veil of a lying absolution, not over penitents, but over men of hardened conscience, who persist in iniquity, remitting the penalties of horrible crimes without any contrition or the performance of any usual penances. They release from vows of chastity, of abstinence, and of pilgrimage beyond seas: they allow heretics to re-enter the Church; and as their power comes from themselves only, nothing checks it, and they use it without let or hindrance.

Boniface went so far as to allege that there were regular associations or guilds of these parasites, and ordered the bishops to make search and inquiry for such people, examine their authorisations and receipts for remittances to headquarters, and if there was any doubt, keep them in prison, without other form of law, until the matter had been referred to Rome.

The Bishop of Durham, in 1340, had taken steps to abate the same nuisance, ordering all

o

vicars and curates in his diocese to prevent all preaching and pardoning by men whose only credentials came from a distance, and to seize from them any money or other articles they had collected.

Pope Urban V., in 1369, tried to suppress the same sort of thing, and especially took notice of the injury done to parish priests and curates; and many other popes and bishops made similar efforts. But the difficulties were great: some men in high places were almost as shameless pardoners as the one in Chaucer's company; and when, in 1414, the University of Oxford moved for the abolition of the whole system, it was found impossible for anything to be done. And nothing was done until the great storm of the Reformation swept the pardoners from one country after another; a storm which was in great part aroused by their doings. At that time the Decree of Reform of the pope (Pius IV., in 1562) stated that there was no further hope of amending the pardoners, therefore their use, and the name of them, were entirely abolished throughout all Christendom.

If much space has been given to the consideration of this character, it is because, while he is one of the least pleasant, he is one of the most important as illustrating a chief feature of the time,—waning faith being gradually overwhelmed by superstition and duplicity.

We shall have a view of the "Poor Parson," whose pure, beautiful life is in charming contrast with those of the luxurious and indifferent monk and friar, and of the degraded summoner and pardoner; but first we have two churchmen, one

connected with the business side of a religious
house, the other unbeneficed.

"A gentle Manciple was there of a temple,
Of which achaatours [1] mighté take exemple

THE MANCIPLE
(*From the Ellesmere MS.*).

For to be wise in buying of vitaille ; [2]
For whether that he paid or took by taille [3]
Always he waited so in his achaat [4]
That he was ay before, and in good state.

[1] buyers   [3] tally, *i.e.* on credit
[2] provisions   [4] buying

Now is not that of God a full fair grace
That such a lewéd [1] mannés wit shall pace
The wisdom of a heap of learned men ?
Of masters had he more than thriés ten,
That were of law expert and curious,
Of which there were a dozen in that house
Worthy to be stewárds of rent and land
Of any lord that is in Engéland,
To make him livé by his proper good [2]
In honour debtéless, but [3] he were wood, [4]
Or live as scarcely [5] as him list desire ;
And able for to helpen all a shire
In any case that mighté fall or hap ;
And yet this Manciple set hir aller cappe." [6]

The picture is so complete that nothing need be added to it. This unlettered man knew that he that is diligent in business shall stand before kings, and made himself the master of his many masters. A similarly estimable character, though one absolutely lacking in business acumen, is the Clerk of Oxford.

" A Clerk there was of Oxenford also
That unto logic haddé long y-go. [7]
As leané was his horse as is a rake,
And he nas [8] not right fat, I undertake,
But lookéd hollow, and ther-to [9] soberly [10]
Full threadbare was his overest [11] courtepy ; [12]
For he had getten him yet no benefice,
Ne was so worldly for to have office ;
For him was lever [13] have at his bed's head
Tweénty bookés clad in black and red
Of Aristotle and his philosophy,
Than robés rich, or fithele, [14] or gay sautrie : [15]

[1] uneducated
[2] within his means
[3] unless
[4] mad
[5] frugally
[6] set all their caps, *i.e.* was able to out-wit and manage them
[7] gone
[8] was not
[9] moreover
[10] poorly
[11] uppermost
[12] cape
[13] would rather
[14] fiddle
[15] psaltery

But all be that he was a philosopher,
Yet haddé he but little gold in coffer;
But all that he might of his friendés hente [1]
On bookés and on learning he it spent,
And busily 'gan for the soulés pray
Of them that gave him where-with to scoleye [2]
Of study took he most care and most heed,
Not one word spoke he moré than was need,

THE CLERK OF OXENFORD
(*From the Ellesmere MS.*).

And that was said in form and reverence,
And short and quick and full of high senténce.
Sowning [3] in moral virtue was his speech,
And gladly would he learn and gladly teach."

This admirable young scholar stood little chance of preferment in competition with such successful self-seekers as were represented even in

[1] obtain   [2] study   [3] tending to

the small company of pilgrims. His best prospect was that he might obtain some small country parsonage, such as was held by the last pilgrim of the original company, of whom we have Chaucer's description. Before passing to him, however, it may be well to note the contrast between this Clerk of Oxenford and two others. The one who became the fifth husband of the Wife of Bath, by whom he was courted while her fourth husband still lived, was a very different sort of person ; and so, too, was the clerk Nicholas of the Reeve's tale, who beguiled the carpenter.

The Poor Parson of a Town, with his brother the Plowman, whom we have already discussed, form a very charming pair, of whom little need be said beyond what is given in Chaucer's own words. "A town" evidently means quite a small country village, for we are expressly told that his parish was wide, and houses far asunder ;—he was, in fact, the prototype of the good parson of Sweet Auburn.

> " A good man was there of religioun,
> And was a Pooré Parson of a Town ;
> But rich he was of holy thought and work ;
> He was alsó a learnéd man, a clerk,
> That Christés gospel trewély would preach :
> His parishens[1] devoutly would he teach.
> Benign he was, and wondrous diligent,
> And in adversity full patiént ;
> And such he was y-proved ofté sithes.[2]
> Full loth were he to cursen[3] for his tythes,
> But rather would he given,[4] out of doubt,[5]
> Unto his pooré parishens about,
> Of his off'ríng, and eke of his substánce ;
> He could in little thing have suffisance.[6]

[1] parishioners
[2] times
[3] curse or excommunicate (the non-payers)
[4] give
[5] without doubt
[6] sufficiency

Wide was his parish and houses far asunder,
But he ne lefté nat [1] for rain nor thunder,
In sickness nor in mischief to visíte
The furthest in his parish, much and lite, [2]
Upon his feet, and in his hand a staff.
This noble ensample to his sheep he yaf [3]
That first he wrought and afterward he taught.
Out of the gospel he those wordés caught,
And this figúre he added eke thereto,
That if gold rusté what shall iron do ?
For if a priest be foul, on whom we trust,
No wonder is a lewéd [4] man to rust ;

THE POOR PARSON
(*From the Ellesmere MS.*).

And shame it is if a priest také keep,
A shiten [5] shepherd and a clené sheep.
Well ought a priest ensample for to give
By his cleannéss how that his sheep should live.
He setté not his benefice to hire
And left his sheep encumbered in the mire,
And ran to Londoun, unto Saínt Poules, [6]
To seken him a chantery for souls ;
Or with a brotherhood to be withhold,
But dwelt at home and kepté well his fold,

[1] never failed   [3] gave   [5] befouled
[2] great and small   [4] ignorant   [6] Paul's

So that the wolf ne made it not miscarry,—
He was a shepherd, not a mercenary :
And though he holy was, and virtuous,
He was to sinful man not despitous,[1]
Nor of his speeché dangerous nor digne,[2]
But in his teaching discreet and benign,
To drawen folk to heaven by fairnéss,
By good ensample, this was his business :
But it were any person obstinate,
What so he were, of high or low estate,
Him would he snybben[3] sharply for the nonys.[4]
A better priest I trow that nowhere none is ;
He waited after no pomp and reverence
Nor maked him a spicéd[5] conscience,
But Christés lore, and His Apostles twelve,
He taught, but first he followed it himselve."

At this point one would gladly leave the pilgrims ; but there are two more, described in the *Canterbury Tales*, though not in the prologue. They are the Canon-alchemist, and his Yeoman, who overtook the other pilgrims on the fourth day at Boughton-under-Blean. They represented the scientific delusion of the age, and the Yeoman began by lying as shamelessly as ever did any Pardoner. Describing his master, he says :—

"That all this ground on which we be riding,
  Till that we come to Canterbury town,
  He could all cleané turn it upside-down,
  And pave it all of silver and of gold."

In feigned astonishment the Host cried, "Benedicite!" but expressed wonder that so great a man should care so little for his appearance, and pointed out that his cloak was dirty and ragged. Whereat the Yeoman admitted that his master, like other great men, was somewhat

[1] unsympathetic
[2] haughty
[3] reprove
[4] nonce ; time being
[5] pampered

GATEWAY BUILDING (INTERIOR), HYDE ABBEY, WINCHESTER.

slovenly.   Further pressing and leading from the
Host induced the Yeoman to tell the story of his
experiences as an alchemist, and to decide on
leaving his master's service; and the story, as

THE CANON'S YEOMAN
(*From the Ellesmere MS.*).

given by Chaucer, is a wonderful exposition of
the methods of mediæval alchemy.   The list of
drugs, chemicals and elixirs, the names of vessels
and tools, and the descriptions of methods, form a

short but very full treatise of greatest possible interest, and the story of the hopes and fears, the self-deceptions and deceptions of others that made up the alchemist's lot, is full of instruction. The doings of the Canon, who was apparently an honest investigator, spending his own money and all that he could raise from others in experiments from which he constantly expected great returns, are even more interesting than those of the fraudulent teacher of alchemy whose tricks were exposed. In the days before modern methods of exact observation, the alchemists did much good pioneer work in chemistry, and if their time and money were often wasted on wild-goose chases, their beliefs and hopes were on a par with the general ignorance of the period. The story of their doings, introduced as by an afterthought, tends greatly toward the completeness of Chaucer's picture of mediæval life.

CHAPTER X

TALES OF THE FIRST DAY

"When that Aprillé with his showerés soote [1]
The drought of March hath piercéd to the roote,
And bathéd every vein in such liquor
Of which virtúe engendered is the flower;
When Zephirus eek with his sweeté breath
Inspiréd hath in every holt and heath
The tender croppés, and the youngé sun
Hath in the Ram his halfé course y-run,
And smallé fowlés maken melodye,
That sleepen all the night with open eye,—
So pricketh them Natúre in their couráges,—
Then longen folk to go on pilgrimages,
And palmers for to seeken strangé strands,
To ferne [2] halwes,[3] kowthe [4] in sundry lands
And specially from every shirés end
Of Engéland, to Canterbury they wend,
The holy, blissful martyr for to seek
That them hath holpen when that they were sick."

Before we take our staffs in hand to follow
Chaucer's pilgrims' road, it may be well to
consider the nature of the country through which
we are to travel. Fortunately, in Lambarde's
"Perambulation," Kent possesses the earliest
County History, and one which may well be
taken as a model for its thoroughness and its

---

[1] sweet   [2] ancient   [3] shrines   [4] known; celebrated

219

discrimination. Although Lambarde wrote in 1570, two hundred years after Chaucer's day, and thirty years after the final blow had been given to the pilgrimages by Henry VIII., his work affords most valuable glimpses of the state of Kent even in the pilgrims' times. He tells us that "the soil is for the most part bountiful, consisting indifferently of arable, pasture, meadow and wood land," of which "wood occupieth the greatest portion even till this day. . . . In fertile and fruitful woods and trees, this country is most flourishing also, whether you respect the mast of oak, beech and chesten for cattle : or the fruit of apples, pears, cherries and plums for men, for . . . it hath whole woods that bear chestnut (a fruit whereof even delicate persons disdain not to feed), not commonly seen in other counties. As for orchards of apples and gardens of cherries, and those of the most delicious and exquisite kinds that can be, no part of the realm (that I know) hath them, either in such quantity and number, or with such art and industry set and planted." Of horses, cattle and sheep, Lambarde says the only peculiarity of Kent is that, "it bringeth forth the largest of stature in each kind," and reminds us that even in the time of Polydorus, the Kentish poultry was notable for its size. Parks of fallow deer and warrens of grey rabbits were very numerous, though we are told that half the parks had been disforested within living memory, while the rabbits (being sources of profit, and the deer merely for pleasure) had fully held their own or even increased. Of the gentry, mention shall be made anon. Of the yeomanry, Lambarde says that they are nowhere more free and jolly than in this shire, for that "there were never any bondmen (or villaines, as the law calleth them) in Kent." The tenure of the yeomen was (as it still is) freehold, "and in this their estate, they please themselves, and joy exceedingly, insomuch, as a man may find sundry yeomen (although for wealth comparable with many of the gentle sort) that will not change their condition, nor desire to be apparelled with the titles of gentry. Neither is this any cause of disdain, or of alienation of the good minds of one sort from the other; for nowhere else in all this realm is the common people more willingly governed. To be short, they be most commonly civil, just and bountiful, so that the estate of the old franklins and yeomen of England either yet liveth in Kent or else it is quite dead and departed out of the realm for altogether."

The industries of the county were husbandry and its kindred arts, seafaring, working in stone, iron, and fuel wood; and, most importantly, the making of coloured woollen cloths, "in which last feat they excel, as from whom is drawn both sufficient store to furnish the wear of the best sort of our own nation at home, and great plenty also to be transported to other foreign countries abroad."

Nearness to London, and situation on a great national highway (the Dover Road, or the Watling Street), were noted by Lambarde as affecting the men, as well as some of the industries of Kent. The land supported no red deer, because it had no "great walks of waste ground," and it had no black conies (or as we should now say, silver-grey rabbits), for black conies are kept partly for their skins, which have their season in winter; and Kent, by its nearness to London, "hath so quick a market of young rabbits that it killeth this game chiefly in summer." Of the gentry, he tells us that "the gentlemen be not here (throughout) of so ancient stocks as elsewhere, especially in the parts nearer to London, from which city (as it were from a certain rich and wealthy seed-plot), courtiers, lawyers, and merchants be continually translated, and do become new plants amongst them. Yet be their revenues greater than anywhere else; which thing groweth not so much by the quantity of their possession, or by the fertility of their soil, as by the benefit of the situation of the country itself . . . by the sea, the river, a populous city and a well-traded highway, by the commodities whereof the superfluous fruits of the ground be dearly sold, and consequently the land may yield a greater rent. These gentlemen be also acquainted with good letters and trained in the laws. They manure[1] some large portion of their territories as well for the maintenance of their families, as also for their better increase in wealth. So that they be well employed both in the public service and in their own particular, and do use hawking, hunting, and other sports, rather for their recreation than for an occupation of pastime."

Thus rich in every way, by natural and by industrial circumstance, Kent well maintained at the close of the pilgrimages, that old reputation of which she has long been proud. She was

---

[1] Manuring, at this time, indicated tillage and cultivation rather than the application of fertilisers.

famous, as Dickens tells us by the lips of Jingle, for "apples, cherries, hops,[1] and women," famous for her free-born, free-soil yeomen, of whom Scott makes Wamba sing :

> "For a yeoman of Kent, with his yearly rent,
> There ne'er was a widow could say him nay,"

and little less famous for her seventy miles of the most important portion of the greatest Roman road, along which the commerce, the culture, and the diplomacy of Europe have rolled for a couple of thousand years toward Westminster and London.

Of this seaward portion of the Watling Street, the fifty-six miles from London to Canterbury form Chaucer's Pilgrims' Way, and, with the exception of some twelve miles between Dartford and Strood, the modern Dover Road follows the same line. Let us try to trace the way as Chaucer's pilgrims saw it. We will join them at the Tabard, in the borough of Southwark, where we hear that a goodly party is assembling to start on the morrow. Thus, in Chaucer's words :—

> "Befel that in that season on a day,
> In Southwark at the Tabard as I lay,
> Ready to wenden on my pilgrimage
> To Canterbury with full devout couráge,
> At night were come into that hostelry
> Well nine-and-twenty in a company,
> Of sundry folk, by áventure[2] y-fall[3]
> In fellowship, and pilgrims were they all,
> That toward Canterbury woulden ride.
> The chambers and the stables weren wide,
> And well we weren easéd atté best.
> And shortly, when the sunné was to rest,

[1] Hops began to be freely used in the reign of Henry VIII.
[2] chance   [3] fallen ; thrown

> So had I spoken with them everyone
> That I was of their fellowship anon,
> And madé forward early for to rise,
> To make our way, there as I you devise."

The Tabard, of which nothing now remains, save the name, attached to a modern inn on the same site (No. 85 Borough High Street), was orginally built as a London House for the Abbot of Hyde, Winchester, in 1307. It stood in the Borough High Street, the busy market-road leading from London Bridge into Kent, and until long after the close of the pilgrimages, was surrounded by good gardens and orchards, which broke the line of houses on both sides of the Borough, while thick plantations of trees ran along the river side below London Bridge. The house was large and rambling, many-gabled, built of huge timbers with lath-and-plaster between, extended around three sides of a great square, with storehouses, brewhouse, harness-rooms, and rooms for the horse-keepers on the fourth side, and beyond that again a second great square surrounded by stables. The first square was entered by an archway through the front portion of the house itself, and another archway led through the far side of the square to the stable yard. The first duty of the travellers was to see their horses well bestowed, then to partake of the meat and drink set before them—great loaves of bread, thin oaten cakes, huge joints, meat pies and mutton pasties, washed down with nut-brown ale. For men of the Kentish weald, and others who loved the apple-drink, there was pomage or cider made from the fruit of the very orchards through which they were about to pass; and

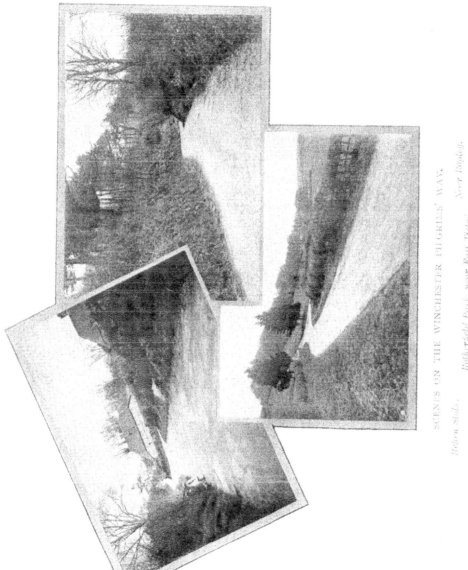

SCENES ON THE WINCHESTER PILGRIMS' WAY.

Bclacn Stoke.   Rotherfield Park, near East Tisted.   Near Ropley.

wines of foreign lands were also on the generous
board. Chaucer says :—

> " Great cheeré made our Hoste us everyone,
> And to the supper set he us anon,
> And servéd us with victual at the best ;
> Strong was the wine and well to drink us leste [1]
>   A seemly man our Hosté was withal.
> For to have been a marshal in a hall.
> A largé man he was, with eyen [2] stepe, [3]
> A fairer burgess is there none in Chepe ; [4]
> Bold of his speech, and wise, and well y-taught
> And of manhood him lackedé right naught.
> Eke thereto he was right a merry man,
> And after supper pleyen [5] he began,
> And spake of mirth amongés other things,
> When that we haddé made our reckonings ;
> And saidé thus : ' Now, lordings, trewély, [6]
> Ye be to me right welcome heartily ;
> For by my troth, if that I shall not lie,
> I ne [7] saw this year so merry a company
> At onés [8] in this harbour as is now ;
> Fain would I do you mirthé, wist I how.
> And of a mirth I am right now bethought,
> To do you ease, and it shall costé naught.
> You go to Canterbury—God you speed,
> The blissful martyr quité you your meed !
> And well I woot, [9] as ye go by the way
> Ye shapen you to talen and to play ;
> For trewely comfort ne mirth is none
> To ridé by the way dumb as a stone ;
> And therefore will I maken you disport,
> As I said erst, [10] and do you some comfort.
> And if you liketh all, by one assent,
> Now for to standen at my judgément,
> And for to worken as I shall you say,
> To-morrow when ye riden by the way,

[1] " us leste " = it pleased us	[6] truly
[2] eyes	[7] not
[3] bright	[8] once
[4] Cheapside	[9] know
[5] jesting	[10] before

P

Now, by my father's soulé, that is dead,
But ye be merry, smité off my head !
Hold up your hand, withouten moré speech.'
Our conseil was not longé for to seche ;[1]
Us thought it was naught worth to make it wíse,
And granted him withouten more avise,
And bade him say his verdict, as he leste.[2]
    ' Lordings,' quoth he, ' now hearken for the best ;
But take it naught, I pray you, in disdain ;
This is the point, to speaken short and plain,
That each of you, to shorté with your way
In this viage[3] shall tellé talés tweye,[4]—
To Canterburyward, I mean it so,
And homeward he shall tellen other two,—
Of aventúres that whilom[5] have befall.
And which of you that beareth him best of all,
That is to say, that telleth in this case
Talés of best senténce[6] and most soláce,
Shall have a supper at our aller[7] cost,
Here in this placé, sitting by this post,
When that we come again fro Canterbury.
And, for to maké you the moré merry,
I will myselven gladly with you ride
Right at mine owén cost, and be your guide ;
And whoso will my judgément withsay
Shall pay all that we spenden by the way.
And if ye vouchésafe that it be so
Tell me anon, withouten wordés mo,
And I will early shapé[8] me therefor.'
    This thing was granted, and our oathés swore
With full glad heart, and prayden him also
That he would vouchésafe for to do so,
And that he wouldé be our governour,
And of our talés judge and réportour,
And set a supper at a certain price,
And we would ruléd be by his device[9]
In high and low ; and thus, by one consent
We been[10] accorded to his judgément.

[1] seek	[6] judgment
[2] pleased	[7] of all
[3] journey	[8] prepare
[4] two	[9] plan ; scheme
[5] once upon a time	[10] did be ; were

And thereupon the wine was fet[1] anon ;
We dronken, and to resté went each one,
Withouten any longer tarrying."

As was the custom of the time, the guests disposed themselves to sleep in those chambers which "weren wide," and not in the small private rooms that would be expected nowadays. Grooms and horse-keepers slept in the stables and barns, the serving-men found beds amongst the rushes or straw of the hall and other downstairs rooms, the general guests lay on couches, or benches, or on the floor in the great upper rooms, with or without beds, that were practically long, wide sacks, stuffed with straw, rushes, or hay. The women had their separate rooms, and possibly some guest of great importance or fastidiousness would be accommodated with a bedstead, and a room reserved for himself. Bedsteads and couches were not necessities in those days. Great folk, when they visited the distant houses of their friends, quite frequently carried their beds with them, and did the same when changing from one to another of their own houses. Bedsteads, as we know them, were introduced in the fifteenth century, and at about the same time, night-clothes, and the habit of discarding the day-clothes before sleep, were noticed as luxurious innovations.

Whatever may have been the accommodation, we may hope that the pilgrims all slept soundly, for they made an early start next morning. The sun rose about five o'clock, and at an even earlier hour the men and maids of the period were

[1] fetched

expected to be up and about their work, in stable or field, in washhouse, bakehouse, or brewhouse. The Host of the Tabard probably roused his guests before sunrise :—

> "Up rose our Host and was our aller cock,
> And gathered us together all in a flock,
> And forth we riden, a little more than paas,[1]
> Unto the watering of Saint Thomas."

The speed, "a little more than pace," reminds us that the pilgrimage was in the day of horses noted for strength rather than for speed, over a way which had fallen into much neglect since the time of the road-making Romans, while this first part would not be over the Roman road, since that ran direct to Westminster, passing to the south of the borough. Moreover, a party of thirty men and women, variously mounted, of very varied abilities in the saddle, and with the need for stopping to repair minor mishaps and to keep the whole company together, would necessarily move slowly. A royal pilgrim, the queen-mother Isabella, on her pilgrimage in 1358, slept the first night at Dartford, fifteen miles from London, the second at Rochester (thirty miles), the third at Ospringe (forty-seven miles), and on the fourth day arrived at Canterbury. John of France, a couple of years later, spent the nights of his pilgrimage at Dartford, Rochester, and Ospringe, dining at Sittingbourne on the third day; and other records show that these were the usual stages on journeys of state or business, as well as on pilgrimage. This slow progress would give ample time for long rests, during which the

---

[1] pace; a walk

tales of Chaucer's pilgrims could be enjoyed : and although it is clear that parts of the stories were told while the cavalcade was in motion, it seems reasonable to suppose that most of them were given during halts by the way—or they could not have been heard by so large a party. Other considerations bearing upon this point will be seen anon.

Meanwhile, by ways of which no semblance remains to-day, and very little record (save in the name of Tabard Street, which runs along the first half-mile of their route), the pilgrims reached the first " Watering of St Thomas," a name given to many wells, springs, and streams along the roads to Canterbury. This particular watering was a stream near the second milestone on the Dover Road, commemorated to-day by the name of St Thomas Street, on the south side of the Old Kent Road, and by the Thomas à Becket Inn. Here a pause was made :

> " And there our Host began his horse arrest
> And saidé, 'Lordings, hearken, if you leste
> Ye woot[1] your foreword and I it you record.
> If even-song and morrow-song accord
> Let see now who shall tell the firsté tale.
> As ever mote[2] I drinké wine or ale,
> Whoso be rebel to my judgément
> Shall pay for all that by the way is spent.
> Now draweth cut, ere that we further twynne[3]
> He which that hath the shortest shall begin.
> Sire Knight,' quoth he, 'my master and my lord,
> Now draweth cut, for that is mine accord.[4]
> Come near,' quoth he, 'my lady Prioress,
> And you sir Clerk, let be your shamefacedness,
> Ne studieth naught ; lay hand to, every man.'
>   Anon to drawen every wight began,

[1] know   [2] may   [3] proceed   [4] agreement

> And shortly for to tellen as it was,
> Were it by áventúre, or sort,[1] or cas,[2]
> The sooth[3] is this, the cut fell to the knight,
> Of which full blithe and glad was every wight :
> And tell he must his tale, as was reasoun,
> By foreward[4] and by composicioun,[5]
> As ye have heard ; what needeth wordés mo ? "

The lottery of "drawing cut" was by one person (in this case the Host) breaking a number of pieces of straw or grass to about the same length, and one appreciably shorter. Gathering them all in his hand, so that only the ends were seen, he allowed his companions to draw, the lot falling upon him who drew the short piece. In this case the Knight, drawing the short cut, at once accepts fate's decision :—

> " And when this good man saw that it was so,
> As he that wise was and obedient
> To keep his foreward by his free assent,
> He saidé, 'Since I shall begin the game,
> What, welcome be the cut in Goddés name !
> Now let us ride and hearken what I say.'
> And with that word we riden[6] forth our way ;
> And he began with right a merry cheer
> His tale anon, and said in this manére."

The Knight's tale of the fates of Palamon and Arcite is characteristic of the man by whom it is supposed to be told, with his love of chivalry and martial matters. Its language and construction agree well with the culture of the man who—

> " . . . never yet no villainy ne sayde,
> In all his life, unto no manner wight
> He was a very perfect, gentle knight."

[1] fate	[4] prearrangement
[2] chance	[5] undertaking
[3] truth	[6] rode

All through the story, to its last line of benediction :

"And God save all this fairé company.
                    Amen,"

the tone suitable to the knight is well preserved. It is a long poem of some two thousand two hundred and fifty lines, and for a reason that we shall see shortly, Chaucer meant that most of it should be told during a rest. At its ending "there was not young or old" in all the company but said it was a noble story, well worth remembering. The Host—

"... laugh and swore, "So may I gon,
This goeth aright ; unbuckled is the male ;[1]
Let see now who shall tell another tale ;
For trewely the game is well begun."

He called upon the Monk for the next story, but the Miller, who was so drunk that he could scarce sit his horse, and could not keep hat or hood upon his head, interrupted "in Pilate's voice," or in the harsh, ranting tone used by Pontius Pilate in the miracle plays. He insisted on telling the second story, but the Host, seeing his condition, tried to pacify him, and only when the effort proved fruitless, bade him proceed in his own devil's way. Thereupon the Miller said :—

"That I am drunk, I know it by my sound ;
And, therefore, if that I mis-speak or say,
Wyte[2] it the ale of Southwark, I you pray ;"

and proposed to tell the story of a carpenter, his wife, and her lover, whereupon the Reeve interfered, bidding him refrain from tales of harlotry.

[1] a pedlar's wallet   [2] blame

The Miller, far from being dissuaded, replied at some length to the Reeve, and forthwith commenced his tale, for the inclusion of which the poet makes this apology to the reader :—

> " What should I moré say, but this Millér
> He nolde [1] his wordés for no man forbear,
> But told his churlés tale in his manére.
> Methinketh that I shall rehearse it here :
> And therefore every gentle wight I pray,
> For Goddés love, deemeth not that I say
> Of evil intent, but for I moot [2] rehearse
> Their talés allé, be they bettre or worse
> Or ellés falsen [3] some of my mattere :
> And therefore, whoso list it not y-hear,[4]
> Turn over the leaf and choose another tale ;
> For he shall find enow, both great and smale,
> Of storial thing that toucheth gentilesse,
> And eke morality, and holiness,—
> Blameth not me if that ye choose amiss.
> The Miller is a churl, ye know well this,
> So was the Reve, and other many mo,
> And harlotry they tolden bothé two.
> Aviseth you, putteth me out of blame
> And eke men shall not maken ernest of game."

The Miller's story of the rich churl who was a carpenter in Oxford, and of the poor scholar, Nicholas, is full of incidental touches redolent of the period. The poor scholar was learned in astrology, and could predict rain or drought. The fact that he had a separate sleeping-room is noted :

> " A chamber had he in that hostelry
> Alone, withouten any company,"

and we are told that it was daintily decked with sweet herbs, while the scholar himself was as " sweet as is the root of licorice or any cetewale "

---

[1] would not   [2] must   [3] falsify   [4] cares not to hear it

REMAINS OF BOXLEY ABBEY.

St. Andrew's Chapel.   Brewhouses and Bakehouses.

Interior of the Abbey Church.

(valerian). His clothes press was covered with a red cloth ; his bed was neat, and on shelves at its head he tidily arranged his astrolabe and the counting-stones then used in arithmetic. A psaltery hung above the press, and at nights he sang sweetly, now the Angelus to the Virgin, and again the music of the king.

The descriptions of the costumes of the carpenter's wife and of Absolon, the parish clerk, are very full and interesting : we are told that the latter chewed grain and licorice to sweeten his breath, and placed under his tongue a comfit known as a "true-love" for the same purpose ; and that the carpenter swore by St Thomas, while his wife's oath was "by St Thomas of Kent."

The gist of the story need not be given here, for it is not of the kind now popular in drawing-rooms. Chaucer tells us that the company received it with varying degrees of approval, "but for the moré part they laughed and played," with the exception of the Reeve, who was annoyed that the coarse joke went against the carpenter, because he also "was of carpenteris craft." He began a long statement—aimed at the Miller—about the folly of trying to continue the ribaldries of youth when the hair was grey, but was cut short by the Host, who cried :—

.   .   .   .   .   .

"Say forth thy tale, and tarry not the time,
Lo, Depéford, and it is half way prime,
Lo, Greenéwich, ther many a shrew is in,
It were all time thy talé to begin."

From this passage we may feel that the tales were told at rests, rather than while riding, for otherwise Deptford and Greenwich would have come in sight long before the Knight's and the Miller's tales were completed. From the Watering of St Thomas, where the lots were drawn, to Blackheath Hill is not much more than two miles, traversed, in Chaucer's day, by a country highway, between farms and cottages, and with Deptford and Greenwich nestling between it and the river.

It is a little difficult to understand exactly the idea Chaucer wished to convey. "Half way prime" meant 7.30 A.M., and if the pilgrims only intended to reach Dartford on the first day, one wonders why the Host should be in such a hurry. Probably his real wish was to check the Reeve's preaching and induce him to begin his story. It may be that the party had just come in sight of Deptford and Greenwich, or that they had just reached the top of Blackheath Hill, from which there would be a good view of these villages. In any case, their way from the "Watering" had lain along the Old Kent Road and the New Kent Road, through Deptford Broadway and over Deptford Bridge, which spans the Ravensbourne. This little stream still supplies some power to factories, as it did to the grist mills of the pilgrims' days, and at the top of Blackheath Hill the open Heath, continuous with Greenwich Park, is still preserved. Somewhere about this spot we may imagine the Reeve beginning his tale, which, in revenge for and in contrast to the Miller's, made its victim a miller, who suffered at the hands of clerks (or scholars) of Cambridge. Like the Miller's tale, it opens with a good description, for it tells us that the

miller of Cambridge was proud and gay as any
peacock, that he could pipe, fish, mend nets, turn
cups (drink), wrestle and shoot, and went well
armed. At his belt he carried a long knife as
well as a "full trenchant" sword, while his pouch
held a short dagger, and "a Sheffield thwitel"
(yet another knife) "bore he in his hose," as
Highlanders still wear the skeen dhu. After
such an armoury, one is not surprised to hear
that this miller had a round face, flat nose, and
skull as bald as an ape's ; or that he was jealous,
a braggart, a thief, and a coward. The
Cambridge scholars were two North-country
men, from the town of Strother, whose saints,
for swearing purposes, were Cuthbert and James,
and whose dialogue is in the northern speech
throughout. We learn incidentally that wild
mares roamed in the fens around Cambridge ;
and that the miller, with his wife and grown-up
daughter as well as a baby son, all occupied the
one great sleeping-room of the mill. For the
story itself readers may be referred to the original.
It is certainly as "broad" as the Miller's, and the
Reeve concludes, religiously but triumphantly—

> " And God, that sitteth high in Trinity,
> Save all this companye, great and smale.
> Thus have I quit the Miller in my tale."

We have seen that after the Knight had begun
the story-telling, the Host had no difficulty in
inducing others to continue. When the Reeve
had finished, the Cook of London was so delighted
that he "clawed him on the back," declared that
never since he was called Hogge of Ware had he

heard a miller so well taken to task, and volunteered—

> "If ye vouchésafe to hear,
> A tale of me, that am a pooré man,
> I will you tell, as well as ever I can,
> A little jape that 'fel in our citee."

The Host accepted the offer, in a few lines that must be quoted for the light they throw upon the trade of a cook—

> "Now tell on, Roger, look that it be good
> For many a pasty hast thou letten blood,
> And many a Jack of Dover hast thou sold,
> That hath been twiés hot and twiés cold ;
> Of many a pilgrim hast thou Christés curse,
> For of thy parsley yet they fare the worse
> That they have eaten with thy stubble goose :
> For in thy shop is many a flyé loose."

Then, fearing lest he should offend the cook, begged him not to be angry at his jest, but the cook admitted the truth of the charges—even including the twice hot-and-cold jack-pudding— but added that a true jest is a poor jest—

> "And therefore, Harry Bailly, by thy faith,
> Be thou not wroth, ere we departen here
> Though that my tale be of a hosteleer :
> But nathéless I will not tell it yet ;
> But ere we part, I wis, thou shalt be quit."

He began the story of a London apprentice, whom he calls Perkin Revelour, who was ready to sing and hop at every bridal, who "lovéd bet the tavern than the shop," and who would rush from his work whenever there was a procession in Cheapside. He diced and danced and robbed his master, until suddenly he was discharged, and had no resort but to send "his bed and his array" to a compeer of his own kind, at which point the story concludes—"of this Cokes Tale maked Chaucer na more." It is the last that remains of the tales of the first day—probably Chaucer never completed the series he intended.

It is impossible to connect the tales with any definite part of the day or the way. From Blackheath, six miles from London, the road dips to what was then the pleasant hamlet of Kidbrooke, just beyond which it bends into the long straight line of the Watling Street, rising gradually for the first mile or so, and then more steeply to the top of Shooter's Hill, which is still richly bowered in trees. To Welling is a pleasant down grade, followed by a gradual rise to Bexley Heath, a place which has been much spoiled by recent building, then down again to Crayford, thirteen miles from London, where the road crosses the little river Cray. Here we are told that Hengist finally defeated the Britons, and founded the Saxon kingdom of Kent, in A.D. 457; and here the pilgrims would find a little church. They probably pushed on, however, to the next, and much more important ford, where the road crossed the river Darenth, thus giving rise to the name of Dartford for the place of crossing. Here was ample entertainment for man and beast —every comfort, physical and spiritual, In the Bull Hotel, built and galleried around a courtyard, there may still be portions which go back to somewhere near the pilgrims' days, and the church, which still shows an ancient fresco of St George and the Dragon, and brasses of as early date as 1402, has parts of great antiquity. Dartford had long been a populous and famous place, probably largely because it was a recognised stage on the way from London to the coast. Here, in 1235, the Archbishop of "Colein," sent by the Emperor Frederick, met, and married to the Emperor, Isabel, the sister of Henry III., for, as Lambarde says, "Princes may wooe by picture, and marrie by proctor"; and another proof of the importance of the place is given by the holding of a great tournament to celebrate the home-coming of Edward III. from France in 1331. Much more interesting to the pilgrims, however, would be the fact that the same king, Edward III., had five years later founded a priory of the order of St Augustine for one prioress and thirty-nine sisters. At the time of their visit this priory was wealthy and prosperous, and so continued until the dissolution under Henry VIII. The present Priory Farm, to the left, just before entering Dartford, preserves the memory and the few small ruins of what Chaucer saw as a noble building. Just beyond the little river, on the brow of the hill to the left of the road, stood a Chantry of St Edmund, a place of great sanctity and power, visited not only by pilgrims passing to the greater shrine of St Thomas, but also by so many of its own devotees that the road from London to Dartford was at one time familiarly known as St Edmund's Way. The offerings at this shrine formed part of the endowment of the priory, and although no part of the shrine remains, its site is marked in the cemetery which surrounded it and which is still used for burial purposes, by the memorial to the Protestant martyrs burned on Dartford Brent in the time of Queen Mary.

After the pilgrims had made their devotions at the shrine of St Edmund, they might well discuss (at the Bull, or other hostelry) the stirring doings of Wat Tyler, Jack Straw, John Ball, and John Hales, whose "Peasant Revolt" had come to a head in Dartford only six years before.   They would talk over the doings of the "petie collectors in every quarter," who "with great extremities raked much money from the miserable people," and would remind each other of the divine wrath of the tyler of Dartford (whether he were really Wat or John) who slew the "naughtie fellowe who dishonestly intreated a young Damosell," daughter to that same tyler, and thereby caused the whole seething cauldron of discontent to boil over.   They would tell of how the great army of a hundred thousand desperate Kentish men and men of Kent had stormed the jail at Maidstone to release their prophet, John Ball; how they sacked the palace of the Archbishop of Canterbury; and how they marched by Blackheath, slaying every lawyer they met by the way, to London town, where they were joined by the great army from Essex, with recruits from Norfolk and Suffolk, Cambridge and Hertfordshire, Surrey and Sussex.   Some of the pilgrims may have seen that brief dramatic scene in Smithfield when Wat Tyler was slain by Walworth, and when the crowd, shouting for vengeance for the death of their captain, were taken by the bold front of the boy-monarch, who rode forward, crying: "What need ye, my masters, I am your captain and your king."

At least Harry Bailly must have seen the

Kentish crowd surging past his door to London bridge; and returning, as they had done from their memorable defiance of the Conqueror, with pledges of freedom, of redress for their grievances, and of maintenance of their ancient rights. And while some of the pilgrims quoted the rhyming epistles of John Ball, some local man may have capped them with the doggerel which is preserved to this day as referring in its last line to the "naughtie fellowe" who was slain by the Dartford tyler :—

> "Sutton for mutton,
>   Kirby for beef,
> South Darne for gingerbread,
>   And Dartford for a thief."

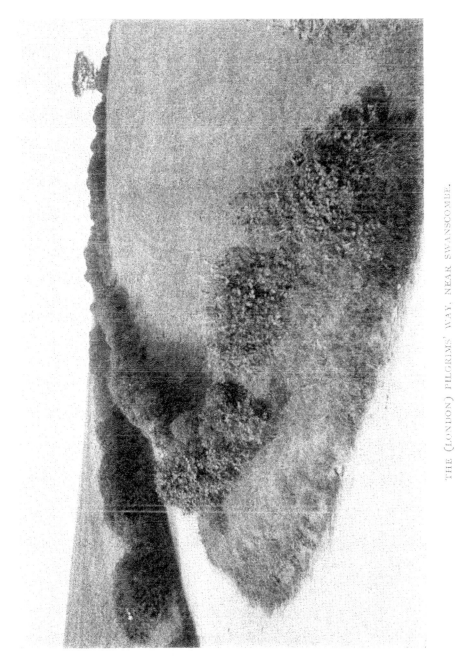

THE (LONDON) PILGRIMS' WAY, NEAR SWANSCOMBE.

The Way from Ingress Abbey and the Eastern Counties Join on the Watling Street.

CHAPTER XI

WE are not told how early the pilgrims started
from Dartford.   Probably they rose betimes and
spent some hours in the little town, for the
thread of the narrative was taken up at ten
o'clock in the morning, when the Host pointed
out that a quarter of the day was gone, and
called upon the Man of Law for the next tale.
To this the Man of Law at once agreed, but
prefaced his story by saying that he knew no
thrifty tales save those which Chaucer—

> " Though he kan [1] but lewedly,[2]
> On metres and on rhyming craftily,
> Hath said them, in such English as he kan,
> Of oldé time, as knoweth many a man."

Which statement he followed with a partial list of
Chaucer's works, and also of other stories which
Chaucer had not made into English, and which
the Man of Law considered unworthy of such
treatment.   A prologue, praising wealth and
lamenting poverty, led up to a statement that the
"tale" had been learned from a merchant; and
forthwith he launched into the dramatic and
wonderful story of Constance, founded by

[1] knows   [2] ignorantly, clumsily

Chaucer upon part of the Anglo - French Chronicle of Nicholas Trivet, an English Dominican friar who lived in the beginning of the fourteenth century. In following his original, Chaucer introduces religious reflections which are, perhaps, more proper to the Friar than to the Man of Law, and once he makes the slip of forgetting that the tale is supposed to be told in words, from memory, for he speaks of a castle, "of which the name in my text naught I find."

At the end of this story the Host called upon the Parson, adjuring him "for Goddés bones," and again, "by Goddés dignity," to tell the next tale. The Parson gently reproved him for sinfully swearing, whereupon the Host exclaimed to the whole company that "I smell a Lollard in the wind," and announced that the Parson would "preachen us somewhat." At this point the Shipman interfered—

> " ' Nay, by my father's soul ! that shall he not !
> . . . Here he shall not preach :
> He shall no gospel glosen¹ here nor teach
> We liven all in the great God,' quoth he.
> ' He wouldé sowen² some difficulty,
> Or springing cockle in our cleané corn ;
> And therefore, Host, I warné thee biforn,³
> My jolly body shall a talé tell,
> And I shall clinken you so merry a bell
> That I shall waken all this companý ;
> But it shall not be of philosophý,
> Nor of physík, nor termés quaint of law ;
> There is but little Latin in my maw.' "

The Shipman's tale was commended by the Host, who considered a moment before calling upon the next teller.

---

¹ expound   ² sow   ³ at the outset

" ' But now pass o'er, and let us seek about,
Who shall now tellé first of all this rout
Another tale,' and with that word he said,
As courteously as it had been a maid,
' My lady Prioressé, by your leave,
So that I wist [1] I shouldé you not grieve,
I wouldé deemen that ye tellen should
A talé next, if so were that ye would.
Now, will ye vouchésafe, my lady dear ? '
' Gladly,' quoth she, and said as ye shall hear."

She prefaced her tale by a devout supplication to Christ and His virgin mother to guide her song that she might worthily speak in their honour ; then told the story of a little Christian boy, murdered by a Jew for singing "O Alma redemptoris mater," as he passed through the Jewish quarter of his town, and how he continued singing loud and clear, although his throat was cut, and ceased not until a holy abbot had received him as a martyr, and had removed from his tongue a grain laid thereon by the blessed Virgin.

For a while the company remained solemn, after the relation of the miracle, until the Host again began jesting and thus addressed Chaucer—

" ' What man art thou ? ' quoth he ;
' Thou lookest as thou wouldest find a hare ;
For ever on the ground I see thee stare.

   .   .   .   .   .   .

Say now somewhat, since other folk have said ;
Tell us a tale of mirth, and that anon.'
' Hosté,' quoth I, ' be ye not ill y-paid,
For other talé certés kan [2] I none
But of a rhyme I learned long agone.'
' Yes, that is good,' quoth he, ' now shall we hear
Some dainty thing, methinketh by this cheer ! ' "

        [1] knew   [2] know

At this, Chaucer began the tale of Sir Thopas, evidently a skit upon the stories told by the romancers of the time, from some of which he quoted many phrases and expressions. In brisk rhyme he began the tale, but he had only finished the first "fit" of twenty-seven verses and was telling the fifth verse of the second fit, when the Host rudely interrupted—

> "'No more of this, for Goddés dignity!'
> Quoth ouré Hosté, 'for thou makest me
> So weary of thy very lewédness[1]
> That, also wisely[2] God my soulé bless
> Mine earés aken[3] of thy drasty[4] speech
> Now such a rhyme the devil I biteche[5]!'"

Chaucer protested against being hindered, since it was the best rhyme he knew; but the Host would not be pacified, further condemned his poetry, and continued—

> "'Thou dost naught ellés[6] but despendest[7] time;
> Sir, at a word, thou shalt no longer rhyme
> Let see wher[8] thou canst tellen aught in jest,
> Or tell in prosé somewhat, at the least,
> In which there be some mirth, or some doctríne.'"

To this suggestion Chaucer gladly assented, and began the tale of Melibeus, after a short prologue, in which he asked pardon in case his version should be slightly different from other renderings of this well-known story. Though he gave it in prose, many of its sentences carry the lilt of his verse, thus—

> "A daughter which that callèd was Sophie.
> His wife and eke his daughter hath he left.
> Of which the dorés weren fast y-shette.
> Three of his oldé foes have it espied."

| [1] ignorance | [3] ache | [5] commit to | [7] wastest |
| [2] surely | [4] rubbishy | [6] else | [8] whether |

All of these lines occur within the first seventy
words. The story proved a long and very dreary
sermon on the forgiveness of enemies, but the
excellence of its moral won the full approval of the
Host, who heartily wished that his wife might
have heard the tale. At some length he told of
the woes arising from his wife's frequent fear that
she was being insulted, and her taunting references
to his own cowardice when he refused to avenge
her fancied wrongs—

> " ' But let us pass away fro this matteer.
>   My lord the Monk,' quoth he, ' be merry of cheer,
>   For ye shall tell a talé trewélý.
>   Lo ! Ro-uchéstre stant here fasté by !
>   Ride forth mine owené lord, break not our game.' "

Whereat the Monk was nothing loth, but volunteered to do even more than was required—

> " And said, ' I will do all my diligence,
>   As far as sowneth [1] into honesty,
>   To tellé you a tale, or two, or three ;
>   And if you list to hearken hitherward,
>   I will you say the life of Saint Edward,
>   Or elles,[2] first, tragédies will I tell
>   Of which I have a hundred in my cell.' "

Eventually he started upon a series of tragedies
—of Lucifer, Samson, Hercules, Nebuchadnezzar,
Cenobia, Nero, and others, including some of
about his own time. For a long time the company listened with more or less attention, but at
last the Knight peremptorily checked the tales of
of disaster, contending that it is better to tell of
poor men raised to great estate and (as we say

[1] tendeth   [2] else

nowadays) "living happily ever after," than to dwell upon misfortune. The Host agrees—

> " ' Yea,' quoth our Host, ' by Sainté Paulés bell !
> Ye say right sooth,' this Monk he clappeth loud ;
> He spak how ' Fortune covered with a cloud '
> .   .   .   .   .   ' it is a pain,
> As ye have said, to hear of heaviness.
> Sir Monk, no more of this, so God you bless !
> Your tale annoyeth all this company ;
> Such talking is not worth a butterfly,
> For therein is there no disport or game.
> Wherefor, Sir Monk, or don[1] Piers by your name,
> I pray you heartily, tell us somewhat else,
> For sikerly[2] nere[3] clinking of your bells,
> That on your bridle hang on every side,
> By heaven's king, that for us allé died !
> I should ere this have fallen down for sleep
> Although the slough had never been so deep.
>
> .   .   .   .   .   .
>
> Sir, say somewhat of hunting I you pray.'
> ' Nay !' quoth this Monk, ' I have no lust to play ;
> Now let another tell, as I have told.' "

We saw that " Rochester stant here fast by " before the Monk's tale was begun. That may have been when the first glimpse of the cathedral city on the Medway was obtained from the hill near Cobham Park; and the reference to the " slough had never been so deep," indicates that the low-lying ground, now occupied by Strood, had been reached. On the Monk's refusal to tell a merrier tale—

> " Then spake our Host with rudé speech and bold,
> And said unto the Nuné's Priest anon,
> ' Come near, thou priest, come hither thou Sir John.

[1] contraction of dominus ; a title familiarly applied to churchmen
[2] surely
[3] were not = but for clinking, etc.

> Tell us such thing as may our heartés glad ;
> Be blithé though thou ride upon a jade.
> What though thine horse be bothé foul and lean ?
> If he will serve thee, recké not a bene ;
> Look that thine heart be merry evermo.' "

And the obedient Nun's Priest at once began the story of Chanticleer and his wife Partlet—the tale of the cock who was deceived by the flattery of a fox, and who saved his life by his wit.

At the end of this story some of the old manuscripts give certain words of the Host to the Nun's Priest, but it seems doubtful whether they were written by Chaucer. They are more in keeping with what we might expect to be addressed to the Monk than to the Nun's Priest, and they contain one line which is exactly the same as one already used to the Monk. Further, they end with the lines—

> "And after that, he with full merry cheer
> Said unto another as ye shallen hear."

It seems impossible that Chaucer should have made the Host address "another," instead of giving his title; and from the fact that this fragment makes reference to the Nun's Priest's story, it seems probable that its writer had mistaken the address to the Monk for that to the Nun's Priest and had confounded the two persons.

In any case, the fragment tells nothing of who was to be the next speaker, or of where the day was to end.

We imagine, therefore, that it ended in Rochester, a city by the bank of the Medway, a much fairer river in those days than it has been since the pestilential breath of immense cement works have filled its valley. The city was full of interest for all travellers, and while our pilgrims are admiring its wonders, we may review their course from Dartford. On leaving that town they continued straight along the Watling Street, from which the present Dover Road bends to the northward, and does not rejoin the older line until just before reaching Rochester. The old road strikes across Dartford Heath, which is still a pleasant breezy bit of rough moorland and runs in a straight line for about three miles, then curves very slightly to reach Springhead, the site of an important Roman station, believed to have been Vagniacæ. From several points along the hillside we have wide-sweeping views across the fertile fields and hop-gardens of a rich valley, stretching away to the great woods of Shorne and Cobham, clothing the northward slope of the downs, over a low shoulder of which we are to reach Rochester. Through this peaceful tract the old Roman road and pilgrims' road runs as a good country lane, passing one or two hamlets, one or two sleepy wayside public-houses, and an occasional small prosperous-looking farm-house. High thick hedges of hawthorn here conceal and there reveal the smiling fields and well-pruned orchards, and the only passengers likely to break our meditations are the slow herdsman or shepherd, the waggoner with his stout team and heavy Kentish wain, built as large and ample, and with the same graceful curving lines as the prairie schooner of a new country, or perchance the farmer or his wife, driving to market in a general-utility gig. The road gently rises and

THE PILGRIMS' WAY FROM LONDON, SKIRTING COBHAM PARK.

falls, passes through the little village of Singlewell or Ifield, and continues in almost an absolutely straight line until it climbs into the green mazy recesses of Shorne Wood, a place of gnarled trunks with undergrowth of bracken. The fine old churches of Cobham and Shorne lie at least a mile away from the road, and Cobham Park, through part of which it runs, shows us nothing of the very interesting Roman remains which it contains. Passing through Strood the road is rejoined by the Dover Road, and for the rest of the way to Canterbury they are identical. Here also it is joined by a branch of the Winchester Pilgrims' Way, coming down the north bank of the Medway by Halling and Cuxton, and here it seems quite likely that the London stream of pilgrims would receive many recruits.

Strood itself was a place of much interest for the pilgrims, for it belonged to the Templars, and it had a hospital for wayfarers, founded by Gilbert Glanville, Bishop of Rochester, and pupil of Thomas of Canterbury, about 1190. It was familiarly called Newark or Neworke, and the name is still preserved in connection with houses on the site, which also have some fragments of the ancient building. Some memories of the Templars and fragments of their buildings are preserved in the Temple Farm, near the riverside; and Strood-born people are still roughly chaffed as being born with tails, a libel founded in a legend which is thus quoted by Lambarde from Polydore Vergil :—" Becket (being at the length reputed for the king's enimie) began to be so commonly neglected, contemned, and hated, that when as it happened him upon a time to come to

Stroude, the inhabitants thereabout (being desirous to despite that good father) sticked not to cut the taile from the horse on which he roade, binding themselves thereby with a perpetual reproach : For afterward (by the will of God) it so happened, that every one which came of that kindred of men which had plaied that naughty pranke, were borne with tailes, even as brute beasts bee."

Our pilgrims crossed the Medway to Rochester by the ancient wooden bridge which stood in the same position as the bridge of to-day, and they would look with interest at the works of the new bridge of stone which was then being built a few yards further down the river (where the S. E. Railway bridge now crosses). This new bridge, about 560 feet long and 15 feet broad, and "equal to any in England, excepting the bridges of the metropolis," was opened in 1392. Though all traces of its structure have disappeared, the lands given by good Sir Robert Knolles for its support still bring revenue to the Bridge Wardens, and there are still some remains of the Bridge Chapel founded by John of Cobham for the use of way-farers, endowed out of the bridge estates, with three chaplains who were to say three masses every day, at five o'clock, at eight o'clock, and at eleven o'clock, "that travellers might have an opportunity of being present at these offices." It is not absolutely certain that this chapel was open when Chaucer's pilgrims passed in 1387. If not, it was probably building, and, later it was so largely used by pilgrims as to have acquired the local name of the Pilgrims' Chapel. The city was then completely walled and had a Broadgate,

Southgate, and Cheldegate. Parts of the wall may still be seen in bye-lanes on both sides of the High Street beyond the cathedral. The castle, said to have existed long before Norman times, and greatly strengthened by Gundulph the building archbishop, who erected most of what remains to-day as the finest piece of Norman domestic architecture in England, would attract attention before Rochester was reached. The cathedral, rebuilt, and the priory founded by the same Gundulph, who " never rested building and begging, tricking and garnishing, till he had advanced this his creature to the just wealth, beautie, and estimation of a right Popish Priorie," were full of interest. There was the tomb of St Paulinus, though its great silver shrine had been coined into money to pay the expenses of the house in time of trouble; there was the tomb of the Saxon St Ythamar, and the shrine of St William of Rochester, canonised in 1256, "with indulgence to all such as would offer at his tomb." In the beautiful undercroft or crypt were many chapels and altars, including those to St Mary, St Catherine, and St Edmund. Of churches, Rochester had St Clements, of which nothing now remains, St Nicholas, a fine old building, still nestling under the shadow of the north-west corner of the cathedral, and St Margaret's, which still has records as far back as A.D. 1272, though the present building only dates from 1824. St Catherine's hospital for poor folk, founded by Symond Potyn, of the Crown Inn, in 1316, and standing in Eastgate, near the foot of Star Hill, would also attract the pilgrims' attention. Of inns for the accommodation of travellers there was probably good choice, for we know that there was a "Crown" on almost the same site as the present inn of that name in A.D. 1316, and that the names of the Bull and of the King's Head have been used continuously for hostelries on the same sites since at least as early as A.D. 1450.

CHAPTER XII

As the tales of the second day finished, so those
assigned to the third day begin without any
local reference. From evidence suggested at the
beginning of the record of the second day we
may imagine that the pilgrims' habit was to rise
early and devote the first morning hours to sight-
seeing and religious exercises. For this there
was ample scope in Rochester.

The first story of the third day (supposing
the generally accepted arrangement to be correct)
is that of the Doctor of Physic, which has no
introduction save the words—" heere folweth the
Phisiciens Tale." Compared with some of the
others it is short (less than three hundred lines),
and gives a straightforward version of the slaying
of Virginia by her father, to save her virtue.

At its ending, the Host broke into strong
invective against the unjust judge and all who
had plotted against Virginia; praised the Doctor
for his tale; and invoked the blessing of God
and St Mary upon all his medicaments. At

253

the same time he lamented the sorrow of the story—·

> " ' But well I woot [1] thou doost [2] my heart to erme [3]
> That I almost have caught a cardynacle.[4]
> By corpus bonés ! but [5] I have triacle,[6]
> Or else a draught of moist and corny ale,
> Or but [5] I hear anon a merry tale,
> Mine heart is lost, for pity of this maid.
> Thou *beel amy*,[7] thou Pardoner,' he said,
> ' Tell us some mirth, or japés right anon ! ' "

The Pardoner was nothing loth, and replied—

> " ' It shall be done,' quoth he, ' by Saint Ronyon !
> But first,' quoth he, ' here at this alé stake
> I will both drink and eaten of a cake.'
>   And right anon the gentles 'gun to cry,
> ' Nay ! Let him tell us of no ribaldry ;
> Tell us some moral thing, that we may leere [8]
> Some wit,[9] and thenné will we gladly hear.'
>   ' I grant, y-wis,' [10] quoth he, ' but I may think
> Upon some honest thing, while that I drink.' "

One would gladly have a clue to the "ale stake" which the pilgrims were passing just at this time, and know whether any successor stands in the same spot, to refresh the weary traveller. But no information remains save that it was somewhere between Rochester and Ospringe.

In his long prologue the Pardoner very frankly told the fraudulent means by which he drew an ample living from a religious and credulous people, as has been set forth, in Chaucer's own words, in Chapter IX. With the words—

> " For though myself be a full vicious man
> A moral tale yet I you tellé can,"

[1] know	[5] unless	[8] learn
[2] makest	[6] medicine	[9] wisdom
[3] grieve	[7] bastard French — good	[10] certainly
[4] heart disease	friend	

he began a story of three riotous youths who, hearing that Death was in a neighbouring village, swore to meet and kill him. An old man whom they questioned pointed out a tree under which they would find Death lying, but they really found great store of money. The two elder youths decided to watch the treasure, while the third went to the city for food and drink, that they might carry home the money after nightfall. The two planned to stab the third, on his return, that they might have all the treasure, while their messenger decided to poison his two fellows, that all the wealth might be his own. Thus they all died before benefiting by their unexpected wealth, and so gave point to the moral, " *Radix malorum est Cupiditas* "—cupidity is the root of all evil—which the Pardoner declared was his invariable text. At the end of his story he began (as was his wont) to beg for money in return for the privilege of kissing his relics and receiving absolution. He pressed the Host to come first—

> " For he is most envelopéd in sin,"

whereupon the Host answered very emphatically and very coarsely, until, seeing the Pardoner was vexed—

> " So wroth was he no word ne would he say
> 'Now,' quoth our Host, 'I will no longer play
> With thee, ne with none other angry man.'
> But right anon the worthy Knight began,
> When that he saw that all the people lough,[1]
> 'No more of this, for it is right enough !
> Sir Pardoner, be glad and merry of cheer ;
> And ye, sir Host, that been to me so dear,

[1] laughed

I pray you that you kiss the Pardoner ;
And Pardoner, I pray thee draw thee near,
And as we diden, let us laugh and play.'
Anon they kissed, and riden [1] forth their way."

No connecting link has been preserved between this scene and the Wife of Bath's tale, which is nowadays placed immediately following. The order is probably correct, but connecting matter may have been lost, or perhaps was never written.

The Wife of Bath began her story with the longest prologue or preachment allowed to any of the pilgrims. Stating that she had already had five husbands and was looking out for a sixth, she took up with much vigour and some skill, the case of Matrimony *versus* Celibacy. Some interesting side-lights were thrown upon the lady's character and experiences, and although the prologue was really a long socio-religious dissertation, its frankness and *naïveté* relieved it from any possible suggestion of dulness. Through a talk recorded in eight hundred and thirty lines she met with no interruption : but when she reached the conclusion and said,

"Now will I say my tale, if ye will hear,"

the Friar laughed, and suggested that the talk had been rather long for a mere preamble— whereupon the Summoner turned upon him :—

" ' Lo,' quoth the Summoner, ' Goddés armés two !
A frere [2] will intermit him ever-mo.
Lo, goodé men, a fly, and eke a frere, [2]
Will fall in every dishé and mateere [3]
What speak'st thou of " preambulatioun ? "
What ? amble, or trot, or peace, or go sit down !

[1] rode   [2] friar   [3] affair

SIDE GATEWAY, DAVINGTON PRIORY.

DAVINGTON PRIORY, NEAR FAVERSHAM.

Thou lettest[1] our disport in this manere.'
' Yea, wilt thou so, sir Summoner ? ' quoth the Frere ;
' Now, by my faith ! I shall, ere that I go,
Tell of a summoner such a tale or two
That all the folk shall laughen in this place.'
   ' Now ellés, Freré,[2] I beshrew thy face,'
Quoth this Summoner, ' and I beshrewé me
But if I tellé talés two or three,
Of frerés[2] ere I come to Sittingbourne,
That I shall make thine hearté for to mourn
For well I woot[3] thy patiénce is gone.' "

The Host authoritatively interfered at this point,
telling them that they are behaving like drunken
men, and bidding them let the woman tell her
tale ; and turning to the lady, he added—

  " ' Do, dame, tell forth your tale, and that is best.'
  ' Al ready, sir,' quoth she, ' right as you list ;
  If I have license of this worthy Frere.'
  ' Yes, dame,' quoth he, ' tell forth, and I will hear.' "

The important point in this link is the mention of
Sittingbourne, as if there were time to tell at least
a tale or two before reaching there. Thus the
Wife's tale must have been early in the third day
(if our four-day supposition is correct), and it
must come after the Monk's tale, which is introduced by a reference to Rochester. As there is a
Cold Arbour[4] about two miles west of Sittingbourne, it is just within the possibilities that its
name recalls the very halting-place where Chaucer
intended to lay this scene ; and it is possible to
read the Summoner's injunction to " go sit down "
as evidence that this part of the story, at any rate,
was at a halting-place. However that may be,
the Wife of Bath's tale, though only half the

---

[1] hinderest   [2] friar   [3] know   [4] See Chapter XV.

length of her prologue, was an interesting, well-told story of a knight of King Arthur's court, justly condemned to death, and respited for a year at the Queen's urgent petition, on condition that at the end of the year he should return and say what women most desire. He sought through many lands, and at last obtained the answer from an old and ugly woman, on his promise that if the answer proved acceptable he would grant her first request. The request was that he would marry her ; but after doing so, he lamented his fate, whereupon she reasoned with him at some length, and finally bade him choose to have her, old, ugly, and virtuous ; or young, fair, and a wanton. At length he said she was so wise that he would leave the choice to her, whereupon she told him that as he had thus given her the mastery, she would change herself into a young and beautiful woman, and would be virtuous also. This was one of the "happy ever after" stories, which the teller finished with a wish that Christ would give good husbands to us all, and grace to bear with those we wed—

> " And eke, I pray Jesu to short their lives
> That not will be govérnéd by their wives ;
> And old and angry niggards of dispence,[1]
> God send them sooné very pestilence ! "

Through all this story, the "worthy limitor, this noble Friar," had made a kind of "lowering chiere" upon the Summoner ; but confined his ill-temper to black looks until the tale was done, and "no villain's word as yet to him spake he." As the story ended, he turned to compliment the

[1] expenditure

Wife of Bath on the way in which she had handled matters of great dialectical difficulty—

> " ' But, dame, here as we ridé by the way,
>   Us needeth not to speaken but of game,
>   And leave authoritees, in Goddés name,
>   To preaching and to scholé of clergye,
>   And if it liké to this companye
>   I will you of a summoner tell a game.
>   *Pardee*, ye may well knowé by the name
>   That of a summoner may no good be said.
>   I pray that none of you be ill apaid,[1]—
>   A summoner is a runner up and doun
>   With mandéments [2] for fornicatioun,
>   And is y-beat at every townés end.'
>   Our Host then spake, ' A, sir, you should be
>   hende [3]
>   And courteous, as a man of your estate,
>   In company ; we will have no debate !
>   Telleth your tale, and let the Summoner be.'
>   ' Nay,' quoth the Summoner, ' let him say to me
>   What so him list,[4]—when it com'th to my lot,
>   By God ! I shall him quiten every grot !
>   I shall him tellen which a great honóur
>   It is to be a flattering limitour ;
>   And his office I shall him tell y-wis.' [5]
>   Our Host answerdé, ' Peace ! no more of this !'
>   And after this he said unto the Frere,
>   ' Tell forth your tale my leevé [6] master dear.' ' "

With right good-will—or, rather, ill-will—the Friar then began the story of a rascally summoner who met and communed with a fiend in the form of a yeoman and was eventually carried to hell. The Summoner listened with such patience as he might, but at its close—

> " This Summoner in his stirrups highé stood
>   Upon this Frere his hearté was so wood,[7]

---

[1] pleased, satisfied	[3] polite	[5] certainly	[7] mad
[2] summonses	[4] wills	[6] loved	

> That like an aspen leaf he quook [1] for ire.
>   'Lordings,' quoth he, 'but one thing I desire—
> I you beseech that of your courtesye
> Since you have heard this falsé Freré lie,
> As suffereth me I may my talé tell.
> This Freré boasteth that he knoweth hell,
> And God it woot [2] that it is little wonder
> Frerés and fiendés be but lyte [3] asunder ' "

And so forth, with certain unsavoury details— and concluded—

> "God save you allé, save this curséd Frere!
> My prologue will I end in this manere."

He told a story, wherein a greedy friar was befooled by a sick man from whom he was endeavouring by threat or persuasion to secure contribution of money or goods. The last line runs—

> "My tale is doon,—we been almoost at town."

From previous indications and from the fact that Sittingbourne is two-thirds of the way from Rochester to Ospringe, we may presume that the town in question was Sittingbourne. Probably a halt was made there, and the party was again in motion before the Host addressed the young Clerk of Oxford, chiding him for being as silent as a newly-wed maid at table, and asked him for his story in due turn. In this case the Host specified the nature and treatment of tale suitable for a pilgrimage—

> "But preacheth not, as frerés do in Lent,
>   To make us for our oldé sinnés weep.
>   Ne that thy talé make us not to sleep.

---

[1] quaked   [2] knows   [3] little

Tell us some merry thing of áventúres—
Your termés, your coloúrs, and your figúres
Keep them in store till so be ye indite
High style, as when that men to kingés write :
Speaketh so plain at this time, I you pray,
That we may understandé what you say."

The Clerk replied that he would tell a story—

"Learned at Padua of a worthy clerk,
As provéd by his wordés and his work ;
He is now dead and nailed in his chest,
I prayed to God to give his soulé rest !
    Fraunceys Petrak, the lauriat poete,
Highté [1] this clerk whose rhetoriké sweet
Illumined all Ytaille of poetrie."

This reference to Petrarch is especially interesting, in view of the fact that Chaucer went on a political mission to Genoa in 1373, and may have met Petrarch, who spent his last months in Arqua, some twelve miles from Padua, who was certainly there during most of 1373, and who died there on July 18, 1374. He was crowned poet laureate in Rome on Easter Sunday of 1341.

The Clerk's tale is Chaucer's rendering of the story of Griselda, as written by Petrarch, after the original in the Decameron of Boccaccio, and a very beautiful, dignified, and poetical rendering it is. Though most of it is a fairly close translation, there are passages in which Chaucer gives his own views or slightly elaborates upon his model. He evidently felt that the submissiveness of Patient Griselda to the whims of her relentlessly cruel husband was like the extreme chivalry of the knight, old-fashioned and unjustifiable. At the end of Part V. he inserts a

---

[1] was called

verse which shows (as do many other lines in various tales) that this story was not originally written for the character to whom it is attributed when stringing the series together. A clerk would not be made to say :—

> " Men speak of Job, and most for his humblesse,[1]
> As clerkés, when them list, can well indite,
> Namely of men, but as in soothfastness,[2]
> Though clerkés praisé women but a lite,[3]
> There can no man in humblesse[4] him acquite
> As women can, nor can be half so true
> As women be, but [5] it be fall of new." [6]

He introduces two stanzas which may give his own opinion of the changeful populace, and of which we quote a portion :—

> " O stormy people ! unsad,[7] and ever untrue !
> Ay undiscreet,[8] and changing as a vane,
> Delighting ever in rumbul [9] that is new ;
> For like the moon ay waxé ye and wane !
> Ay full of clapping,[10] dear enough a jane ! [11]
> Your doom [12] is false, your constance evil preeveth [13]
> A full great fool is he that on you leeveth [14]
>   Thus saiden saddé [15] folk in that citee
> When that the people gazéd up and down,—
> For they were glad, right for the noveltee
> To have a newé lady of their town."

Chaucer completed the story with a couple of stanzas on the rarity of Griseldas nowadays, and offered to say a song, which proved to be a

[1] humility
[2] truth
[3] little
[4] humility
[5] unless
[6] " it be fall of new " — it is a hitherto unknown thing
[7] unstable
[8] thoughtless
[9] rumour
[10] chatter
[11] a small coin, used in Italy
[12] judgment
[13] proveth
[14] believeth
[15] reliable

summing up of advice based on Griselda's story :—

> "But one word, lordings, hearken, ere I go :
> It were full hard to findé nowadays
> In all a town Griseldas three or two ;
>
> . . . . . .
> For which hear, for the Wifé's love of Bath,—
> Whose life and all her secté[1] God maintain
> In high maistrie,[2] and ellés[3] were it scathe,[4]—
> I will with lusty hearté, fresh and green,
> Say you a song, to gladé you, I ween ;
> And let us stint of earnestful[5] matere :
> Hearken my song that saith in this manere.
> Griselde is dead, and eke her patiénce,
> And both atonés[6] buried in Ytaille ;[7]
> For which I cry in open audience,
> Ne wedded man so hardy[8] be t'assail
> His wifé's patiénce in hope to find
> Griselda's, for in certain he shall fail.
>
> O noble wivés, full of high prudence,
> Let no humility your tongé[9] nail,
> Nor let no clerk have cause or diligence
> To write of you a story of such mervail.[10]
>
> . . . . . .
> If thou be fair, there[11] folk be in présence
> Shew thou thy visage and thine apparail ;
> If thou be foul, be free of thy dispence,[12]
> To get thee friendés ay do thy travail ;[13]
> Be ay of cheer, as light as leaf on lynde[14]
> And let him care and weep, and wring and wail ! "

At this point the Merchant broke into the conversation, and, taking his text from Chaucer's last words, began :—

> " 'Weeping and wailing, care and other sorrow
> I know enough, on even and a-morrow,'

[1] sex
[2] mastery
[3] else
[4] misfortune
[5] pensive
[6] at once
[7] Italy
[8] foolhardy
[9] tongue
[10] marvel
[11] where
[12] expenditure
[13] endeavour
[14] linden tree

Quoth the Merchánt, 'and so do other mo
That wedded be, I trow that it be so ;
For well I woot[1] it fareth so with me.
I have a wife, the worsté that may be.
For though the fiend to her y-coupled were,
She would him overmatch, I dare well swear.' "

He admits that all wedded men have not the
same sad experience, but protests that it is
general, and says that although he has only been
married two months his sorrows in that time can
not be equalled by a lifetime's troubles of any
unmarried man. The Host suggested that out
of his full experience he should tell something for
the benefit of the company, but he answered that
his heart was too sore for telling of his own tale.
Wherefore he began the pitiful story of a wedding
between old Januarie and "fresshé May," in the
beginning of which Januarie quoted from ancient
authors on the dangers of matrimony, but made
his own decision in its favour. The story told
how the old knight was beguiled by his young
wife and her young lover ; which caused the
Host to make comment on the failings of women,
concluding :—

"I have a wife, though that she pooré be ;
But of her tongue a labbing[2] shrew is she ;
And yet she hath a heap of vices mo,

.   .   .   .

For an[3] I shouldé reckon every vice
Which that she hath, y-wis[4] I were too nyce ;[5]
And causé why, it should reported be,
And told to her of[6] some of this meynee,[7]

[1] know
[2] babbling
[3] if
[4] I guess
[5] foolish
[6] by
[7] large party

PORTIONS OF ANCIENT HOSPICE, ON BOTH SIDES OF WATER LANE, OSPRINGE.

Of[1] whom it needeth not for to declare
(Since women konnen[2] outen[2] such chaffare),[3]
And eke my wit sufficeth not thereto,
To tellen all, wherefor my tale is do."

By this time we imagine that the pilgrims had reached Ospringe, the third sleeping-place of their journey. The close of the last chapter told of the things which would interest them in Rochester, and as Friday was market day, they probably chaffered awhile at some of the stalls, after attending early mass at the Bridge Chapel and seeing the sights. When they left the little city (for it was almost exactly half a mile long by a quarter-mile wide within the walls) they passed through a short stretch of low swampy ground toward Chatham, where their road made a curve to the left, parallel with a winding of the river, then bending sharply to the right, sought the straight line loved by the Roman engineers. Chatham, in the pilgrims' days had a hospital of St Bartholomew, founded by Gundulph, with altars to St James and St Giles. But it had also a much more wonderful matter in the shape of a statue of the Virgin Mary, known as Our Lady of Chatham, of which the following story is condensed from Lambarde :—The dead body of a man, probably shipwrecked, was washed ashore in Chatham parish, and buried in the churchyard. Whereupon the effigy rose at night, went to the house of the parish clerk, and awakened him, telling him "that there was lately buried (near to the place where she was honoured) a sinful person, which so offended her eye with his

---

[1] by   [2] are known to publish   [3] matter

ghastly grinning, that unless he were removed, she could not but (to the great grief of good people) withdraw herself from that place, and cease her wonted miraculous working amongst them. And therefore she willed him to go with her, to the end that (by his help) she might take him up and cast him again into the river."

The clerk consented, "but the good Lady (not wonted to walk) waxed weary of the labour, and therefore was enforced for very want of breath to sit down on a bush by the way, and there to rest her. And this place (forsooth), as also the whole track of their journey (remaining ever after a green path), the town dwellers were wont to shew."

The corpse was duly disinterred and thrown into the river, and "Our Lady shrank again into her shrine." The sinful body floated about for some days and at length was taken up by the people of Gillingham, and buried in their churchyard. "But see what followeth upon it: not only the rood of Gillingham (say they), that a while before was busy in bestowing miracles, was now deprived of all that his former virtue, but also the very earth and place where this carcase was laid, did continually for ever after, settle and sink downward."

Leaving Chatham we climb the height of Chatham Hill, from which there is an extensive view of the mouth of the Medway and its marshes, the valley of the Swale and the Isle of Sheppey, and take a pleasant but not very eventful course for four miles to Rainham. The "chapel of Rainham" was a place of some sanctity, and the church still preserves some old

brasses and monuments, though not of such early
date as the pilgrims' times. Another mile brings
us to Moor Street, a tiny hamlet where our
thirsty pilgrims probably found an "ale-stake,"
and in another three miles we reach Newington,
with a large and interesting church, in which
traces of good fourteenth century frescoes are
still to be seen. Here, in the early Norman
days a priory for nuns was established, but was
suppressed when the prioress was found strangled
in her bed. According to historians, the nuns
were removed to Minster, in Sheppey; but the
local folk will have none of this, and point out
Nunpit, a mile west of the church, where they
say that the nuns were buried alive.

Just beyond Newington the road ascends the
small height of Keycol Hill, from the top of
which there is a fine view over some of the most
richly cultivated land in Kent, and half a mile or so
further we pass within sight of one of those Cold
Arbours which are sometimes supposed to be
especially connected with pilgrims' ways, and
which actually are very often associated with
Roman roads, drovers' roads, and other ancient
highways. A couple of miles further bring us to
Sittingbourne, with a church that is (except the
tower) of eighteenth century date, though on a
very ancient site, and with a Red Lion Inn that
claims to be the direct descendant in uninter-
rupted succession, of the house of same name at
which Henry V. was sumptuously entertained on
his return from Agincourt. Other ancient inns
still greet passing guests, though two of the
most important have been converted to other
uses.

Half a mile north of Sittingbourne is Milton, a "royal villa" in the days of Alfred the Great, and a place of importance until 1052, when the partisans of Earl Godwin burned the king's house and ransacked the district. Of more importance, from the pilgrims' point of view, would be the fact that Milton owned, and owns to-day, as it did in Roman times, a famous oyster fishery.

Bapchild, a village a mile and a half beyond Sittingbourne, is believed to be the place where in 694 Wihtred, King of Kent, held a great conference "to consult about repairing the churches of God." It has a church which is principally Norman, and until the beginning of last century had some remains of a chapel, built by Archbishop Brightwald about 694, and probably in memory of the above-mentioned conference, but converted, as the shrine of St Thomas became popular, into a pilgrims' rest-house. Beyond this place the road is beautifully undulating, rising to a Beacon Hill, which was furnished with its beacon, its watchman, and its messenger in our pilgrims' days, and falling again toward Ospringe, a famous resting-place for all travellers. Before reaching the village we pass, on the left, some small remains of an ancient chapel. At the end of Water Lane, Ospringe, stands a half-timbered house marked Maison Dieu, and at the other corner of the lane is the Crown Inn, the lower part of which belongs to the same foundation. It was a hospice for travellers, founded by Henry II., in which he reserved a Camera Regis, a private apartment for his own use when journeying to Canterbury or Dover, and the local people say that the two parts were anciently joined by an archway across the lane. At the corner of the next lane on the right stands Chapel House, a modern building above ground, but with remains of a second hospice in its cellars and lower walls. Both these travellers' rests were in the hands of the Knights Templars, but they do not seem to have been used by Chaucer's pilgrims, for the Canon's Yeoman says he saw them ride from their " hostelry."

CHAPTER XIII

TALES OF THE FOURTH DAY

The first thing we hear about the stories of the fourth day (perhaps when the pilgrims were at or near the village of Preston, just beyond Ospringe) is that the Host called upon the young Squire for a tale of love, alleging that he knew as much as any man on that subject.

> "'Nay, sir,' quoth he, 'but I will say as I can
> With hearty will—for I will not rebel
> Against your lust.[1]   A talé will I tell.
> Have me excuséd, if I speak amiss,
> My will is good, and lo, my tale is this.'"

The story was of Cambuscán (not Cambúscan as Milton afterward made it), a great king, to whose feast on the twentieth anniversary of his accession, came a strange knight, from the lord of Araby and Inde, with wonderful magical gifts. These were a marvellous steed of brass; a sword which was irresistible, and which had the power of healing wounds made even by itself; a mirror which would show coming disaster, tell truly who was friend or foe, and reveal the constancy or otherwise of absent lovers; and a ring which

---

[1] desire

enabled the wearer to understand the talk of birds, and to know the virtues of all plants and roots, whereby all wounds might be healed.   The mirror and the ring were for Canace, the daughter of Cambuscán, who was so delighted with her magic gifts that she must rise early the next morning and walk in the park.   There she met a distressed falcon, weeping and wounding herself for sorrow at the desertion of her lover, and after hearing her sad tale, bore her to the castle, to salve her wounds and comfort her grief.   At this point the Squire proposed to leave this portion of his story, telling later how the falcon recovered her repentant lover by the mediation of Cambalus, son of the king of Araby and Inde.   Meanwhile, he would speak of Cambuscán's victories ; of how Algarsif was helped in his wooing, and saved from great perils by the brazen horse ; and of how Cambalo fought in the lists with two brethren in order to win Canace.   He just commenced on Part III. of his narrative, and had spoken but two lines, when the Franklin broke in with praise of the young Squire's eloquence, hoped for his long life and continuance in virtue, said he would give twenty pounds' worth of land to have his own son such a discreet young man, but regretted that that same son---

> " To virtue listeth [1] not entend [2]
> But for to play at dice, and to despend [3]
> And lose all that he hath, is his usage ;
> And he had lever [4] talken with a page
> Than to commune with any gentle wight,[5]
> There he might learné gentilesse [6] aright."

[1] pleaseth	[3] squander	[5] person
[2] to attend	[4] rather	[6] courtesy

The Host interrupted, crying "a straw for your gentilesse."

"'What! Frankelin, *pardee*, sir, well thou woost [1]
That each of you must tellen atté least
A tale or two, or breaken his behest.'
'That know I well, sir,' quoth the Frankéleyn,
'I pray you haveth me not in disdain
Though to this man I speak a word or two.'

. . . . . .

'I will not you contrarien [2] in no wise
As far as that my wittés will suffice ;
I pray to God that it may pleasen you,
Then woot [3] I well that it is good y-now.' [4]
    'These oldé, gentle Britons in their days
Of divers áventurés maden lays
Rymeyéd [5] in their firsté Briton tongue,
Which layés with their instruments they sung,
Or ellés [6] redden [7] them for their pleasaunce, [8]
And one of them have I in rémembraunce,
Which I shall say with good will as I can.
    'But, sirs, because I am a burel [9] man,
At my beginning first I you beseech,
Have me excuséd of my rudé speech.
I learned never rhetoric certain ;
Thing that I speak it moot be bare and plain.
I sleep never on the Mount of Pernasso [10]
Nor learnéd Marcus Tullius Cicero.
Colours [11] ne know I none, withouten dread,
But suche colours as growen in the mead,
Or elles suché as men dye or paint
Colours of rhetoric be to me quaint ; [12]
My spirit feeleth naught of such mateere,
But if you list my talé shall you hear.'"

This ancient British or Breton story—of which no old original is now known—told of a good knight, Arveragus, and his faithful wife, Dorigen ; how

[1] knowest	[5] rhymed	[9] untaught
[2] oppose	[6] else	[10] Parnassus
[3] know	[7] read	[11] flowers of rhetoric
[4] enough	[8] pleasure	[12] unfamiliar

THE LAST STAGE OF THE WINCHESTER WAY, DOWN HARBLEDOWN HILL.

THE BLACK PRINCE'S WELL, HARBLEDOWN.

Last of the " Waterings" of St Thomas for both the London and the Winchester Ways.

that when the knight had been a couple of years away from home, a squire, Aurelius, told Dorigen that he was dying of love for her, and she replied that she would ever be true to her husband. In confirmation of her decision, she declared that she would be the sweetheart of Aurelius when he was able to remove all the rocks of the Breton coast—but not until then. After a time Aurelius secured a magician who made all the rocks disappear, whereupon the lady was distressed nearly to death. Her husband asked the reason, and hearing of the vow, said that troth must never be broken, and sent Dorigen to Aurelius. He, struck by the high chivalry of the knight, declared that a squire must at least do as much, and bade her return, unharmed. Aurelius then went to the magician, offering all the money he could raise, which was only half what he had covenanted to pay, and begged for a year or two in which to pay the rest. In their conversation the magician learned the facts, and in emulation of the high-mindedness of the knight and the squire, refused to receive any payment for his services; whereupon the Franklin concluded :—

> " Lordings, this question, then, would I ask now,
> Which was the mosté free,[1] as thinketh you ?
> Now telleth me, ere that ye further wend.
> I know no more, my tale is at an end."

The Second Nun's tale, which followed, has no introduction by the Host. It begins with a discourse on the sin of idleness, and says that to prevent such idleness she has spent time in trans-

---

[1] liberal

lating the story of St Cecilia. Then follow eight verses of a very beautiful hymn to the Virgin, from which the fifth may well be quoted as a specimen of the work, and also as showing one of the many minor slips made by Chaucer in stringing together the *Canterbury Tales*, for he makes the nun speak of herself as an unworthy son of Eve.

> " Now help, thou meek and blissful fairé maid,
> Me fleméd [1] wretch in this desért of gall ;
> Think on the woman Cananee, that said
> That whelpés eat some of the crommés [2] all
> That from their lordés table been y-fall,
> And though that I, unworthy son of Eve,
> Be sinful, yet accepté my bileve." [3]

Next follow five verses on the meaning of the name Cecilia, and thereafter the story of the life, martyrdom, and canonisation of the saint. Then Chaucer continues :—

> " When told was all the life of Saint Cecile,
> Ere we had ridden fully fivé mile,
> At Boghton-under-Blee, us 'gan atake [4]
> A man that clothéd was in clothés blake,
> And underneath he had a white surplys ; [5]
> His hackney, which that was all pomely [6] grys,[7]
> So swatté [8] that it wonder was to see ;
> It seemed as he had prickéd [9] milés three.
> The horse eke that his Yeoman rode upon
> So swatté [8] that unnethé [10] might it gon ; [11]
> About the peytrel [12] stood the foam full high
> He was of foam all fleckéd as a pie.[13]
> A male [14] twofold upon his crupper lay,
> It seeméd that he carried lite [15] array.
> All light for summer rode this worthy man,
> And in mine hearté wond'ring I began

[1] exiled
[2] crumbs
[3] faith
[4] overtake
[5] surplice
[6] dappled
[7] grey
[8] sweated
[9] spurred
[10] scarcely
[11] go
[12] breast-piece
[13] magpie
[14] wallet
[15] little

What that he was, till that I understood
How that his cloak was sewéd to his hood,
For which, when I had long adviséd me,
I deeméd him some Canon for to be.
His hat hung at his back down by a lace,
For he had ridden more than trot or pace ;
He had ay prickéd[1] like as he were wood.[2]
A cloté[3]-leaf he had under his hood
For swoot,[4] and for to keep his head from heat ;
But it was joyé for to see him sweat !
His forehead droppéd as a stillatorie[5]
Were full of plantain and of pellitory ;
And when that he was come he 'gan to cry,
God save, quoth he, this jolly company !
Fast have I prickéd, quoth he, for your sake,
By causé that I wouldé you atake[6]
To ridden in this merry companye.
His yeoman eke was full of courtesie,
And saidé, sirs, now in the morrow tide,
Out of your hostelry I saw you ride,
And warnéd here my lord and my sovereign,
Which that to riden with you is full fain,
For his desport ; he loveth dalliance."

These were the Alchemist and his man. The
Host suggested that the Alchemist should tell a
tale, but after some conversation, the Yeoman
told the experiences of honest and dishonest
alchemists, as has been mentioned in Chapter IX.
The next point at which the thread is resumed
(there is a gap after the Canon's Yeoman's tale)
is at Harbledown :—

"Woot ye not where there stant a little town,
    Which that y-clepéd[7] is Bobbe-up-and-down,
Under the Blee[8] in Canterbury way ?
    There 'gan our Hosté for to jape and play."

[1] spurred
[2] mad
[3] a name used for the yellow water-lily: (?) also for the docken
[4] sweat
[5] still
[6] know
[7] called
[8] the Blean Hills

He asked for a volunteer to wake up "our fellow all behind"; then noticing that the fellow in question is the Cook, declared he should tell another tale. As he approached he looked pale and ill, and excused himself on account of a great drowsiness. The Manciple took pity on him and offered to tell a tale in his stead, but as he drew nearer, noted that the indisposition was due to drink, and began to abuse him as a "stinking swine." The Cook, becoming angry, fell from his horse, and—

> "There was great shoving, bothé to and fro,
> To lift him up, and muchel care and woe,
> So unwieldy was this sorry, pallid ghost."

The Host excused him his tale and accepted the Manciple's instead, but said that the Manciple had been "too nice" in openly reproving the Cook, and warned him that the latter might retaliate some day, by speaking of reckonings that were not honest. The Manciple feared or pretended to fear such exposure, so he gave the Cook a draught of wine from his own gourd, which made peace at once; whereafter the Manciple began his tale of how Phœbus kept a wonderful talking crow, which was white, as were all crows in those days. The wife of Phœbus was untrue to him, and when the crow told his master, he at once shot his wife. Repenting suddenly, when too late, he swore that his wife must have been true, abused the crow as a traitor, and—

> ". . . pulled his whité featherés everyone,
> And made him black, and refte [1] him all his song,
> And eke his speech, and out at door him slung
> Unto the devil!"

[1] robbed him of

Wherefore all crows are black and have lost their sweet voices. By this time it was four in the afternoon ; they were entering at "a thorp's end," and the Host said, "now lacketh us no talés more than one," and, turning to the Parson, said "every man save thou hath told his tale," and called upon him for a fable. The Parson, quoting Paul's Epistle to Timothy, said he would tell no "fables and such wretchedness," for why should he sow chaff when there is a chance to sow wheat. They all agreed that it was well to end the journey and the day (and the week ?) with "vertuous sentence," so the Parson began what was really a very good, very moral, and very long sermon, dealing mainly with the seven deadly sins and their cures or antidotes, and having none of the vivacity of Chaucer's ordinary work.

The sermon is followed by a section : " Here taketh the maker of this book his leave," which is so contrary to the whole spirit of Chaucer that we are tempted to credit the suggestion that it was interpolated, after his death, by the monks of Westminster, who may have arranged his manuscripts. The allocation of the tales to this day is unsatisfactory in many respects. We can scarcely believe that Chaucer intended to end his book with anything so solemn as the Parson's tale, but think it must have been intended as a foil to some brighter incident introduced by some one met on the way (like the Canon's Yeoman), or to a brilliant epilogue of Chaucer's own, describing the entry into Canterbury and visit to the shrine.

From the incident of the Canon and his

Yeoman, we imagine that the pilgrims started right away from Ospringe without any exploration of the wonders of Faversham. Possibly they had seen them in the evening, after reaching Ospringe, or perhaps they intended to do so on returning from Canterbury. At any rate, most of the real pilgrims along this way must have visited Faversham to see its very famous Abbey of Cluniac monks, founded by King Stephen and Matilda ; worshipful for having a portion of the true cross, which was presented by Godfrey of Bouillon, and notable for being the burial-place of Stephen, Matilda, and their son Eustace. In the abbey farm, some pieces of wall and considerable foundations still remain ; the bailiff's house is now a public-house (the Globe, in Abbey Street), and a small portion of the abbey gateway is included in the house, No. 80. Abbey Street, where Arden of Faversham lived in the sixteenth century, and was murdered. The Priory of Davington, some half-mile away, founded by Henry II. and Fulke de Newenham, in 1153, is still in large part preserved, as a private house. It was a Benedictine foundation for nuns, but its properties were so small that it was known as the house of "the poor nuns of Davington," and it escaped confiscation at the time of the dissolution by having previously escheated to the king for failing to keep its proper number of nuns. The church of Faversham, which was in the patronage of the monks of Augustine's, was, and still is, an unusually large, fine and interesting church, with architectural details, brasses, carved miserere seats, and remains of some frescoes of Early English date. In this church, too, was a

CANTERBURY FROM HARBLEDOWN HILL.

The joint Way of the London and the Winchester Pilgrims, and first View of the Cathedral.

chapel of St Thomas of Canterbury, and there were altars to St Erasmus and the Saints Crispin and Crispianus. The two last-named were especially honoured in Faversham, to which town they fled in the Maximinian persecution.

If the pilgrims visited these wonders of Faversham, they would have more than one possible way back to their main road, but they probably rejoined it directly and passed the little church of Preston, which then belonged to Christ Church, Canterbury—the cathedral to which they were wending. For the next three miles or so, the road undulates a good deal, and at Boughton-under-Blean, where the pilgrims were overtaken by the Canon's Yeoman, it begins to rise to Boughton Hill, the highest point on this part of the road, from which the view, looking backward, is particularly fine, embracing much of fertile Kent and a portion of sea. For over a mile the road is fairly level and runs through a richly-wooded country, part of the old royal forest of Blean. Until 1840, when it was made into the parish of Dunkirk, this district was extra-parochial, and had an evil reputation as a haunt of highwaymen, footpads, and smugglers, and possibly this was the real reason why the Canon hurried after a large party, for safety. Passing through the hamlet of Upper Harbledown, we soon come to a long descent, beyond which is a very sharp steep rise to Harbledown. Here was the leper hospital, founded about A.D. 1080 by Lanfranc (now used as alms-houses), with its chapel on the hill just above, which still shows much of its original structure. Both chapel and hospital will gladly be shown to visitors by the sub-priors of the hospital, who will also point out the Black Prince's Well. This, the last of the Waterings of St Thomas, is neatly built over, and surrounded with an approach of flagged steps, and is said to have been last restored by Edward the Black Prince. On the keystone of the arch are his three ostrich feathers, and, curiously enough, the water is still in some repute for its curative powers. The sub-prior of the hospital told us that he still occasionally receives small remittances from various parts of the Continent, with requests that he will forward a few bottles of the water, for the curing of diseases of the eyes.

At the leper hospital was preserved a slipper of St Thomas, described by Erasmus as decorated with copper and crystal, and presented to every pilgrim to kiss. The slipper has disappeared (it was lately said to be in the possession of one of the Canterbury photographers), but a crystal, which is believed to have been the one used in its decoration, and the collecting-box which was always shown with the slipper, may still be seen in the hospital. Here also are an ancient chest, said to have been one of the treasure-chests brought over by the Conqueror, and many interesting old utensils, treasured from the early days of the foundation.

Just beyond Harbledown, the towers of Canterbury Cathedral come into view, down a straight stretch of road; and what first sight could be more impressive or gratifying to pilgrims who had travelled weary leagues with earnest and devout purpose? Striking as is the sight to-day, especially when the great mass of the cathedral is touched by the very early morning, or the evening sun, it was still more beautiful in the pilgrims' days, when there was a central spire surmounted by a great golden angel.

At this point, devout pilgrims dismounted from their horses, to complete the journey on foot; and if they were under penance, would remove their shoes, and even change their garments for the penitential hair-shirt, as we have seen was done by Henry II. On the right, as we continue toward Canterbury, is the ancient church of St Dunstan, where Henry made his change, and half a mile further brings us to the fine west gate.

Though Chaucer did not complete his story of the pilgrimage, there is preserved to us the Tale of Beryn, in which we are informed that the pilgrims stayed at the Chequers of the Hope, an old hostelry, of which some of the lower portion still remains, in the shop at the left of the entrance to Mercery Lane.

CHAPTER XIV

THE FALL OF THE CULT OF ST THOMAS

THE excessive zeal, the exaggerated enthusiasm, the marvellous cures, and the lavish gifts that arose around the early memory of Thomas the Martyr fostered a great cult, but they bore the seeds of decay and ruin. It was inevitable that interested and self-seeking people should largely supplant the humble and earnest in any position where gifts flowed so freely that life could be lived in ease, luxury, and ostentation. It was inevitable that the decay of faith amongst the ministers of holy things should lead to indifference or open scoffing and ridicule amongst the slightly-educated laity; that pilgrimages should attract the merry, restless, reckless ne'er-do-weels; and that the real or fancied powers of saintly images should be magnified for the obtaining of pecks of grain, fat pullets, and cockerels, or more valuable offerings from credulous people.

The story of the fall of the cult is a part of the story of the Reformation in England, and with that mixture of pious protest, unexampled plunder, and hypocritical sacrilege this book cannot deal. It is necessary, however, to touch upon some of the fourteenth-century factors, those which influenced or were influenced by the work of Chaucer, especially since these affect the underlying currents of honest faith and honest scepticism, which prepared the great fabric of Romanism in England for the direct assaults of the royal power.

We have seen how the cult began, without the help of, and rather against the best efforts of, the influential men in the Church. We have seen how at the Translation every resource of unlimited wealth and power, every artifice of the very highest kind of advertisement and stage-management, were used to impress the people. We have seen, if only in an inadequate glimpse, something of the spirit in which two humble earnest pilgrims wandered from the heart of Hampshire to the heart of Kent. And in Chaucer's vivid painting we have seen the mixed motives, characters, and mental attitudes of nearly two score men of the world and of the Church, at a time when the cult had lost much of its original religious fervour, but still remained highly popular. We must now briefly consider some of the contemporaries of Chaucer who affected the movement.

The *Vision of William (Langland) concerning Piers Plowman* came before the publication of Chaucer's best - known work. This was Langland's principal (and probably his only) book, and appeared in manuscript, in three modifications or editions about 1362, 1377, and 1392. It tells of a blameless ploughman, like the one drawn as the brother of Chaucer's Poor Parson, who acts as a guide to the Temple of

Faith; and in the second part he is Jesus the son of the Nazarene carpenter, who alone can guide to God the Father. It is in English, in unrhymed verse, it not only attacks the vices of evil priests and monks, but also the injustice and greed of the rich, the oppression and cruelty of the powerful. It took a great hold upon the common people. Great numbers of MS. copies were distributed, but its widest circulation was given by ballad-singers and reciters, travelling preachers, pedlars and chapmen, who used the latest popular news and politics as helps to sell their wares. A short description of covetousness; slightly modernised in the spelling, may be interesting to compare with the work of Chaucer, already given :—

> " And then came coveitise,
> Can I him not discryve,[1]
> So hungrily and hollow
> Sir Hervy him looked.
> He was beetle-browed,
> And baberlipped[2] also
> With two bleared e'en
> As a blind hagge ;
> And as a leathern purse
> Lolléd his cheeks
> Well[3] sidder[4] than his chin
> They chyveléd[5] for elde ;[6]
> And as a bond-man('s) of[7] his bacon
> His beard was bedravelled,
> With a hood on his head,
> A lousy hat above
> And in a tawny tabard[8]
> Of twelve winter('s) age."

This writer's advocacy of the claims of the poor was on the same lines as that of John Ball, " the

[1] describe	[3] much	[5] wrinkled	[7] by
[2] thick-lipped	[4] wider	[6] old age	[8] coat

mad priest," whose work in connection with the Peasants' Revolt has already been mentioned in Chapter X. It was strongly socialistic, but it also popularised that early free-thinking which was more classically associated with the names of Roger Bacon, Duns Scotus, William of Ockham, and others. The spread of these doctrines amongst the poor folk was greatly aided by the "simple priests" of John Wycliffe, who, in 1378, were sent wandering over the land; and thus the socialists became tinged with certain religious ideas, while Wycliffe, probably against his own wish, became identified with the political revolt. Wycliffe was for a long time supported by John of Gaunt and his party, who were bent on spoliation of the Church, and who found his doctrines serviceable, although he was a reformer and not a confiscator. The Peasants' Rising, supposed to be partly the result of Wycliffe's teaching, lost him the support of the nobles, but still he went on with his work, and by the issue of many tracts in the common tongue, as well as by the translation of the Bible into English, did good service to the English language as well as to English thought. Some of the complaints he brought against the Church were that "the brokers of the sinful city of Rome promote for money unlearned and unworthy caitiffs to benefices of the value of a thousand marks, while the poor and learned hardly obtain one of twenty. So decays sound learning. They present aliens who neither see nor care to see their parishioners, despise God's services, convey away the treasure of the realm [in tribute to Rome], and are worse than Jews or Saracens. The pope's revenue from England alone is larger than that of any prince in Christendom. God gave his sheep to be pastured, not to be shaven and shorn."

It is to be remembered that these charges were brought by one who was himself a churchman, and that Roger Bacon, William Langland (probably), John Ball, and others, were men within the Church aiming at the removal of abuses. Thus, the agitation was not against the Church itself, but rather by the Church, against certain definite and very serious evils. Many of the common folk, however, could not discriminate very finely ; they began to regard the Church as a mass of corruption, and faith as a subject for ridicule, so that the doings of Henry VIII., more than a century later, had a great measure of popularity, although they did much injury to some of the poores tpeople.

Though the cult of St Thomas suffered somewhat from the general odium heaping upon the Church, it had also its own special vices, follies, and shortcomings, and its own protesters. Notable amongst these was Simon of Sudbury, afterward Archbishop of Canterbury, who, in 1370, when he was Bishop of London, met and addressed a great crowd of pilgrims going along the Watling Street to the fourth Jubilee of Thomas. He roundly rebuked their folly, idleness, and levity, told them that they were guided by mischievous superstition, and that the plenary indulgence promised to devout pilgrims would be no good to such as they were. They all felt that he had uttered blasphemy ; one gentleman rode up to him, saying, " My Lord Bishop, for stirring the people to sedition against

St Thomas, I stake the salvation of my soul that you will die a most terrible death"; and the people cried, "Amen, Amen." Eleven years later Simon of Sudbury was dragged from the Tower and slain by Wat Tyler's force, and people remembered the prophecy.

A similar story was told of Wycliffe, that on December 29, 1384, he meant to preach in his church at Lutterworth against the commemoration of the martyrdom on that day, but was prevented by the stroke of paralysis from which he died a couple of days later. In spite of these supposed judgments of the incensed saint, there was a growing feeling against the luxury and idleness of the life connected with the great shrines, a growing disbelief in the miracles. Yet the pilgrimages continued. In quite the later years of the cult the gifts were great, and it is interesting to compare those at the shrine of St Thomas with those at the other principal altars. They were: Christ's Altar, £3, 2s. 6d. ; Altar of the Virgin, £63, 5s. 6d. ; St Thomas, £832, 12s. 3d. And in the next year : Christ's Altar, *nil;* Altar of the Virgin, £4, 1s. 8d. ; St Thomas, £954, 6s. 3d. ; in addition to which there was great wealth of gold and silver vessels and ornaments, and of jewels. Henry VII., considered one of the wisest princes of his age, and a great supporter of religion and learning, left in his will a kneeling likeness of himself, life-size, of silver gilt, "to be set before St Thomas of Canterbury, and as nigh to the shrine of St Thomas as may well be." In 1520, at the time of the last great jubilee, when there was some fear that the pope might not grant the usual indulgences, it was pleaded at Rome that no man since the death of St Peter had done more for the liberties of the Church than St Thomas. In that year Henry VIII., on his way to the Field of the Cloth of Gold, stayed and fared sumptuously at the archiepiscopal palaces of Otford, Charing, and Canterbury. At the cathedral city he was entertained, with the Emperor Charles V. and the great nobles of England and of Spain, in a style that had never been equalled since the great feasts of the Translation. In 1532, when James Bainham, member of the Middle Temple, was brought to the stake at Smithfield, one of the charges against him was that he had said that Archbishop Becket was a murderer, and that if he had not repented of his crime, he was rather a devil in hell than a saint in heaven. And the sincerity of Sir Thomas More, who was the principal instrument in securing Bainham's death, is shown by his letter when, on the eve of his own execution some three years later, he wrote: " I should be sorry that it should be any longer than to-morrow; for it is St Thomas's Eve and the Octave of St Peter, and therefore to-morrow I beg to go to God. It were a meet day, and very convenient for me."

Between the deaths of Bainham and More, Henry had struck his first great blow at the Church, and at the cult of St Thomas, by the Act of Supremacy, which provided that King Henry and his heirs were the only supreme head on earth of the Church of England, with power to redress all heresies and abuses which may lawfully be reformed. In the next year came the commission for the visitation of religious houses,

GATES AND GUEST-HOUSES OF CANTERBURY.

Mystery Lane and the Chequers of the Hope.   Gate of St. Augustine.   West Gate of City.
Norman Stairs and Hostelry Hall.   Infirdmary and Treasury-house of Monks.

which reported great licentiousness and immorality
in some of the smaller monasteries.   As a result,
all houses having revenues of less than £200 a
year were suppressed.   Thus three hundred and
seventy-six establishments, of which it might be
said that whatever their faults, they had always
fed the starving and sheltered the homeless, were
destroyed at one blow.   And their great funds,
left by pious people for religious and philanthropic
purposes, merely served to add £32,000 a year
to the purse of a licentious king, with an
additional lump sum of £100,000 as the value of
plate and jewels.

At the end of 1536, all superfluous holidays
which fell in term-time or in harvest-time were
forbidden, the principal feast at which this was
aimed being the Translation of St Thomas.   In
1539 came the Bill suppressing the greater
monasteries, with confiscation of all their
property to the king's use, and in 1547 there
was a royal injunction that all objects of
devotion should be so utterly destroyed "that
there should remain no memory of them in wall,
glass windows, or elsewhere within churches."
That this last injunction was especially rigorous
against St Thomas and his memory, we may
judge from the fact that on April 24, 1538,
Henry sent summons, "To thee, Thomas Becket,
sometime Archbishop of Canterbury," to appear
within thirty days to answer a charge of treason,
contumacy, and rebellion against his sovereign
lord, King Henry II.   When the saint appeared
not, the case was argued with the Attorney
General appearing for King Henry II., and an
advocate, provided at the public expense, for

T

Thomas. The dead king proved his case, and on June 10, 1538, Thomas was condemned to have his bones publicly burned, and the offerings of his shrine forfeited to the crown.

Of the spoiling of the sanctuary there is no complete contemporary record. We know that the jewels and gold of the shrine itself filled two coffers of such a bigness that each required seven or eight men to lift it; that the other valuables filled twenty-six carts, and that the greatest jewel, the Regale of France, was set in a ring to grace the fat thumb of the King.

The royal commissioners naturally found that all the miraculous images, pictures, wells, etc., were frauds, and the mob, incensed at their stories of deception, were prepared to dance around and applaud while the objects of their recent worship were being desecrated and destroyed. St Thomas's Well, in Canterbury, lost its healing virtue when the shrine was destroyed, and now we do not even know its position. Cranmer asked for a commission to examine the "blood of St Thomas," which he "suspected to be red ochre." The king declared of Thomas that "notwithstanding the canonisation, there appeareth nothing . . . whereby he should be called a saint; but rather esteemed a rebel and traitor to his prince. Therefore, his grace straitly chargeth and commandeth, that henceforth the said Thomas Becket shall not be esteemed, named, reputed, nor called a saint, but 'Bishop Becket,' and that his images and pictures throughout the whole realm shall be put down and avoided out of all churches and chapels, and other places; and that from henceforth the days used to be festivals in his name shall not be observed—nor the service, office, antiphonies, collects, and prayers in his name read, but rased and put out of all books."

The records of Canterbury were completely destroyed, so far as they dealt with Thomas, and all through the country, images and windows were broken, frescoes were scraped away or whitewashed over, dedications of churches were changed, and even incidental references to the saint were obliterated. In some few places, as in the chapel of the Guild of the Holy Cross at Stratford-on-Avon, the pictures were pre-served, or were only covered with a whitewash which was afterwards removed; but even in this case the words "the translation of Saint Thomas the Martyr" were obliterated in the Constitution of the Guild.

The reports of the commissioners are full of interest, but we can only briefly mention a couple of facts directly connected with the Pilgrims' Way from Winchester. From Hyde Abbey they report, on a Saturday: "About three o'clock A.M. we made an end of the shrine here at Winchester. . . . We think the silver thereof will amount to near two thousand marks . . . the altar we purpose to bring with us . . . such a piece of work it is, that we think we shall not rid it, doing our best, before Monday next or Tuesday morning. Which done, we intend, both at Hyde and at St Mary's, to sweep away all the rotten bones that be called relics, which we may not omit, lest it should be thought that we came more for the treasure than for avoiding the abominations of idolatry."

From Boxley Abbey (see p. 137) the commission reported, with regard to the famous Rood of Grace, that they "found therein certain engines of old wire, with old rotten sticks in the back of the same, that did cause the eyes to move and stare in the head thereof like unto a lively thing; and also the nether lip in like wise to move as though it should speak." This, with the other "soteltie" was carried into the market-place at Maidstone on a market day, when the people held "the false, crafty, and subtle handling thereof in wondrous detestation and hatred." Thereafter these images were publicly destroyed in St Paul's Churchyard, London.

CHAPTER XV

THE PILGRIMS' WAYS: TO-DAY

A GOOD deal of mystery and speculation has been woven around pilgrims' roads in general, and "the" Pilgrims' Way from Winchester to Canterbury in particular. A lonely road, clinging to the side of the Downs through a distance of thirty or forty miles, carefully just avoiding most of the villages it passes, marked with a series of chapels and rest-houses, and with place-names that suggest the one-time existence of others, is an object of interest around which sentiment and poetry can freely play. And when we find it familiarly, lovingly known by the common people as The Pilgrims' Way, the one perfecting touch is added to the romance.

For bringing this old track-way before the public, and for the preservation of any record of its line in certain places, we are indebted to the engineers of the Ordnance Survey. It is to be regretted, however, that they kept no notes of the evidence on which they adopted the name and the line in various places, and that they do not seem to have always recorded such parts of the Way as are at present out of use. We have taken considerable pains to check the observations of the Survey and of several writers who have done much good work in tracing the Way, only to find that many doubts are raised which cannot at all easily be settled.

It is not necessary here to attempt to trace the Ways in full. That has been done incidentally in Chapters VI. and X. to XIII. These, with the maps, will answer most of the purposes of the modern pilgrim who wishes to walk, cycle, or drive over one of the routes.

The Way from Winchester is shown on the ordnance maps in portions from Guildford to Bigberry Wood, near Harbledown. West of Guildford it is easily recognisable by any one who has explored the undoubted parts of the Way, as far as Farnham; but beyond there it is very uncertain. It is well to remember that pilgrims to Canterbury came from "every shire's end," and that, therefore, every road which existed during the thirteenth, fourteenth, and fifteenth centuries, and which can still be traced, is in a sense a Pilgrims' Way. Therefore, any old road that ran to Farnham was a continuation and a feeder of "the" Pilgrims' Way. In our special sense, however, we need a road which is traditionally known, or is especially likely, to have been the main route from the great landing-place of Southampton, and the great sanctuary of Winchester, to Canterbury.

It is well to remember that the pilgrims did not make their roads, but merely chose the "through" routes, avoiding as far as possible the tortuous network of lanes spread all over the country and uniting village to village. The best of such "through" roads, almost the only

WINCHESTER CATHEDRAL, FROM THE SOUTH-EAST.

ones in fact, were the Roman roads; some of which (if not most) were built on roads already existing when the Romans came.

In Roman times there was a road from their port at Bitterne (Clausentum) straight through Otterbourne to Winchester, and the modern road, starting from the other side of the Itchen, and not running quite so straight as far as Otterbourne, follows the older road for the rest of the distance. Therefore, from Otterbourne we may be sure of the road, and to that place it is a little uncertain.

From Winchester a great Roman road ran northerly to Silchester. It is followed by the modern Basingstoke road for about thirteen and a half miles, after which the modern road bears a little to the east. From Basingstoke to Farnham there is not a very direct road now, but there are lanes which only require the bridging of one or two short gaps to make a good connection, and there may have been an old, direct way by Greywell Hill, North Warnborough, Mill Lane, and Heath House. An alternative road, possessing some of the characteristics of the true Pilgrims' Way, runs from beyond (west of) Basingstoke, passing a mile or so to the south of that town and going to Coombehurst, The Grove, along the north side of Hackwood Park, by Polecat Corner, Four Lanes End, Long Sutton, south of a "Roman intrenchment," and by Dippenhall. The name of Ridgeway House, close to Dippenhall, probably indicates a Roman road.

The modern road from Winchester to Farnham runs through the Worthies, Itchen Abbas,

Itchen Stoke, Alresford, Chawton, and Alton, and as this was a thickly-settled district in early Saxon times, there is no reason why this road should not have been used by the pilgrims. In our Chapter VI. we have followed Mrs Ady (Julia Cartwright), who in her book, *The Pilgrims' Way*, gives this route, with a detour through Ropley and East Tisted, which is based on local tradition and the fact that there was a Pilgrims' Place, between Tisted and Chawton, where Pelham now stands. We have been unable to obtain any confirmation of the tradition from local people or from such antiquarians as we have been able to consult.

From Farnham the Way follows the London road for about three miles, to near Whitewaysend House, then one road goes forward along the Hog's Back to Guildford, while the other goes through Seale, over Seale Common, past Shoelands (said to be derived from shooler, a beggar), and through Puttenham, to which point it is an easily distinguishable country road. At Puttenham, opposite the Jolly Farmer Inn, it strikes across the heath, between a tumulus marked with a flagstaff and a tiny cemetery chapel. It is only a cart track, which in about a mile divides, right, to Compton, with its pilgrims' church, and left to wander a quarter of a mile and then strike the end of a well-marked lane crossing the Compton - Guildford road half a mile further, where are the home and picture-gallery of the late Mr G. F. Watts, R.A. From here it skirts and runs through some beautiful woodland for just over two miles, passing Brabœuf Manor, and striking the

CIDERHOUSE COTTAGES, GUILDFORD.

Anciently the Pest-house.

ANCIENT HOSTELRY AT COMPTON, SURREY.

Godalming road at the foot of the hill on which stands St Catherine's. St Catherine's Well is passed in going to the ancient ferry, from which a track across two fields leads to the end of Ciderhouse Lane. A hundred yards up this, on the left, are two cottages, once the Pesthouse, and from them the path is straight through the Chantries (a wood) to the height crowned by St Marta's Chapel. The path down the hill is clear for half a mile, then breaks into a lane to Albury.

Probably along this piece there were many ways, for the hillside was unenclosed and uncultivated; the old road (probably older than the pilgrims' time), may have followed the line up Pewley Hill, north of Tyting Farm, along Albury Downs, Netley Heath, and Hackhurst Downs, past The Roughs, Newlands, and Combe Bottom. Probably some pilgrims went through Albury and Shere; in which case they would continue through Abinger Hammer, Wotton, and Dorking. Those who took the Downs road we have suggested would go forward by Oaken Grove, White Down, and Denbies, skirt Ashcombe Wood, and pass Chapel Farm (where traces of a chapel yet remain), and so to Burford Bridge, where we know there is a "Way Pool."

From here, again, there were more ways than one. Those who have followed the pilgrims' route and written on the subject, have supposed they went up Box Hill, and along the road at the top, past the Hand-in-Hand Inn, to Pebble Combe: there, bending eastward, below Walton Heath and above the Hermitage, past Margery Wood, Reigate Hill, White Hall, and Gatton Park to above Merstham. Thence we get over two miles practically straight and clear. Below Quarry Hangers and above Whitehill Farm it looks as if the Ordnance Survey had set the next scrap of the Way a little too high; but from here for the next three miles or more the Way is speculative, and little trace remains. It probably went by Marden Castle, Chaldons Farm, and Oxted Chalk Pits, for at Flinthouse Farm we pick it up again with certainty.

To return to Burford Bridge. Though the line above given may be correct, there are ample traces of an old lane, running along the lower slopes of Box Hill, the Betchworth Hills, and the Buckland Hills, and having the exact characteristics of "The Pilgrims' Way," so far as it is preserved. In places it runs as a lane, with hedges on both sides; in others, it continues across cultivated fields just as a ledge or shelf, falling away to the south; and again it is continued by three or four fine old yews in a line. In places, a modern road or lane has been run along it for a distance, and in some places there is trace of another track, parallel, a couple of hundred yards away. We have not been able to follow up these fragments as we wish, but suggest it as well worth doing by a local antiquary.

Resuming at Flinthouse Farm, we think there is much to be said for the line by Botley Hill, past Cold-harbour Green, the highest point hereabout, to Tatsfield Church. A piece may be missing just beyond here, but our line comes out at The Mount, a little further up Westerham Hill than is shown by the ordnance map or identified by local fame. Our reason for this can be seen on the ground, though it is difficult to give in words or on a map. Walking along the pilgrims' road of the ordnance map, along the section above Brasted, one can plainly see, half a mile or so further up the hill, the remains of an old straight lane. At places, for a field-width, it is missing, but again it becomes plain; it touches Pilgrim House, which, suspiciously enough, is half a mile *above* the Ordnance Surveyors' Pilgrims' Way, and from there to above the rifle butts the hedgerows are preserved, grown together into a thicket.

About this part of the line we have no doubt whatever. The road of the ordnance map may have anciently inherited the name, but it is not the old Pilgrims' Way; and if any one doubts this, we suggest that he study the ground, in the late afternoon when the sun is well westering, from the Sevenoaks road, a little way out of Westerham. The contour of the old way then throws a shadow even in those parts where it has no hedges.

It is not necessary that this amended line should be continued by way of Tatsfield. Even when crossing Titsey Park and Pilgrims' Lodge Farm (which is one, and probably the principal, of the ways) the line continues with a truer direction and a better level if carried above the rifle butts and Pilgrim House than if taken on the accepted road.

Taking the road from Titsey Park. however, which is a cycling or driving road ranging from "fair" to excellent, it runs a straight course to Chevening Park, where it has been completely stopped, and we must turn south for a mile, east for a mile, and northward again for nearly a mile, to get around the park. Even then we are a quarter of a mile below the old Way, which ran through what are now fields. So we keep the road half a mile eastward, then turn left up the Knockholt road, alongside one large field, and the next turn to the right puts us in the Way again, from which we soon get one of the most diversified views on its whole course.

Through Otford, and to a little beyond St Clere (mansion on right) the old Way has been adopted as "the London Road" and is in good condition, but beyond this point to where it crosses the London-Wrotham road it is a narrow lane, degenerating into a mere bridle-path and with the twigs of the hedges brushing a foot-passenger from both sides. Above Wrotham, there is a quarter of a mile excellently surfaced, then it becomes a good country lane, degenerating gradually. Beyond Trotterscliffe it crosses the Stansted road at a Pilgrims' House, and a mile beyond, it runs above the Coldrum stone circle, which still has some of its great uprights in position, reminding us of a pre-Christian time when the pilgrims' road may have been in use. Above Birling Place, past Bunker's Farm, and to Lad's Farm the Way is a bridle track, crossed by various roads and lanes, in one place being merely a cart track through fields, but never losing its direction and identity. At Lad's Farm it

OTFORD: CHURCH AND REMAINS OF ARCHBISHOPS' PALACE.

ST THOMAS'S WELL, OTFORD.

becomes a metalled road again, and at Upper
Halling passes Chapel Houses, where the tops
of two lancet windows may just be seen above
a lean-to addition. These houses or cottages
are diagonally opposite the Black Boy Public-
house, and are not where marked on the
ordnance map. Beyond this the Way runs
nearly to Cuxton, where its individuality
becomes lost in the Rochester road.

The question of where the pilgrims crossed
the Medway has given rise to much discussion,
and some have been biassed, no doubt, by an
attempt to keep them on "the Pilgrims' Way"
as much as possible. We know that great
crowds of the pilgrims crossed at Maidstone,
and remembering the archbishops' palaces at
Wrotham, Malling, Maidstone, Leeds, and Charing, this seems a likely line for the greater number
of pilgrims who could afford to make reasonable
offerings along the way. Some may have
crossed at Aylesford, where there was a good
bridge, others at Snodland, where there is a
line of churches—Snodland, Burham Court, and
Burham—connected by a ferry and by a lane
that soon joins the next part of undoubted
Pilgrims' Way. Others may have crossed the
ferry from Lower Halling to Wouldham; and
an intelligent navvy tells us that the pilgrims
crossed at North Halling, where a stone causeway still remains across the river, and is practic-
able for active youths when the tide and the
river are very low.

There is no apparent reason why any pilgrims
should have gone further north than Aylesford,
even if they wished to visit Boxley Abbey and

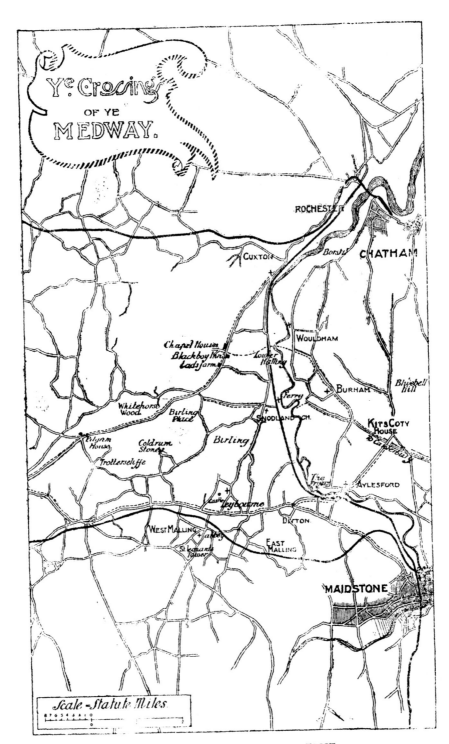

SKETCH MAP OF MAIDSTONE DISTRICT.

KIT'S COTY HOUSE.

had no interest in Maidstone, and we think that those who study the question on the spot (not merely on the map) will be forced to the conclusion that whatever the pilgrims may have done, *the people who made the Pilgrims' Way were aiming for Rochester, or, at least, some point as far north-east as Cuxton.* Following the Way westward from (say) Boxley Abbey, the same idea is confirmed, that the Way is pointing to Borstal (opposite Cuxton) or to Rochester.

We know little of the mediæval interest taken in Kit's Coty House, which may have attracted people north of Maidstone, but that would not take them further than Aylesford.

Joining the Way above Kit's Coty House, we find it run plainly, and almost in a straight line, just above the churches, past Boxley Abbey, Boxley, Detling, Thornham, Hollingbourne, Harrietsham, Lenham, and so to Cobham Farm, beyond which it has been destroyed by cultivation to the width of two or three fields. Here we must diverge half a mile right, and about three-quarters of a mile along the Ashford road, bear left to Hart Hill, from which the Way is clear again, above Charing. Here it is a good road, and continues so until near Burnt House, where it takes a slight bend to the left, passes the mouth of a small chalk quarry and continues as a shady footpath (for about a mile, two footpaths separated by a few feet of distance, and by a hedge of sapling trees). Above Westwell it has bits of well-made roadway, and at the keeper's cottage at the edge of Eastwell Park it seems to disappear. Five different people who lived within half a mile of this point, told us that the Way did not exist beyond here; and, as a matter of fact, any one who wants a pleasant walk, from here to Boughton Lees, would be wise to take the foot-path through the park rather than to attempt the ancient Way. But it does exist. Its mouth is choked with mighty nettles, above which the bushes grow together. For a few yards the path is cumbered with the bottles, cans, and other refuse of the cottages, and as it proceeds it is crossed by fallen trees and partly filled with rank weeds and creepers. But the old Way is there; and it would be a gracious act for the noble owner of the park to make it clear, if the local authorities neglect to do so.

Beyond Eastwell Park our evidence is the Ordnance Survey, based on local information. It takes us by Boughton Lees, and above Chilham, with an unaccountable bend around Old Wives' Lees, and so to Harbledown. It is difficult to find, in places, and when found, is not quite convincing. To Boughton Lees the path is its own demonstration, but Charing is the last point in which we know the pilgrims to have been interested. The main road from there to Canterbury went up Charing Hill, by Challock Lees, Mollash, and Chilham, and there is no obvious reason why the bulk of the pilgrims should not take it, even if they wished to see Harbledown and St Thomas's Well before reaching the cathedral city. Again, as in the case of the Medway portion, dealing with the Way, as apart from the pilgrims, we suggest that the old road was not aiming at Canterbury, but ran (and still exists in fairly

PART OF THE TITHE-BARN, MAIDSTONE.

continuous state) by Springrove, Wye, Brabourne, and Stowting Court, falling at Horton Park into the Stone Street from Canterbury to Lymne. This would agree with the idea that it was part of an ancient trade road, used for bringing the much-prized tin of Cornwall (in a time when bronze was *the* metal of the civilised world) to the narrow seas for shipment. This way is called "th' old lane" by inhabitants of Boughton Lees, who say that they always consider it a continuation of "th' old lane" on the other side of Eastwell Park (our Pilgrims' Way). At Brabourne it is known as "the old Roman road."

We are aware that Mr Grant Allen, and Mr Charles Elton, whom he quoted, took the "Tin Road" through Canterbury to Sandwich or Richborough, but they did so after quoting authorities to show that there were roads to and from Lymne, and calling Cæsar and Strabo to witness that the emporium of the Gallic merchants was opposite Boulogne. They seem to have been quite carried away by the desire to take the road through Canterbury, or they would not have used evidence pointing directly to Lymne in support of a conclusion, "consistent with the tin mart being near Thanet." "Opposite Boulogne" is surely more likely to have been Lymne, some thirty-two miles distant, than Sandwich, which was twice as far.

We may now consider some general characteristics of "the" Pilgrims' Way. It has been said to be a "made" Roman road, but this seems to be quite a mistake, though it may have crossed a Roman causeway, or even have

U

run along one for a short distance in places. In its whole course, both where still in use and where deserted, we have seen no evidence of roadmaking earlier than quite modern times. In some places the old Way runs alongside the modern road, within a few paces, plainly traceable as a mound or as a hollow. Had it been a "made" road, the modern one would have been made over it. We have seen some three miles of a most typical portion of the Way torn up, where there was absolutely nothing but grass and a few loose flints from the chalk, above the solid chalk itself. At several other points we have confirmed this, and where it goes over sandstone rock, the same thing occurs.

In the day when this road was laid out, but little of the land was cultivated, and probably still less was fenced; for cattle had herdsmen instead of hedges to guide them.

The road was merely the shortest and most convenient way from point to point. It aimed at keeping on the sandstone or chalk, to avoid the worse footing and the denser herbage of the clays. It kept as level as it conveniently could without long detours, and it aimed for good crossings of the rivers (originally fords). At first the Way would be very wide, straggling and undefined, probably needing a guide or old experienced packman with every party. As cultivation pushed up from the valleys and men began to fence, they naturally took a line along the way, and thus it first became defined—on its southern side. It became a lane when its northern side was fenced:—not for the sake of defining the Way, but for preventing the

CHARING CHURCH, AND REMAINS OF ARCHBISHOPS' PALACE.

straying of cattle into the crops. That the fencing was done after the making of many of the roads that cross the Way at right angles, we have evidence in the fact that in many cases where the Way crosses such a road, its line drops down the hill a distance of from five or ten to perhaps thirty yards. And this drop is almost invariably made on the eastern side, suggesting that the travellers who first defined the Way came from the west.

The yews along the Way have had much comment; it has been suggested that they were planted as way-marks, and it is said that they are commonly called "palms" along the Surrey and some of the Kentish portions of of the Way, and prominently used in church decoration. There are some fine yews along the Way, but there are few places where they are so thick along the Way itself as on the hillside a little above; no part of the Way has such a fine line of yews as may be seen in some of the hedges running up the hill at right angles from it; and there are many parts of the Way where there is scarce a yew to the mile, though they grow well in neighbouring hedges. At the same time, there are places where fine, old, almost equidistant yews continue the line of two old lanes across a field or fields, and where they doubtless indicate that the lane once ran. Our inquiries along the Way have failed to find any one who ever heard the yews popularly called palms; and not one of the clergymen along the Way knows of this, or of the use of yews (except amongst all other evergreens) in church decoration.

There is said to be, or to have been, a tradition that the Roman snail, or Apple snail (*helix pomatia*), was introduced by the Norman pilgrims; but of this we can find no memory remaining. Jeffreys, in *British Conchology*, 1862, makes no mention of this tradition, though he gives and criticises other stories of the introduction of the species, which occurs in many places in Kent, Surrey, Hertford, Oxford, Wilts, and Gloucester.

The connection of the name of Cold-harbour, and its variants, Cold Arbour, Windy Arbour, Cole-kitchen, etc., with the Pilgrims' Way seems entirely fanciful: and the suggestion that the name "always" occurs along a Roman road seems much too sweeping. The name almost certainly means what it simply implies, namely, a harbour (shelter or refuge) which was not warmed. But the things to which the name was applied may have been various, and we think there is probability that it meant in at least one case a harbour for shipping, in others a house or shelter-place for travellers, in others a camping-place for herdsmen travelling to the fairs, and in others a cattle-pen or sheep-fold on a hillside. As to the second meaning, it has been suggested that the shelter was merely a grassy sward, provided with water, and shaded by trees, comforting in the heat of summer. In the alternative, it is said that there were wayside rest-houses like those in the Alps and in India, without any landlord or attendant; but this is surely not a tenable idea on the Pilgrims' Ways, which were well provided with inns, ale-stakes, and free board and lodging at

CHARING : PART OF THE ARCHBISHOPS' PALACE.

the monasteries, etc. Another suggestion, that the name applies to places where Roman villas, deserted about the fourth century, long remained as unwarmed rest-houses for travellers, belongs to a time earlier than our pilgrims, and need not be considered here.

Many place-names along the road directly connect it with the pilgrims — Pilgrim House, Pilgrim Place, etc.—and others, such as Chapel Houses, will record, even after the buildings are gone, the one-time existence of a wayside shrine. Other names indicate the extensive use of the road in old times, and may, in some cases, be connected with the riff-raff of people drawn in the wake of the pilgrims. A few of these interesting place-names, taking them in order from west to east, are—Shoelands (shooler, a beggar), near Puttenham; Tyting (tithing) Farm, St Marta's; Chapel Farm, near Burford; the Way Pool, Burford Bridge; and Chapel Houses, Halling. Near Puttenham are Roberds' (robbers') Moor, and Beggars' Corner.

In addition to place-names, there are a few words in the general language which are said to be derived from the pilgrimage. A "canterbury" was a traveller's tale or fable; and the word is given in this sense in certain good American dictionaries as being still used in the United States. The Canterbury bell (campanula medium), a flower growing freely in the wild state in Kent, is said to have taken its name from the little metal bells which competed with the ampullæ and the leaden "heads of Thomas," as signs of the Canterbury pilgrim. The pace known as a canter is a contraction of Canterbury gallop; and "cant" is said to have been originally applied to the hypocritical religious dissertations of those who had been to the martyr's shrine.

Of the minor ways to Canterbury, which had some special connection with the pilgrims, little need be said. Many came from the eastern counties, concentrating on West Thurrock, whence they crossed the Thames by ferry to Greenhithe, landing close to the grounds of Ingress Abbey, which was a grange of the Priory of Dartford. By more than one road, a couple of miles would bring the pilgrims into the Watling Street a little to the west of Springhead.

There are traces of two "Pilgrims' Roads" marked on the ordnance map as coming from the south-east. One (working from Canterbury) goes past Barton Fields, Hoad Farm, Patrixbourne, Shepherd's Close, and forward until it is lost in Ileden Wood. The other is first marked near Great Bossington, five miles from Canterbury, whence it runs a mile to Uffington, then in "traces" through Goodnestone Park, beyond which it bends below Chillenden. Other maps continue its line from a point a mile west of Tilmanstone to East Studdal. Both these seem far from convincing. We would like to know the evidence on which they were called pilgrims' roads; and we are reminded that in one place, at any rate (Eastwell Park), we met an intelligent gamekeeper who, while knowing a good deal about "the" Pilgrims' Way, uses "pilgrim way" as a generic name for any horse road which is scarce good enough for a cart. With him the term was equivalent to

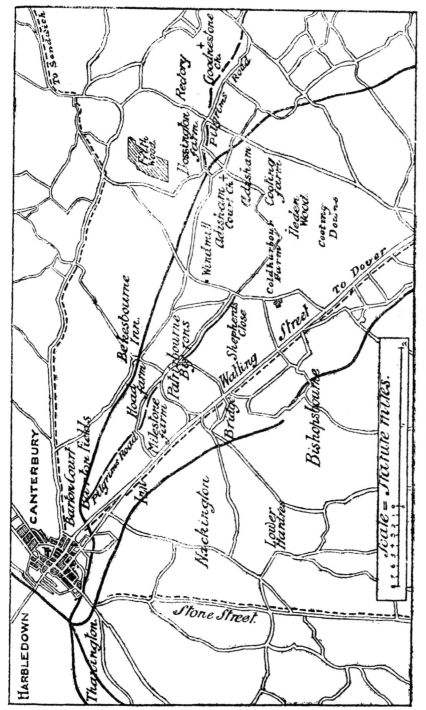

SKETCH MAP OF CANTERBURY DISTRICT.

bridle-path ; and he described several lanes as " only a short cut, or pilgrim way."

From Sandwich and from Dover the pilgrims followed the high roads with which we are acquainted, and from Lymne or West Hythe, they took the line of the old Roman Stone Street, which was followed from Saltwood Castle by the murderers.

INDEX

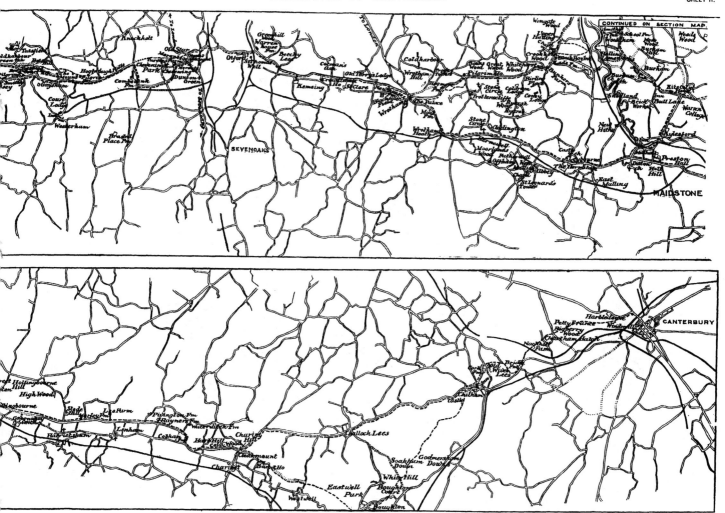

PUBLISHED BY ADAM & CHARLES BLACK, SOHO SQUARE, LONDON

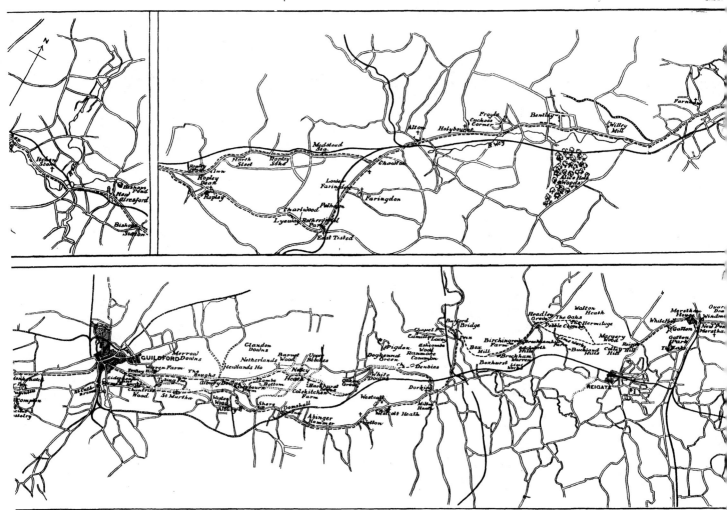

PUBLISHED BY ADAM & CHARLES BLACK, SOHO SQUARE, LONDON